INSIDE THE ROYAL WARDROBE

DRESS AND FASHION RESEARCH

Series Editor: Joanne B. Eicher, *Regents' Professor,*
University of Minnesota, USA

Advisory Board:

Vandana Bhandari, *National Institute of Fashion Technology, India*
Steeve Buckridge, *Grand Valley State University, USA*
Hazel Clark, *Parsons The New School of Design New York, USA*
Peter McNeil, *University of Technology Sydney, Australia*
Toby Slade, *University of Tokyo, Japan*
Bobbie Sumberg, *International Museum of Folk Art Santa Fe, USA*
Emma Tarlo, *Goldsmiths University of London, UK*
Lou Taylor, *University of Brighton, UK*
Karen Tranberg Hansen, *Northwestern University, USA*
Feng Zhao, *The Silk Museum Hangzhou, China*

The bold *Dress and Fashion Research* series is an outlet for high-quality,
in-depth scholarly research on previously overlooked topics and new
approaches. Showcasing challenging and courageous work on fashion
and dress, each book in this interdisciplinary series focusses on a specific
theme or area of the world that has been hitherto under-researched,
instigating new debates and bringing new information and analysis to
the fore. Dedicated to publishing the best research from leading scholars
and innovative rising stars, the works will be grounded in fashion studies,
history, anthropology, sociology, and gender studies.

ISSN: 2053-3926

Published in the Series
Angela M. Jansen, *Moroccan Fashion*
Angela M. Janson and Jennifer Craik (eds), *Modern Fashion Traditions*
Heike Jenss, *Fashioning Memory*
Paul Jobling, *Advertising Menswear*
Annette Lynch and Katalin Medvedev (eds), *Fashion, Agency,*
and Empowerment
Maria Mackinney-Valentin, *Fashioning Identity*
Magdalena Crăciun, *Islam, Faith, and Fashion*
Kate Strasdin, *Inside the Royal Wardrobe*
Daniel Delis Hill, *Peacock Revolution*
Elizabeth Kutesko, *Fashioning Brazil*

Forthcoming in the Series
Nancy Fischer, Kathryn Reiley, and Hayley Bush, *Dressing in Vintage*
Alessandra B. Lopez y Royo, *Contemporary Indonesian Fashion*

INSIDE THE ROYAL WARDROBE

A dress history of Queen Alexandra

KATE STRASDIN

BLOOMSBURY VISUAL ARTS
LONDON • NEW YORK • OXFORD • NEW DELHI • SYDNEY

BLOOMSBURY VISUAL ARTS
Bloomsbury Publishing Plc
50 Bedford Square, London, WC1B 3DP, UK
1385 Broadway, New York, NY 10018, USA

BLOOMSBURY, BLOOMSBURY VISUAL ARTS and the Diana logo are trademarks
of Bloomsbury Publishing Plc

Hardcover edition first published 2017
This paperback edition first published 2019

Cover design: Untitled
Cover image: Francois Flameng portrait of Queen Alexandra (©Royal Collection Trust /
Her Majesty Queen Elizabeth II 2016)

A catalogue record for this book is available from the British Library.

Library of Congress Cataloging-in-Publication Data
Strasdin, Kate, author.
Inside the royal wardrobe: a dress history of Queen Alexandra / Kate Strasdin.
New York: Bloomsbury Academic, An imprint of Bloomsbury Publishing Plc, 2017. |
Based on the author's thesis (Ph.D.–University of Southampton, 2013)
under the title: Fashioning Alexandra. | Includes bibliographical references.
LCCN 2017042931 | ISBN 9781474269933 (hardback)
LCSH: Alexandra, Queen, consort of Edward VII, King of Great Britain,
1844-1925–Clothing. | Queens–Clothing–Great Britain. | Costume—Great Britain–
History–19th century. | Costume–Great Britain–History–20th century. |
Queens–Great Britain–Biography.
LCC DA568.A2 S73 2017 | DDC391/.0220941–dc23
LC record available at https://lccn.loc.gov/2017042931

ISBN: HB: 978-1-4742-6993-3
PB: 978-1-350-10234-7
ePDF: 978-1-4742-6994-0
eBook: 978-1-4742-6995-7

Series: Dress and Fashion Research

Typeset by Deanta Global Publishing Services, Chennai, India
Printed and bound in Great Britain

To find out more about our authors and books visit www.bloomsbury.com
and sign up for our newsletters.

CONTENTS

LIST OF ILLUSTRATIONS

LIST OF PLATES

ACKNOWLEDGEMENTS

In the almost decade of research that has resulted in this publication, following a part-time PhD pathway, there are many people to whom I am enormously grateful for their wisdom and support. I am indebted to the curators in the museums and archives I have visited over the years, sharing their time and knowledge with such generosity: Alexandra Kim and Deirdre Murphy, Historic Royal Palaces; Pauline Rushton at National Museums, Liverpool; Kevin Jones and Christina Johnson at the FIDM Museum, Los Angeles; James Sherwood at the Henry Poole archive on Savile Row; Pam Clark at the Royal Archive; Lisa Heighway and Frances Dimond, Royal Photographic Collection; Beatrice Behlen, Museum of London. A special thanks to Shelley Tobin for starting me along this career path in the first place and to Julia Fox and colleagues at the Totnes Fashion and Textile Museum for their unflagging interest.

I was lucky to receive two awards that were invaluable to my research. My thanks always to Rosemary Harden and Elaine Uttley at the Fashion Museum Bath and their generous award of the Keith Ponting Bursary. To the committee of the Veronika Gervers Foundation I offer sincerest thanks for supporting my application and awarding to me the 2011 Gervers Fellowship allowing me time and expertise at the Royal Ontario Museum, Toronto. Karla Livingston and Alexandra Palmer made this a wonderful research trip.

I had an incredibly supportive supervisory team – at the University of Southampton Professor Maria Hayward, Barbara Burman and Jane McDermid were wonderful and I cannot thank them enough.

Finally to my family. I undertook this research with a toddler and a new baby and so all thanks and love to my husband Stuart for encouraging me to continue when it seemed crazy to do so and my parents for being there always.

INTRODUCTION

For over half a century, Alexandra, Princess of Wales and Queen Consort (1844–1925), reigned as one of the most stylish women in Britain. From her twenties to her matriarchal and still youthful sixties, Alexandra's legacy has been defined through dress. She was not, according to contemporary accounts, a brilliant woman, but she was a canny one and she had an innate sense of the fitness of her appearance for any given occasion. In a new world of an increasingly powerful and influential media, Alexandra recognized that how she presented herself to the world mattered.

Now, almost 150 years later, this book offers the opportunity to study in depth and detail, some of those garments, which helped to make Alexandra one of the most popular public figures of her day. It is an interdisciplinary study using objects of textiles and dress, alongside written sources, to gain an understanding of how Alexandra's working royal wardrobe operated. There have survived, in museums across the world, a variety of gowns, shoes, shawls, fans, coats, stockings, gloves, petticoats and nightgowns that once formed part of a vast working wardrobe that required its own department within the royal household and half a dozen full-time staff just to ensure it ran smoothly. The survival of these objects, disparate and random though they are, allows an attempt at an analysis of a life through dress, for clothes 'can reflect in fabric and stitches, the factual and emotional story of their life' (Taylor, de la Haye, Thompson 2005: 14). This then forms the premise for the research which follows, the story which objects, in this case clothes, can tell of a life; the contextualization of a period of history through its surviving material culture.[1] As Ann Smart Martin, long-time champion of material culture studies, states: 'Material objects matter because they are complex symbolic bundles of social, cultural and individual meanings fused into something we can touch, see and own' (Smart Martin 1993: 141).

Why Alexandra?

From the moment she alighted from the royal yacht at Gravesend to enter Britain and marriage to the heir to the throne, Princess Alexandra of Denmark captured the hearts of a British public starved of royal youth and glamour.

Alexandra married Edward on 10 March 1863 in St George's Chapel Windsor, sealing her fate as one of the most prominent members of the British monarchy. It was in essence an arranged marriage, the couple having met in a prearranged location in Belgium at the request of the Queen Victoria to assess their compatibility, but it was to be a union which, if not a love match, at least evolved into a companionable partnership. Perhaps because her youth and beauty sat in such stark contrast to the reclusive Queen Victoria (1819–1901), Alexandra very quickly became an immensely popular public figure. Fifty years later the widowed queen Alexandra was still a public favourite as witnessed by the crowds that lined the streets of London every year for her annual Alexandra Rose Day, which, although a trial for the ageing queen, was still a testament to the enduring regard felt for her in the public consciousness.

However, less than 100 years after her death, she has become a little known consort – a footnote in the history of Edward VII's own colourful life. While scholars might acknowledge the important role played by Alexandra during her years of influence, the public perception of her is slight. A typical reaction to this research on Queen Alexandra seems to be an awareness that she was Scandinavian, thin and married to a philandering husband. In spite of the many civic reminders of her popularity in the nineteenth century – and there are many Queen Alexandra hospitals, Alexandra Roads and Alexandra Houses around the UK as well as internationally in former colonial locations – her place in the collective memory has faded. This being the case why do her surviving clothes matter? Why Alexandra? Working as an assistant within a large costume collection in the late 1990s, the donation of a number of gowns made by the couturier John Redfern in the early twentieth century set me on the path towards this project. Discovering that one of Redfern's most celebrated customers had been Queen Alexandra, I began to try to find surviving Redfern garments associated with her. While these did not in fact exist any longer I found that many other garments did. It soon became apparent, however, that there was a disparity between the objects I was discovering in museums and the traditional published biographies. Given that her popular public image making was so bound up with her appearance, those objects to have survived that were the embodiment of that public persona were stored in museums undisturbed and unresearched. Here was the clothing of a major public figure scattered around the world, their stories untold.

It can be argued that a detailed study of the clothing of the nineteenth-century super-elite is deeply unfashionable territory for an historian to embark upon, what Fine and Leopold called the description of 'every flounce, pleat, button or bow' (1993: 94). What this book reveals is so much more than that. Not only does it attempt to bridge the gap between the written history, the subject and the object but it also encompasses many classes of experience. The story would therefore not be complete without those men and women whose working lives brought them into the sphere of Alexandra's royal wardrobe.

There is no dearth of published biography about Alexandra. Several accounts were written in her lifetime, and others soon after her death and more sprinkled over the course of the twentieth century. While her appearance and often certain occasions of her dress are noted in each one, there has never been a detailed analysis of how she dressed, why she dressed as she did and the wider impact of her choice of dress. The chance to assess the material objects alongside the rich textual record in what is very much a multidisciplinary approach is still relatively new. In 1998 Valerie Steele wrote:

> Because intellectuals live by the word, many scholars tend to ignore the important role that objects can play in the creation of knowledge. Even many fashion historians spend little or no time examining actual garments, preferring to rely exclusively on written sources and visual representations. (Steele 1998: 327)

This is not just the story of Alexandra's clothes; it is the story of the life that inhabited them. Brenda Maddox wrote about some of the realities of life writing in a review for the *New York Times* in 1999: 'Initial detachment gives way to genuine sympathy after seeing someone through so much' (Maddox 1999). She did not necessarily *like* the subjects of the biographies that she had written but recognized that 'any life is interesting when looked at close up' (Maddox 1999). There have been times during the research and writing of this, when I have felt an irrational need to apologize for my choice of subject. The excesses of royal consumption and the vast sums of money spent upon the appearance of one woman were sometimes uncomfortable facts set in the wider context of nineteenth-century British society. I wasn't altogether sure how I felt about Queen Alexandra at times although I came to admire her in many ways and I felt I 'knew' her better. Trying to better understand a life via the random survival of the person in question's clothing can be an ambitious project. There are many challenges inherent in such an approach that range from access and condition of the garment, geographical location and therefore cost of access and a lack of adequate information relating to the object itself. It is tempting to apply meaning to an object when it is associated with a well-known person when in fact the significance is not so great. It is important to stress that throughout this text, assumptions made on Alexandra's clothing choices are based on the evidence available. As with so much historical discourse, narratives can change, given a different set of sources.

The surviving contents of Queen Alexandra's wardrobe were fascinating from the outset. The interrogation of the object can be a significant moment – one that Jill Lepore discovered when researching the life of the American scholar Noah Webster. Among his family papers in the Amherst College Library, she discovered an envelope containing a lock of Webster's hair: 'That lifeless, limp hair had spent decades in an envelope, in a folder, in a box, on a shelf, but holding it in the palm of my hand made me feel an eerie intimacy with Noah himself. And, against all logic, it made me feel as though I knew him – and, even less logically, *liked* him – just a bit better' (Lepore 2001: 129).

This is a biographical work although it does not cover the entirety of the life in question. The extant garments guide the biographical framework so that it is simultaneously a biography of the objects themselves. However, it has also taken a micro-historical analysis of the person and her clothing, revealing layers of social and cultural complexity involved in the managed appearance of a public figure.

Alexandra's biography has been written before, both during her lifetime and very shortly after her death. And in more recent decades there have been volumes dedicated to her either as an individual or in partnership with Edward. The more carefree childhood that she enjoyed sits in stark contrast to the rigidity of Edward's upbringing, although her Danish roots were to be the subject of great anxiety to Queen Victoria when the marriage negotiations were underway (Fulford: 1968: 53). Following their marriage she was to be subsumed by the British establishment, expected to lay aside to some degree her own national identity. The early years of the royal marriage, so scrutinized by Queen Victoria, the British press and the public alike, lived up to expectations. In spite of the queen's disquiet relating to the social whirl into which Edward and Alexandra threw themselves, the young couple quickly produced an heir and proceeded to enchant the nation with their own brand of visible, glittering monarchy so long denied to the British public. However, Edward's propensity towards boredom and a desire to be constantly entertained in lieu of a more responsible role was to test both his marriage and his relationship with his subjects (Magnus 1964: 107). The scandals that followed the Prince of Wales from the late 1860s onwards, along with the string of mistresses left in his wake, were to dispel the earlier myths of an enduring love match. If it was not true love, however, nor was it necessarily a deeply unhappy union. Displaying a pragmatism that was a feature of Alexandra's general approach to life, she came to accept her husband's failings. At times, and displayed through dress, she might distance herself from his follies. Her choice of white evening wear throughout the 1870s was a display of purity in the face of his transgression and her neat suits spoke of control where Edward's growing waistbands were indicative of excess. She might feel acutely disappointed and angry with him but by the 1880s theirs was a partnership apparently based on mutual respect, sometime frustration, and acceptance. Romantic love there may not have been but a fond companionship appears to have been the defining feature of their almost fifty-year marriage.

Alexandra's role as a mother was also one which divided family opinion. She seems to have been a more relaxed parent than Queen Victoria ever was, allowing her children a far greater degree of freedom more akin to her own childhood experiences. Sandringham was a noisy, happy family home and

Alexandra was not the distant maternal figure that Victoria arguably was. She was to become a tenacious parent as the children reached maturity. Perhaps owing to the loss of her baby in 1871 and then the death of her son Eddy in 1892, Alexandra thereafter was to be an intense presence in her children's lives. For her son George this manifested itself in an infantilized correspondence between mother and grown-up son, in which she often used language suited to a child and signed herself 'motherdear'. For her daughter Victoria it was to result in a life of spinsterhood and servitude to her fond but dominant mother. Unlike her mother-in-law, however, Alexandra could and did show her children love.

This relationship between Alexandra and Queen Victoria is one that features prominently at different points in this book. Undoubtedly there were periods of antagonism between the two women, but the records show that here too Alexandra used dress to mollify and flatter her difficult mother-in-law. From the outset she created a grey poplin gown, worn on her arrival in the UK and chosen to represent Victoria's favourite colour. She wore the royal tartan in ball gowns at Balmoral, although her description of Scotland as 'gloomy' suggests that this was a dutiful act. She patronized many of the same suppliers as Victoria as a comparison of her wardrobe accounts and Victoria's office of robes ledgers confirms. As the years passed there was a growing fondness between the two women but although Alexandra might show a willingness to compromise on occasion, she used dress also to assert her position. Her tailor-mades emphasized the slimness of which Victoria so disapproved. Of course, by 1863 when Alexandra married Edward, Queen Victoria was already growing stouter and her girth was to increase as the years passed. This may account, in part, for the disapproval she expressed towards her daughter-in-law's slender frame. Her evening gowns of Parisian manufacture flew in the face of Victoria's fiercely patriotic consumption. Alexandra presumably wanted to distance herself from the black crape of Victoria and project herself as the antithesis to Victoria's clothed body.

From the 1870s, after her childbearing years were over, the Princess of Wales coped with loss frequently – loss of hearing, loss of mobility following a debilitating bout of rheumatic fever. She suffered the loss of an idealized marriage. She suffered the loss of family members from whom she was geographically distant and then the loss of her son Albert Edward, only a month after his engagement to Princess May of Teck (Fisher 1974: 143). Throughout, she maintained her high-profile public life, attending civic events, society entertainments, travelling in the UK and abroad. For the almost forty years that she was the Princess of Wales she coupled this loss and disappointment with a busy calendar of social diversions and monarchical duty. Following Queen Victoria's death in 1901, the new queen Alexandra largely continued to be both entertaining, entertained and dutiful but with a newly regal edge. Edward took to kingship in a surprisingly effective manner with Alexandra as his majestic companion. Their relationship had reached so amenable a place that Alexandra felt able not only to acknowledge but also to joke about his mistresses.

We cannot know if such levity masked a continuing pain at his infidelity but accounts do seem to support a mutual understanding by the early twentieth century. Although the Edwardian years popularly bask in a halcyon glow, perhaps with the hindsight of the turmoil that was to follow, neither Edward nor Alexandra was carefree young monarchs. In their sixties, they still maintained a relentless schedule until Edward's death in 1910.

Although Alexandra did not play an important political or diplomatic role in the nineteenth and early twentieth centuries, it could be argued that without her the republican movement that had been growing ever stronger in the early 1860s would have flourished and gained a greater foothold in Britain: that in some sense she was the saviour of the British monarchy. In 1862 Queen Victoria was widely criticized for the perceived abandonment of her post. Alexandra's admittance into this inner circle of monarchy breathed life into the institution. As the epitome of a 'princess' her clever clothing choices meant that she was both regal as the event required, or through a general conformity of style she made herself more available as a public figure in a way that Victoria had ceased to be. In a sense Alexandra engaged with the artifice of dress as explored by Joanne Entwistle: 'Public roles as performances put a discreet distance between self and "other" and between public and private life' (Entwistle 2000:118). She used her clothing, judged on the merits of any given event or time of day, to both fit into upper-class Britain and to simultaneously stand out as a prominent public figure. It is easy now to be dismissive of so apparently passive a figure – but her role was arguably multifaceted. Civic duties brought her to the people and served to enhance her popularity. Philanthropic work and charitable causes raised awareness of areas of need. Her role was not about challenging the status quo – her position did not allow hugely reformative acts – but she could support causes and thus make a contribution towards improvement as exhibited by her interest in army nursing conditions.

As dowager queen, Alexandra's social life ceased with the loss of her husband. Aside from the occasional public occasion, she withdrew from society's gaze, lamenting the loss of her youth and secluding herself in Sandringham. The tone of her scant surviving correspondence and of those around her point to some unhappy final years during which her deafness and fragility became a burden that was hard to bear in one who had been so colourful a public character. Her death in 1925 was marked by a surge of national feeling, the notable features of her life once again featuring in the nation's press with a surfeit of memorial issues in her name.

This summary of her life arguably presents that which was already 'known' of Alexandra, as disseminated by published biographies, which begs the question: What does this book add to that biography? These facts are unassailable as the accurate events that shaped the path of Alexandra's life. However, in approaching this biography through the material culture that populated her life, an altogether more rounded picture shall emerge.

1
MANAGING THE ROYAL WARDROBE

On the day that Alexandra actually arrived ashore at Gravesend for her marriage to the future king of England, her chosen attire was not yet that of the wealthy Princess of Wales she was to become: 'Among all this new-found splendour Princess Alexandra still kept her old simplicity: … when at last the day came to leave for England she travelled in a very smart bonnet she had made herself' (Battiscombe 1969: 44). Certainly, Alexandra was at a complete loss when it came to matters of dress deemed suitable to fulfil her new role. One of Queen Victoria's most trusted ladies-in-waiting, Lady Augusta Bruce, was called upon for advice on the matter, who herself first consulted Queen Victoria; 'Three or four trains and *grandes toilettes* will, the Queen thinks, be sufficient.'[1] It soon became apparent, however, that three or four grandes toilettes, while considered sufficient in the eyes of an ageing, monochromatic monarch, was far from satisfactory for a young elegant princess in the possession of a new-found clothes allowance. Certainly by 1869, the Queen felt compelled to warn Edward and Alexandra, prior to a shopping trip to Paris: 'Pray, dear children, let it be your earnest desire not to vie in dear Alix's dressing with the fine London Ladies, but rather to be *as different as possible by great simplicity* which is more elegant.'[2] While Alexandra agreed with the notion of simplicity in dress, the quantity of such simplicity was another matter.

Shopping itself in the manner described by contemporary observers in London was impossible for so popular and easily recognizable a woman as Alexandra. In 1859, Augustus Sala's vivid depiction of one of the metropolis's principal shopping areas draws a scene of social, colourful chaos:

> Regent Street is an avenue of superfluities, a great trunk-road in Vanity Fair. Fancy watchmakers, haberdashers, and photographers; fancy stationers, fancy hosiers, and fancy staymakers; music shops, shawl shops, jewellers, French glove shops, perfumery and point lace shops, confectioners and milliners; creamily, these are the merchants whose wares are exhibited in this Bezesteen of the world. (Sala 1859: 145)

The extension of the omnibus service in the city and the migration of the upper classes to the suburbs extended both the range of shops and the means to get to them for the masses. The act of shopping itself was an ambivalent one among contemporary commentators, some of whom feared for the moral integrity of female consumers in the new department stores (Rappaport 2000: 29).

Given this debate, it could be argued that Alexandra had to play the role of an invisible consumer. In order to avoid the critics that decried 'excessive shopping' Alexandra had to consume from a distance. All of her clothes came from well-known retailers and couture houses and yet her presence as a client was not discussed in the press, preventing open criticism of conspicuous consumption.

Arthur Beavan makes a reference to the means by which Alexandra was able to look as she wished, without a trip to Regent Street. The author was allowed access to Marlborough House and the daily life of its occupants and he noted: 'She has a decided penchant for millinery. As a rule Her Royal Highness designs her own dresses: that is to say coloured pictures of the proposed gown are submitted to her, and she, with brush or pencil, alters the picture to suit her own perfect taste' (Beavan 1896: 84). Brief though this vignette is, of Alexandra 'at home', the description of her private decision making far from the public gaze is instructive. Beavan portrays the confident client, the woman who could take a design and customize it to meet her requirements. If this is indeed an accurate depiction of one of Princess Alexandra's means of acquiring her clothes, it also deals efficiently with any concerns over discretion and privacy. Presumably the dressmaker kept a dress form that matched Alexandra's measurements and, once supplied with her amended design, could undertake the commission with a minimum of fuss.

The Parisian firm of Morin Blossier supplied Alexandra with a large number of her evening dresses from the 1890s until Edward's death in 1910. Since she did not visit Paris with great regularity and there was no UK branch of the establishment, there was clearly a means by which her dresses were supplied that did not require her physical presence, especially since couturier workrooms were such busy places. One syndicated newspaper column described the workshop of Morin Blossier: 'In the corsage department is to be noted a vast wardrobe with pigeon holes, where every client has a fitted lining kept in a numbered and ticketed case.'[3] Presumably this was a common means by which wealthy clients from around the world might order gowns at a distance from the actual premises.

A single folio of Alexandra's wardrobe accounts from the year 1898 reveals the variety of patronage and the geographical spread of the retailers she frequented.[4] The page includes payments made between May and November and lists twenty-nine different payees. Of these, eight are dressmakers including Mme Leclerq-Vigourous whose address listed in trade directories is 105–109 Oxford Street, Berthe & Yeo on Somerset St and four French establishments. Five of the names appearing in the ledger can be described as more generic outfitters – Swan & Edgar who had premises in Piccadilly and on Regent St, Graham & Son found at 26 Portman Square, Woolland Bros whose large Knightsbridge store ran from 1 to 7 Lowndes Terrace, Givry & Co on 39 Conduit St and Howell & James occupying Nos.5-9 Regent St. This page alone contains entries for Brigg & Son the umbrella maker at 23 St James St, Attoff & Norman the bootmakers at 69 New Bond Street, Robert Heath the hatter found on Oxford St, the furrier Poland & Son also on Oxford St, Garrard's the jeweller at 25 & 26 Haymarket and the perfumer Piesse & Lubin at 2 New Bond Street (Figure 1.1). What this sample reveals most significantly is twofold – first, the variety of specific trades that occupied the market for dress and its associated ephemera during the period and secondly the relatively close proximity of these establishments to one another. More pertinent still in this assessment of Alexandra's shopping habits is the location of their London residence, Marlborough House, only two or three streets away from most of those suppliers listed. Not only does this begin to allow an interpretation of Alexandra's strategies of consumption but it amplifies the role of her household, relating the proximity of her home to the location of the retailers and the complexities of fetching ordered goods. Additional duties of the dresser are brought more sharply into focus through such analysis as they managed the collection of goods for the wardrobe.

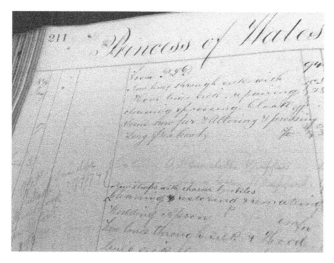

Figure 1.1 Ledger page for Alexandra Princess of Wales 1863, one of many such suppliers' records charting her clothing purchases. © James Sherwood with thanks to Henry Poole and Co.

Royal patronage

Any establishment which was favoured with the Princess of Wale's patronage was certain to capitalize on their good fortune to an unprecedented degree, from the very moment of her arrival to the shores of her new home. W. Fry & Co of Dublin quickly produced an illuminated card, adhered to which was a strip of the lilac poplin they had produced, worn as a mantle by Alexandra as she arrived in Gravesend to be met by Edward. Surmounted by the Prince of Wales feathers, the card reads: 'Part of the Original Piece of Irish Poplin (Her Majesty's Favourite Color), worn by H.R.H. the Princess of Wales when entering London, March 1863, Manufactured by W. Fry & Co of Dublin who forward patterns of Irish poplin post free.'[5] Fry & Co were certainly not going to pass up an opportunity both to herald their association with the beautiful princess and to advertise the rest of their wares.

As with all Royal weddings, gifts were received from every corner of the Empire, but here too manufacturers of textiles and items of clothing were swift in their recognition of a marketing opportunity. Not only were many of the wedding gifts listed in *The Times*, but the gifts went on display in the South Kensington Museum; a wonderful advertisement for those suppliers featured. Clabburn Sons & Crisp, the shawl manufacturers and retailers of Norwich, gave the bride a woven plaid shawl in the Danish royal colours, featuring the traditional motifs of scrolls, sprays and pines. Additionally, they produced souvenir shawls of the same design for their customers to purchase on the tide of popularity for the new Princess of Wales.[6]

The significance of royal patronage cannot be over emphasized in terms of trade benefits. In one example of Queen Victoria's ledger for the office of the robes, the mistress and clerk of the robes deal frequently with requests from suppliers to be awarded the status of a royal warrant holder. Egerton Burnett, a company featured in both Queen Victoria's accounts and Alexandra's too, wrote in 1888 making just such a request. The response was unequivocal: ' Occasional purchase of goods from a tradesman does not entitle him to a Royal Warrant which distinction is reserved for those only who habitually and continually service Her Majesty with goods.'[7] The company, however, did not despair and instead advertised in *The Queen* that they were the 'Holders of Many Royal Appointments' and sold their famous 'Royal Serges'.[8] Similarly, companies would name their products in honour of the Princess and to profit from the association the name might bring, from sewing machines to corsets (see Plate 1).

Unfortunately, the merit of a royal warrant was not a lifetime guarantee. On the death of Queen Victoria, all of her warrant holders received the following letter, which is worth quoting here in full:

> To the Warrant Holders of Her Late Majesty. I am desired by the Mistress of the Robes to inform you that [illegible] on the death of Queen Victoria, the

warrant of appointment granted to you by Her Majesty has ceased to be in force. You are at liberty to apply to Lord Colville, the Lord Chamberlain to the Queen Alexandra for a renewal of the warrant, but the application must state the grounds upon which the request is based and the names of the members of the firms.[9]

The consequences of this cessation of the right to a royal warrant must have been significant to many of the firms concerned. Possibly Alexandra would have awarded the warrants on the basis of former loyalty to the late Queen, but if nothing else there must have been a period of extreme anxiety for those suppliers affected.[10]

Dressers and the royal household

Efficient administration within the household was not in evidence when Victoria ascended the throne in 1837 and contemporary commentators drew attention to the complex bureaucracy that attempted to manage the different departments (Erskine 1916: 145). Thus, the much slicker establishment that operated around the Queen by the time the Prince and Princess of Wales were forming their own household in the 1860s had no longstanding precedent.

The reform of the royal household was in fact a task undertaken by Prince Albert in the early 1840s. The antiquated structure of the household by this date was not only costly but also ridiculously inefficient, separated into the three departments – that of Lord Chamberlain, Lord Steward and master of the horse. The roots of the departments were of medieval origin but by the time Victoria ascended the throne their roles had become mired in impractical tradition. Baron Stockmar recounted one famous example of early Victorian household etiquette. Having noted that one room in particular was always cold, he received the explanation that 'the Lord Steward lays the fire only, and the Lord Chamberlain lights it' (Hibbert 1964: 166). They were complex arrangements made more so as generations passed with no rationalization of the system. This Albert undertook in 1842, bringing order to the chaos and placing the master of the household at the head of the hierarchy, facilitating communications between all concerned.

The office of robes operated within the complex hierarchy of the royal household. While the contents of the wardrobe were paid for out of the privy purse, the practical remuneration of suppliers was overseen by the Lord Chamberlain's department, repair and laundering of garments came under the jurisdiction of the Lord Steward's department while the transport of luggage when travelling was the responsibility of the master of the horse.

The early composition of Alexandra's household had been arranged for her under the autocratic eye of Queen Victoria whose instructions were unequivocal: 'There must be no Danish lady-in-waiting to encourage her to talk in her own language; no little Danish maid even. Ladies-in-waiting and maids alike must be of sound English stock' (Fisher 1974: 47). The identity of these early 'maids' or 'dressers', as they were referred to officially, has not been recorded. Nor indeed have any direct accounts of their work in the household of the new Princess of Wales survived. Given the Queen's dominant role concerning the establishment of this household, however, it is reasonable to assume that its substance in this respect would have mirrored her own. The papers concerning the reign of Queen Victoria are both broad in scope and comprehensive in detail.

In particular, the set of volumes from the Queen's office of robes offers an invaluable insight into the day-to-day maintenance of a unique, busy, working royal wardrobe.[11] Perhaps the strongest sense inferred from the ledgers relating to the office of robes is that of a cohesive, independent department; a large cog in a larger machine running the royal household. At the head of the department, on a monthly salary of £125 was the mistress of robes. More than a purely ceremonial position, this was a role that required a commitment to the smooth running of the Queen's wardrobe. Her duties included the quarterly submission of the department's accounts and expenses to the Treasury, correspondence with existing and prospective warrant holders and suppliers, and the general administration of the dressers and wardrobe maids under her supervision. The hierarchy of the office of robes was as stringent as that experienced at all levels of the household: beneath the mistress of the robes came the groom of the robes, next the clerk of the robes, the messenger John Maclean, three dressers starting with the principal dresser to the third dresser, beneath which came the wardrobe maids.

The inclusion of a messenger salaried to the office of robes may perhaps answer questions as to some of the logistical problems faced by the large numbers of suppliers and the regular requirements of such a large wardrobe. On a monthly salary of £22, the name of John Maclean, messenger, appears on the final line of the administrative posts in the department. 'Messenger's Disbursements' would suggest that he was claiming for travelling expenses and other sundry costs incurred. The suggestion is of daily errands to collect items of clothing from specific retailers, launderers, haberdashery for the dressers, the settling of accounts and a myriad other trips into the city that simply would not have been feasible for the dressers to carry out. He was paid less than the principal dresser who commanded a monthly sum of £37, but more than the third dresser on £17.

The dressers were often hired for their relationship to other known members of the royal household, creating a tight and discreet network of employees. The principal dresser for Queen Victoria outlined in the office of robes volumes was Marianne Skerrett (see Plate 2). A devoted servant, Marianne was entrusted with numerous important tasks, in addition to her daily duties as dresser. There appears too, a salaried dressmaker, Annie Rawlins. Paid at a far lower rate (her annual salary was £64 compared to the £80 per annum of the wardrobe maid) she would presumably have carried out running repairs and adjustments to existing garments in the wardrobe.[12] It seems likely that this was a more practical solution to the perennial issue of garment repair or adaptation rather than regularly outsourcing each piece. The picture that begins to emerge from the copperplate facts and figures is that of a large and complex logistical department dedicated to the purchase, maintenance and transportation of the Queen's clothes from arranging the monograms on her linen and ordering fabric, to the correspondence with warrant holders, suppliers and government officials.

It was as expert shopper that the role of the dresser appeared to fulfil many of the practical aspects in purchasing for royalty. Marianne Skerrett dealt with many of the day-to-day requirements of her mistress's appearance and was commissioned to purchase the Honiton lace for the Princess Royal's wedding dress. Additionally:

> She dealt with the accounts of the silk mercers, milliners, suppliers of lace and embroidery, makers of shawls, linen and corsets, the woollen drapers, the hosiers and glovers, the shoemakers, tailors, plumassiers, perfumers, hatters, straw hat makers, furriers, suppliers of tartan and of Irish poplin, habit makers, soap manufacturers, jewellers, dressing case makers and whip makers who all contributed to her majesty's wardrobe. (Stoney and Weltzien 1994: 7–8)

The role of the dresser within the royal household cannot, it seems, be too highly emphasized in maintaining the appearance of her royal mistress, through her skills as dressmaker, repairer and the cleaning of delicate fabrics. A level of autonomy was expected for those women at the upper end of the wardrobe hierarchy as indicated in an instructional note to wardrobe maids in 1866: 'When new things, shoes, boots and slippers are wanted for Her Majesty they will tell Miss Dittweiler who will order them or in fact whatever is wanted for Her Majesty she will tell Miss Dittweiler of and she will order it.'[13] The implication here is that dressers might order replacement items for the royal wardrobe without recourse to the Queen herself and were trusted to carry out these repeat orders to anticipate the Queen's needs. Thus their intimate knowledge of the wardrobe's contents was invaluable.

The proximity of the dresser to her mistress both physically and mentally placed her in an almost unique position within the household. Unlike the ladies-in-waiting whose weeks in service operated under a rota system, the dressers and wardrobe maids were a permanent fixture of the wardrobe room and therefore the Queen's daily life. Their duties extended into the inner sanctum of the Queen's morning and evening ritual of washing and dressing, preparations for which were minutely outlined in a pencilled note which was presumably written in order to instruct a dresser new to her position:

After the Queen comes in the dressing room the morning I am on duty give the water tepid for the face the eyes with a little camomile tea in it. Then the ears – then the large baisen (sic) with the water for the head – then put down the glass with the water for the ears – then the teeth and then the hands. After this prepare the bath and put out the sheet – then leave the room.

After coming in take the table and the bath away. Afterwards ask if the back would be rubbed with (whisky?) or anything –

Then fasten the stays – put the petticoat over the head – then give the watches to be wound up & put the little chain with the locket & the velvet with the other locket over the head – then give the drawers – then hold the box with the rings then the crinoline & the body petticoat & the tray with the brooches – then the skirt, then the body & the keys with the thinnest chain over the neck, tie the string of the body round the waist, put the brooch in & give the watch.[14]

Contemporary accounts in which the dressers appear at the periphery confirm this elevated position. Lady Eleanor Stanley, one of Queen Victoria's maids of honour for almost twenty years, refers fairly frequently to the dressers in her letters home. On 23 December 1843 she wrote to her mother on being given her Christmas present directly from the Queen: 'It was so nice of her to give them herself instead of sending them by a dresser' (Erskine 1916: 77). In November 1860 she wrote of the often-bewildering rules bound up with mourning etiquette and again referred to the principal dresser, this time seeking her out for advice: 'We were told we might if we like make our mourning a little slighter … this seemed such a confused message that I have just been asking Miss Skerrett about it and she said she would find out, but that the Queen was in black herself this morning, and she was pretty sure HM meant to wear black this evening again' (Erskine 1916: 376). Similarly in the correspondence of Lady Lyttleton, governess to the royal children in the 1840s, there are brief references to the dressers. On 1 March 1848 she records that she received some 'gossip' from Miss Skerrett suggesting a level of regular exchange between the 'Ladies' and dressers (Wyndham 1912: 374).

The daily domain for the dressers was the wardrobe room. In Windsor Castle and Buckingham Palace these were apartments within the Queen's private quarters that had been adapted to meet the requirements of the Queen's dressing, but at Balmoral and Osborne the space had been custom built to meet the Queen's every need. At Osborne House this consisted of a large room next to the Queen's bedroom in which were three vast mahogany wardrobes (Stoney and Weltzien 1994: 9).

The arrangements at Marlborough House seemed to be a more sophisticated affair for what was, by the 1890s, a varied and complex collection of garments for Alexandra. In addition to the chintzy dressing room which by itself measured 25 × 19 feet with a large mirror inlaid into the door, Alexandra had another space set aside for storage:

Her Royal Highness's wardrobe room – that indispensable adjunct of Royalty – is on the second floor over the kitchen; that of the Prince being on the other side of the house over the offices. Ordinary people's garments can usually be stowed away in a comparatively small compass; but to be a Prince or Princess entails the possession of such a variety of State robes and uniforms that it is hardly surprising to find a large apartment devoted to the housing of them, with every imaginable contrivance for this purpose. In connection with this department, it may be mentioned that the Princess has two dressers and a wardrobe woman. (Beavan 1896: 84)

Unfortunately the author does not elaborate as to what 'every imaginable contrivance' may have consisted of.

The duties of the dresser were arduous, remaining 'on call' before the Queen had risen for the day and only resting when she had retired for the night. Frieda Arnold, one of Queen Victoria's dressers in the 1850s, often recorded her weariness in letters home: 'From early in the morning until late at night there are endless preparations to make and adornments for parties to help with, and my poor brain has to know weeks ahead on which day this or that ball, of this or that concert takes place, without my own feet ever dancing a step, or my own ears ever discerning a note of the beautiful music they play!' (Stoney and Weltzien 1994: 147). Lady Eleanor Stanley similarly described the preemptive obligations of life as a dresser when preparing for a royal visit to Cambridge. She wrote on 24 October 1843: 'The dressers start at half past five to be there to have all ready for her to make a toilette as soon as she arrives, but, as we cannot send our maids off so early, they will not arrive till two hours after us, and we must go from here in our finery' (Erskine 1916: 56).

Though the detail has survived outlining the daily duties of the dressers, information concerning the women themselves remains scant. Alexandra's dressers are shadowy figures inhabiting the historical record fleetingly. Three names are known, however: Bessie and Nettie Temple and Harriet Giltrap. The latter served Alexandra as dresser for almost forty years, taking up her post in 1886. Her name features frequently in the wardrobe accounts, her salary recorded in 1898 as £15 per quarter comprising wages and washing allowance.[15] Bessie and Nettie Temple were the daughters of a widowed Sandringham woodsman and so Alexandra rotated their duties to ensure that one of the girls was at home at all times (Battiscombe 1969: 202). The centrality of the dresser's position to the life of her royal mistress is perhaps what emerges most strongly in the brief glimpses gleaned from surviving sources. Of Bessie Temple, Battiscombe describes one occasion that serves to illustrate the bond existing between mistress and maid: 'During a Scottish visit Bessie was given a room inconveniently far from that of her mistress. In the middle of the night the Princess summoned her and for some reason or other desired her to stay in the room till morning. Bessie prepared to lie down on the sofa; the Princess, however, insisted that Bessie must sleep in her bed whilst she herself took the sofa, and it was only with the greatest difficulty that she could be persuaded of the incongruity of such an arrangement' (Battiscombe 1969: 202). In certain informal settings it becomes clear that members of Alexandra's household, particularly her dressers, were included in activities. Travel journals kept by Alexandra over a number of years record trips abroad and in these her dressers occasionally feature. On Saturday 26 August 1893 during a cruise around the fjords of Norway, Alexandra wrote: 'I fear very much that both Charlotte's & my maids Bessy have found a sweet heart amongst them, as the gentleman at arms drove Bessy! And the Sergeant Major, Hutchinson.'[16] Clearly the dresser had accompanied the party on their day trip. A later album records games on board the royal yacht while at sea, one of which involved weighing members of the party. Alexandra's snapshots captured the moment under which image she wrote: 'Maids being weighed – Miss Hill, Harriet & Netty!'[17]

Bessie Temple did indeed marry a crew member of the royal yacht and left her position to live in Gosport with her husband. It is not the last time that Bessie appears in the records, however. In 1905, delayed in Portsmouth by poor weather before another cruise, Alexandra and her daughters took one of the yacht's pinnaces to Gosport on 17 March. A newspaper clipping which the Queen pasted into the album notes: 'From first to last hardly anyone was aware that the Queen was in the town.' In her own hand underneath she wrote: 'We paid a visit to Bessie Sinclair!'[18] While this kind of detail is incidental to their duties within the royal wardrobe, what it highlights is a close working relationship between Alexandra and her dressers which of itself must have facilitated sartorial operations. Her matter of fact inclusion of Bessie, Nettie and Harriet in her journals and personal photographs places them at the heart of daily royal life and underscores their dual importance not only as trusted companion but also as the women who helped to ensure that her reputation for elegance was maintained.

The most lasting legacy of the dressers in a tangible sense was Alexandra's propensity towards giving these women items of clothing. The pattern of these survivals suggests that the recipients never intended that these items would again be worn, conferring an almost talismanic status onto the object. They were relics of their position to be treasured and handed down. Two of the tailored suits in the collections of the FIDM came via descendants of Mrs Giltrap although they are no longer complete, but the more ornate jackets were kept and stored in honour of their royal association. Thus it is thanks to the dressers that so many of Queen Alexandra's garments have survived today, finally donated by their descendants to museums on both sides of the Atlantic.

Royal laundry

Records demonstrate that dressers and wardrobe maids were indeed responsible for a degree of garment cleaning within the royal wardrobe. A document dated March 1866 in Queen Victoria's papers declares of wardrobe maids' duties: 'The one off duty will have to iron and to clean Her Majesty's dress and if there is anything wanting as mending or buttons to be put on, will do it.'[19] Maintaining the cleanliness of a wardrobe as extensive as Alexandra's required time and knowledge. Christina Walkley and Vanda Foster's seminal publication *Crinolines and Crimping Irons* considered in detail the array of cleaning methods available to Victorian women in the pursuit of clean clothes (Walkley and Foster 1978). Through extensive research of household manuals and advice columns the authors were able to demonstrate the varied processes adopted in the care of clothing and accessories to both keep them clean and prolong their wear. The advice given reveals an understanding of a complex range of chemical and domestic ingredients. Dresses were vigorously brushed to remove mud from the hem. The serge suits with which Alexandra was to become particularly associated might also be spot cleaned while the mud from riding habits might require only extensive brushing. This preoccupation with spot and stain cleaning or brushing main garments was simply that surface dirt was more likely to be the issue than body odour. The generous amounts of underwear worn by a woman in Alexandra's position protected these objects from being soiled as a result of being worn next to the skin.

Accessories too could be effectively cleaned 'at home'. The insides of shoes might be sponged periodically with ammonia to prevent odour. Lead sugar, alum, gin, stale bread, chloride of zinc, Epsom salts, cold coffee, dry bran, soda, benzene and turpentine were all elements that featured regularly in popular publications through direct application, steaming, brushing, infusing and ironing.

Accounts also show, however, that the laundering and care of certain elements of the wardrobe was outsourced to other establishments, either as part of a large-scale laundry operation or because the object itself required specialist care. A royal laundry was purpose built by Prince Albert in 1846, situated at Kew Foot Road in Richmond. A conservation study of the area notes that 'the miniature train brought the Queen's washing every day into Richmond Station from London, Windsor and Osborne House and all other royal households excluding Balmoral. It is claimed that 700,000 items a year or 1.5 tons of laundry a day were handled here.'[20] This laundry handled the linens of the royal family from bed linen to undergarments. A small bill in one of the volumes of Queen Victoria's Extraordinary Bills series reveals how such a quantity of washing could be sorted between households. The practice of laundry marking was a common one during the period, a number and set of initials being embroidered onto the object to identify ownership. Within the royal family there was the addition of a monogram, which Walter Capper, linen draper, queries in his invoice (Plate 3). As well as his order for a number of sheets and pillowcases he includes a sketch of the Queen's monogram for approval before his embellishment of the linen.[21] Alexandra also had monogrammed articles of clothing and accessories such as chemises, camisoles, drawers and handkerchiefs as a means of identifying such generic items, examples of which still survive. Within her accounts there are also payments made to two other laundry firms – Rogers & Cook and Davis & Son. While the royal laundry continued to service the royal household until its closure in the 1920s, it may have been more expedient to have another launderer located more centrally. Rogers & Cook were situated at 274 South Lambeth Road in a Georgian building which still stands today and so was much closer than the Richmond establishment.

While in April 1863 the quarterly bill from the royal laundry amounted to £1090.13.4,[22] Queen Alexandra forty years later was making regular but relatively modest payments to Rogers & Cook, such as that of July 1903 for the sum of £5.1.6d.[23] The disparity between these amounts would suggest that Alexandra patronized Rogers & Cook for smaller, more singular tasks.

Given the range of specialist garments whose construction might comprise a range of different fibres and embellishments, certain retailers were paid additional services for the care and cleaning of specific items. Queen Alexandra regularly patronized G Poland & Son, furrier by Royal Appointment, their name featuring with some frequency within the pages of the wardrobe accounts. In addition to purchasing furs, Alexandra also paid Poland & Son for their care. Similarly, Ede & Ravenscroft, the company famed for its ceremonial robe making, was paid the same amount in 1904.[24] Establishments such as Haywards the 'lacemen' who also appear with some regularity in the accounts advertised both their expensive lace and embroidery wares and their ability to expertly clean such goods, a service Alexandra as Princess and Queen perhaps made use of. The picture which begins to emerge from the records and garments is one of ordered variety. Rather than rely on a single establishment to oversee the cleaning and garment care, the dressers and wardrobe maids within Alexandra's household availed themselves of the assorted laundering options from the well-established royal laundry to more local and specialist businesses, thus catering for the full complexity of their mistress's wardrobe.

The true scope of this royal wardrobe has all but disappeared. However, those objects to have survived, when studied in tandem with letters, memoirs, business accounts and photographs, do allow a pattern of consumption to emerge. It is a picture of the super-elite of the late nineteenth century and its many cultural characteristics, surprisingly neglected in academia; of the public and private identities of Alexandra's clothed royal body; of the performativity of royal dress under the frequent scrutiny of the public gaze; and of the agency of a woman in Alexandra's position to dress in such a way that met both wider expectations and satisfied her own private self. Most striking of all, the scrutiny of the royal household, the office of robes and the people employed in the supply and care of Alexandra's clothing reveal what is, in effect, a great machine. All of its constituent parts, with Alexandra at the centre, operated in conjunction with one another from commission to purchase to wear, use and repair. Alexandra, as Princess of Wales and later Queen, was the elegant swan gliding, elegantly clad, on the surface of her public life while beneath her the hard work of her supply chain and household propelled her on her way.

2
ENGAGEMENT AND MARRIAGE

The wedding ceremony

At eight o'clock on 10 March 1863, Windsor's bells started to peal around the town and by ten o'clock the special platforms erected for spectators were filled. The guests were readying themselves at the temporary reception and robing areas by the west door, through which they all began to file into the nave of the chapel. At 11.30 the full state ceremony began. A great procession of carriages arrived outside the chapel as it began to fill with the royalties and dignitaries of Europe. An hour later, a blast of trumpets heralded the arrival of the Prince of Wales, resplendent in his Garter Knight's mantle over a scarlet general's tunic. Magnus wrote that Edward was 'plump and nervous, but radiant' (Magnus 1964: 67). Finally, the longest fanfare of the morning announced the arrival of the bridesmaids and the bride. The bridesmaids were not described favourably. Lady Geraldine Somerset wrote that they were 'eight as ugly girls as you could wish to see',[1] while Lord Granville recorded in a letter to the Duchess of Manchester that 'the bridesmaids looked well – when their backs were turned' (Kennedy 1956: 210). The ceremony was conducted along traditional lines before the archbishop of Canterbury pronounced the final benediction: 'Band, organ and choir joined in Beethoven's "Hallelujah Chorus" from "The Mount of Olives". In a stream of waving plumes and flaming jewels, the whole pageant swept out of the choir at a far less measured pace than that with which it had entered".' After the wedding breakfast inside the castle, the newly married couple left for their honeymoon at Osborne House. Alexandra, in all her bridal finery, was seen for little over an hour' (Maas 1977: 37).

William Russell, *The Times* correspondent charged with the reporting of all subjects royal, closed his long and colourful account of the royal wedding with an hyperbolic summary of the day's significance: 'Thus ends, without a single incident to mar their harmony, the heartiest and most universal rejoicings that we have ever had to record ... the marriage of the Prince of Wales has far more than an ephemeral or personal interest and must be ever memorable in the history of this country' (Russell 1863: 23). His words were the culmination of months of planning and negotiating, the details of which were reported daily in *The Times* – sometimes one or two sentences only, conveying the very latest available detail from the moment the engagement was announced. Although the engagement was agreed upon in September 1862, Queen Victoria delayed the official announcement to her government until November (Figure 2.1). The reason behind the delay was never discussed, but the impending nuptials were circulating in the press from October onwards. Swept along by the spirit of the day, Russell nevertheless captured the sense of a new and vibrant energy this union would bring to the British monarchy.

Figure 2.1 Edward and Alexandra's image taken from one of a series that was commissioned in recognition of the couple's engagement in 1862 (*carte de visite*, author's own collection).

Patriotic planning and patronage – The wedding preparations

Given Alexandra's spirited approach to the planning of her and her ladies' coronation garb forty years later, it is tempting to suggest that, as a relatively unworldly nineteen-year-old faced with the indomitable matriarchy of Queen Victoria, the Princess Alexandra would have accepted with passivity the preparations taking place around her; that her emergence as a matriarch in her own right later on was a linear path from inactive to proactive along an arc of experience. Certainly in the face of only a four-month engagement the speed with which such matters had to be completed required all the weight of the respective royal households but a close analysis of the records, alongside the survival of the dress and accessories themselves, offers some evidence to challenge that path.

The precedent had already been set for Queen Victoria's 'hands on' approach to such matters only five years earlier with the marriage of her eldest daughter Vicky to the Prussian heir. Vicky herself recalled, while assembling her own daughter's trousseau: 'How well I remember all the trouble you took about mine, and how it touched me that you should see into each little detail yourself.'[2]

There are, indeed, at least two contemporary accounts which appear to reinforce the autocratic approach taken by the Queen subsequently for the marriage of her son and heir. Lady Walburga Paget wrote in her memoirs of the attention the Queen gave to the impending event that 'the Queen with her wonderful forethought and knowledge, made all the arrangements for the marriage. I possess a large batch of letters from General Grey, the Queen's Private Secretary, which are simply transcripts of her wishes and orders, and in which she goes into all details with the utmost clearness and method' (Paget 1912: 97). Although the trousseau is not referred to explicitly, the implication is clear that Queen Victoria's wishes were expected to be deferred to in all respects. Her opinion was sought concerning aspects of the trousseau's composition. On the Queen's behalf, Lady Augusta Bruce replied to an enquiry made by Alexandra: 'Three or four trains and *grandes toilettes* will, the Queen thinks, be sufficient.'[3] That the Queen was taking these decisions is of note in itself, but her advice here is even more significant, given the vastly more comprehensive trousseau arranged for Vicky in 1858:

> Along with twelve evening gowns, six ball dresses, three court dresses and fifteen miscellaneous gowns, there was enough velvet silk and summer lawn folded into her trunk to make at least forty more elaborate ensembles. Underwear was ordered by the gross – twelve dozen shifts, twelve dozen pairs of drawers, twelve dozen handkerchiefs (embroidered and plain) and

twelve dozen nightdresses, plus eight dozen petticoats, four dozen dressing
gowns, quantities of mourning dresses, shoes, stockings, shawls, bonnets,
caps, mantillas, mackintoshes and so forth. (Pakula 1997: 75)

Alexandra's position was of course that of daughter-in-law rather than daughter
which might explain Queen Victoria's reluctance to spend too extravagantly.
However, given that Alexandra was to become the Princess of Wales and the
second most prominent female member of the royal family after the Queen, her
recommendation looks paltry next to Vicky's capacious trunk. Of course Victoria
the widow in 1862 was a very different woman to Victoria the wife in 1858, and
so perhaps Alexandra's trousseau was to lack the joie de vivre that Vicky enjoyed
before the death of Albert.

   An early, and it could be argued, authorized biography of Queen Alexandra
appears to contradict Lady Paget's assertion of the future mother-in-law's
complete absorption with the task at hand (Tooley 1902: 23). 'The overwhelming
sorrow of Queen Victoria made it impossible for her to take the personal interest
in her son's young *fiancée* and the preparations for her wedding which she
would have done in happier times' (Tooley 1902: 23). Queen Victoria's grief, writ
large in both contemporary records and in the popular histories of her reign,
was very real, but there is too much evidence of her intervention over matters
as varied as guests, the final selection of the wedding gown and Alexandra's
new ladies-in-waiting to support the idea of Queen Victoria as an uninterested
observer. While Victoria may have believed that she was deferred to in the
decision making as wedding preparations advanced, the reality was perhaps a
different matter.

   While Alexandra doubtlessly lacked the confidence and experience of a
prominent royal figure before her marriage, records suggest that her role in the
marriage preparations was not a passive one. In November 1862, Princess
Alexandra was invited to Windsor for a short stay to become more acquainted
with the Queen and her immediate family. It was here that the execution of
the trousseau began, under the supervision of Alexandra's friend and cousin
Princess Mary Adelaide. Mary was a great favourite of the British public and
she was to maintain her proximity to the throne, when her own daughter, May,
married Alexandra's son George in 1894:

   The friends spent many happy hours together selecting and planning the
   trousseau, the greater part of which was made in London of goods of British
   and Irish manufacture, with the exception of the lingerie which was prepared
   in Copenhagen and Princess Alexandra was greatly assisted in her choice
   of things by the exquisite taste and experienced judgement of the Princess
   Mary. One could not imagine a more delightful counsellor at such a time.
   (Tooley 1902: 23)

The suggestion here is clearly that Alexandra had more than a little influence over the selections for her trousseau. The cost of the bulk of the trousseau appears to have been met by Queen Victoria according to the biographer Duff: 'Finance was a curb on the independence of the Danes, the wedding expenses being on a scale beyond their vision and experience. The Prince of Wales sent Alexandra £3000 for her trousseau and £15,000 in jewels' (Kennedy 1956: 215). That Alexandra was sent this sum of money for her trousseau implies that she and her family retained control over it, asking Queen Victoria's advice over certain of its aspects while maintaining the greater degree of influence over its contents. The Queen was already very admiring of Alexandra's approach to her appearance and asked her to dress more generally as she became more acquainted with the young princess. A contemporary letter seen by the biographer David Duff recorded an early conversation between Alexandra and the Queen. During a visit to Osborne House in November 1862 the Danish princess came down to breakfast dressed in her customary simple jacket: 'My dear', said the Queen, 'you seem very fond of jackets. How is it you *always* wear a jacket?' 'Well', said Alexandra, 'I like them; and then, you see a jacket is *so economical*! You can wear different skirts with it, and I have very few gowns, having to make them all myself. My sisters and I have no lady's maid, and have been brought up to make all our own clothes' (Duff 1980: 47).

The arrangement of the trousseau was to become an operation on two fronts. In London, Princess Mary Adelaide continued to oversee the smooth running of the plans, which she and Alexandra had begun to make in November 1862. On the 25th of that month, she recorded in her journal: 'I saw Mrs James with patterns of Honiton and modèles of gowns for Alix's trousseau.' And nearer the great day, on 25 February 1863, she records briefly: 'Saw Mrs James about the orange blossom for Alix' (Kinloch-Cooke 1900: 398). Meanwhile in Copenhagen the lingerie had been commissioned from a local firm: 'The order for the Princess's wedding trousseau was given to Mr Levysohn of Copenhagen, and so prompt was he in the execution of this honoured duty that the whole was ready in the incredibly short space of four months' (Anon 1863: 16). As a result of his illustrious work for the Princess, Mr Levysohn's premises enjoyed a degree of celebrity in Denmark in the months preceding the wedding: 'Danish ladies flocked day by day to the establishment of Mr Levysohn where the bridal lingerie was on view. Each article was embroidered with the bride's initials below a representation of the English crown. No machine was allowed to touch these fairy-like garments and several hundreds of women and girls were employed on the fine stitching and embroideries' (Tooley 1902: 46). So, with the majority of the costly items of dress in all probability ordered from the UK and the many undergarments, nightwear and accessories stitched in Denmark, the trousseau was finally assembled in its entirety at Windsor. (See Figure 2.2.) The trousseau was laid out in a room adjacent to St George's

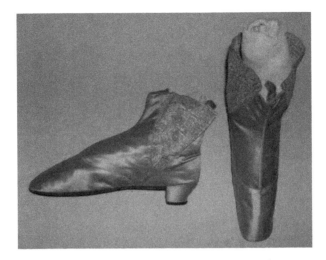

Figure 2.2 Cream silk satin boots made as part of Alexandra's trousseau in either late 1862 or early 1863, The Metropolitan Museum of Art, Gift of Miss Irene Lewisohn 1937, www.metmuseum.org.

Chapel before the wedding day, along with the gifts. It is unclear whether or not anyone outside the court was allowed to see the display. Certainly members of the press must have been given some access judging by the lists published in the newspapers.

Honiton lace

Sadly there are no known records now on the creation of the silver-tissue wedding dress commissioned from Mrs James of Hanover Square. However, there is a detailed account of the manufacture of a feature of this dress which was arguably more visible than the woven silk gown itself. Amid all the frenzy of planning and preparation, a quiet corner of East Devon in the South West of England saw the creation of this most visible and nationally symbolic feature of Alexandra's wedding dress – the swathes of Honiton lace which were to cover the gown almost entirely. These flounces are now a part of the royal collection and so are kept separately to the wedding dress. Queen Victoria herself had commissioned a large flounce of Honiton lace for her own wedding in 1840. The impact of such esteemed patronage was reported at length in the local press:

> The lace intended for Her Majesty's Bridal Dress, though properly called Honiton lace, was really worked at the village of Beer, which is situated near the sea coast, about ten miles from Honiton. It was executed under the direction of Miss Bidney, a native of the village, who went from London, at

Figure 2.3 Honiton lace was enjoying a resurgence thanks to royal patronage. By the early twentieth century it contributed to the tourism industry of Devon as this 1906 postcard demonstrates (author's own collection).

the command of Her Majesty, for the express purpose of superintending the work. More than two hundred persons were employed upon it from March to November, during the past year. These poor women derive a scanty subsistence from making lace, but the trade has lately so declined that had it not been for the kind consideration of Her Majesty in ordering this dress they would have been destitute during the winter. No-one can form an idea of the gratitude they express who has not heard it from their own lips. (Cited in Inder 1971: 5)

Handmade lace had fallen out of fashion from the beginning of the nineteenth century as advances in technology produced the first machine-made laces. Now in the wake of the Queen's patronage, the Honiton workers found themselves in demand once more. By the middle of the century, the manufacture of Honiton lace had become larger than a simple cottage industry (Figure 2.3). John Tucker, whose firm won the commission of Princess Alexandra's wedding lace, employed more than 500 people at the height of his trade. Arguably it was this attention in 1862, only months before the wedding, which led to Tucker's royal commission.

The Tucker family of Devon, charged with the commission of the royal lace, understood the importance of handmade lace keeping pace with changing fashions if it was to continue to flourish as Samuel Tucker, John's son, demonstrated in a letter to his sister in December 1862: 'I fancy your last purls are very nice but they are not quite the style now in fashion, if very nice. All should now be made in the Greek pattern kind and lines and squares somewhat the same as shown in enclosed paper. Please draw some as described and let me have up a sample of each as soon as you can.'[4]

Mary, John's eldest daughter, was particularly skilled in lace design and it was she who designed and oversaw the completion of Alexandra's lace: 'It consisted of four tiers of flounces to be worn round the bridal dress, each bordered by a design of cornucopias from which emerged sprays of rose, shamrock and thistle. There was also matching lace for the train, veil and handkerchief' (Tomlinson 1983: 29). Since Mary Adelaide's journal entries reveal a significant consultation between Alexandra and herself concerning the content of the trousseau and given the evidence for her continued supervision of its progress, the choice of pattern for the lace must also therefore have been approved by Alexandra. Working within the remit of British manufacture, Alexandra ensured that traditional emblems were the most significant feature of the pattern, revealing her acknowledgement of its requirements while simultaneously steering its execution.

On 28 February William Wills, a cousin and agent working out of their London shop at 1 Percy Street wrote to Mary to confirm receipt of their most significant order: 'I have yours of the 27th instant and the box with Royal Lace in to hand and I think looking most beautiful and I hope with you will give satisfaction indeed I do not see how it can do otherwise.' William goes on: 'Can't you come up to see the dress when finished. Perhaps it can be arranged for you to see it on the Princess.'[5] It seems unlikely that this ever happened given the proximity to the day of the wedding and a subsequent letter from her brother Samuel, describing the days leading up to the event. However, the satisfaction anticipated by William in his letter to Mary appears to have been more than adequately achieved. Princess Mary Adelaide was summoned to view the finished article, as she recorded in her journal on 3 March: 'I was called away from my singing lesson with Pinsuti to see the wedding lace and veil for Alix which is of Honiton manufacture and quite beautiful!' (Kinloch-Cooke 1900: 407).

Beneath the lace, the scale of the skirt itself was indicative of Alexandra's own taste. Reporters had early testified to Alexandra's apparent dislike of the very wide cage crinolines. Although the diameter began to shrink by 1864, Alexandra – the bride at the wedding of the year in 1863 – was not afraid to buck the prevailing trend and opt for a vastly more modest silhouette, the bulk of the fullness falling towards the train at the back of the skirt. This preempted by some years the fashionable line of the late 1860s and was to be an early indicator of Alexandra's determination to wear that which both suited and appealed to her. An early London Museum catalogue asserts: 'The dress is in advance of contemporary fashion and anticipates the style of 1870. Queen Alexandra disliked the crinoline fashion and was a strong advocate of a change of style' (Anon 1935: 154). Since the early collection of royal dress that was kept at the then London Museum (now Museum of London) was donated or lent by Queen Mary, this places some authority to the claim.

From the very moment of her alighting from the boat at Gravesend prior to the wedding ceremony itself, Alexandra understood and utilized dress as a tool to win popularity and acceptance. Russell once again reported for *The Times*: 'An instance of the desire of Her Royal Highness to consult the interests of the people of her adoption, and to prepare a pleasant surprise for the Queen was mentioned as resting upon authentic detail. Ascertaining some time ago the favourite colour of Her Majesty, silver grey, she caused a poplin dress of that shade to be manufactured at the well known establishment of Messrs. Fry of Dublin, and appeared in it for the first time on the occasion of her entry' (Russell 1863: 40). It was a significant moment. The furore which accompanied Alexandra's arrival in Britain – the thousands who gathered to see her along the route, into the city of London until their final destination at Windsor, and then the throng of family waiting at the castle meant that Alexandra's appearance on that day was a powerful indication of the role she was set to play. In this, the sense of Alexandra's agency over her own appearance at the start of her new life becomes clearer. A more literal example of Alexandra's control over and choice of her dress, though minor, nonetheless substantiates a more proactive role. On Princes Alexandra's departure from Copenhagen, Lady Paget recalled: 'She wore a dress of brown silk with white stripes and one of those natty little bonnets which seemed to sit better on her head than on anybody else's. Even in those early days I was struck by the extreme neatness and taste of her attire' (Paget 1912: 97).

   At this early stage she knew which battles she could win, and those in which she could bow gracefully in defeat. She chose wisely in co-opting Princess Mary Adelaide to oversee her trousseau as it took shape in England, having spent time in the decision making of its contents in November. She left the execution of the British lace in capable hands, realizing that in this she had little choice but to acquiesce to the wishes of her future mother-in-law but she asserted her preferences for the line her gown should take underneath the profusion of lace. She retained control of the lingerie content of the trousseau, ensuring that at least a little of her own nation's workmanship was represented. She then, as the preparations drew to a close, ensured that the much anticipated first sight of her both from the perspective of the masses and the more intimate welcome of her new family should be as advantageous as possible, clothed as she was both in the Queen's favourite colour and a British-made fabric. Her early induction into the British royal family was not then a tale of sartorial submission, but of quiet and gentle manipulation; of a young woman beginning to understand more fully the impact of her appearance.

Princess Alexandra's wedding dress

Alexandra's wedding dress was contemporarily described by the usually waspish diarist Lady Geraldine Somerset as in 'trés bon gout, light, young and royal'[6] (Figure 2.4).

   Today its description is more problematic. Within days of the wedding, the dress was given over to the dressmaker Mme Elise to be made over into an

Figure 2.4 The profusion of lace was captured much more clearly than the underlying silver tissue of Alexandra's wedding dress (wedding photograph *carte de visite*, Mayall & Co, author's own collection).

evening dress – most probably as a means of enlarging the princess's small trousseau. When William Frith, the artist commissioned to produce the official portrait of the ceremony asked to see the dress in order to paint it he was informed that it had already been cut up and altered.[7] Mrs Bruce, woman of the Bedchamber to the new Princess of Wales, reassured Frith that 'dresser promised to send you all she could' (Maas 1977: 64).

In its current incarnation the wedding dress consists of a bodice and separate skirt. Made from ivory silk, the fabric of both is woven with a silver weft. The bodice is decorated with a panel of vertically ruched net at the neckline to which is attached a deep flounce of lace. The skirt of moiré silk is unadorned and the original skirt was covered with flounces of Honiton lace, all of which is now part of the royal collection and therefore stored at a different location to the rest of the dress. The lining of the skirt features an additional flounce of lace, but in this instance it is a piece of Brussels lace, of which more later.

At the time of the wedding, the ensemble was somewhat different. A closer study of the wedding photographs reveals that the bodice appears to consist of a series of horizontal pleats in the silk, such as many contemporary evening gowns exhibited, while Frith's representation on his vast canvas commissioned by Queen Victoria illustrates the bodice as it is seen today. The skirt presents more of a challenge. Under the copious swathes of Honiton lace in both the photographs and Frith's oil portrait, it is almost impossible to ascertain the exact nature of the silk that lies beneath or how the train may have been constructed. All that may be surmised with any degree of accuracy is that the shape as it appears in the contemporary images and the shape as constructed for the purpose of exhibition is very similar, so that presumably this second skirt, made up from the original train, followed closely the pattern of the first.

The making over of Princess Alexandra's wedding dress so soon after the event is an important element in the tale that such a garment can tell, articulated by Linda Baumgarten in her paper on the significance of altered historical clothing: 'A surviving artefact is full of evidence, not just about its original manufacture, but about its continuing history as well … it speaks eloquently about the nature of human history as a continuum' (Baumgarten 1998: 42).

The path to the creation of Alexandra's wedding dress in the first place was not without issue: 'Princess Alexandra, who had been given a beautiful dress of Brussels lace by King Leopold of the Belgians as a wedding present, found it was considered quite inappropriate for use as a wedding dress' (Arch and Marschner 2003: 10). Leopold, uncle to Queen Victoria, presented Alexandra with the lace dress as part of her wedding gifts from him. It was Queen Victoria's decision that the dress should be of British manufacture and so Leopold's dress was not that which Alexandra wore on 10 March. Instead, the dress of English silk was made by the popular dressmaker Mrs James of Hanover Square. This, then, was the dress so promptly remodelled after the ceremony, much to Mr Frith's frustration. It was not an unusual step to take at this time. Throughout the nineteenth century, many women reused their wedding dress, either through its alteration after the day or through the choice of a coloured dress which was more practical afterwards (Tobin 2003: 48). Social engagements of the new couple in the months following their marriage often record the Princess in white. Lady Knightly described Alexandra at a reception as 'a bit of a thing, with a white gown and a white face, two curls and a tiara' (Cartwright 1915: 36). The biographer Tisdall records similarly: 'The first great official function was a magnificent ball at the Guildhall at which the Prince of Wales was to be presented with the Freedom of the City. Throughout the evening Alix, in plain white satin, was followed intently by every eye' (Tisdall 1953: 58–9). At a ball given by the Brigade of Guards on 26 June in honour of the newly married couple, Alexandra again favoured a lighter palette: 'All the ladies looked beautiful and none more beautiful than Alix, a jewelled diadem glittering on her head, her gown of white lace over mauve looking little like the half-mourning it was supposed to be' (cited in Fisher 1974: 56).

White was, of course, an appropriate colour for the period of mourning in which Queen Victoria's court was still entrenched but it suited the purity and freshness of the new princess's image very well. It was also useful as a means of augmenting her trousseau, which had been criticized in some circles for its sparseness.

If indeed Alexandra's trousseau was smaller than some might have imagined and given the number of social appearances that were expected of the young couple in those early months of their marriage, the reuse of her wedding dress and presumably the going-away dress, which was also recorded as a white gown, was an important addition to her wardrobe.

One of the most interesting features of the remodelled skirt as it exists now can be found hidden, maybe surreptitiously, attached to the lining. A broad band of lace has been attached to the centre front lining of the skirt – it is not a swathe of the Honiton lace which was so profuse elsewhere on the dress, but is rather a band of fine Brussels lace, distinct by its stylized flower motifs. Its position means that it serves no functional purpose and is hidden from view. It is tempting to speculate that this lace may be associated with the sumptuous lace dress given to Alexandra as a wedding present from uncle Leopold, but forbidden as a wedding gown in her new home. If so, its inclusion here, concealed from sight, might hint at just a little subversiveness, that after all her wedding dress, although in not exactly the same state as originally worn, yet contained a vestige of Europe's finest needlework, hidden beneath the tiers of British lace. It is impossible to verify that this was the case but is one interpretation only made possible through a close engagement with the material culture itself. Previous biographers have not ever looked at Alexandra's wedding dress or indeed any of her other surviving garments and so this piece of evidence remained hidden from them. Neither contemporary descriptions nor wedding photographs or portraits could reveal so small, yet possibly so interesting a detail. Thus, in spite of the many familiar images of the wedding day and the dress itself and the extent to which the garment was already 'known', its analysis at first hand 'told' more. It told me that the silver weft woven into the cream silk glittered, in spite of the tarnish of 150 years, and so must have appeared on the day to shimmer in the light. The surreptitious stitching of a seemingly random piece of European lace onto the dress lining which does not serve a practical purpose may 'tell' of an early attempt by Alexandra to achieve a small measure of control, albeit hidden from view at this time. More practically, the dimensions recorded from the wedding dress begin to shape Alexandra in a physical sense. While countless descriptions attest to her slenderness, the waist and skirt measurements reveal that in addition to her slim figure, she was reasonably tall: the bodice measured 17 inches across the shoulders and she had a 21.5-inch waist. The skirt was 42 inches from waistband to hem. Photographs show that the skirt just brushed the ground at the front. While such basic observations may seem incidental to a serious academic study, the benefits of making and drawing upon these figures is eloquently described by Kay Staniland who remarks that the object 'offers an actual contact with its original owner, an outer skin which is still strongly permeated with the bodily characteristics of that personality' (Staniland 1997: 64). In other words, the dress can tell part of the story of its wearer.

Conclusion

For decades, the expectations of dress history were bound up in the minutiae of shape and form – the fullness of a skirt, the tightness of a sleeve – the 'hemline history' that placed surviving objects into their chronological place. While this

Figure 2.5 Alexandra's going-away dress was a bridal affair as so many of the dresses in the early months of her marriage were – a white dress with veiled hat. The photograph captures Alexandra facing the photographer while Edward and Victoria both look away (*carte de visite*, author's own collection).

kind of study was invaluable in contextualizing garments for the generations of historians that followed, material culture methodologies can demand more of historic dress than simply its place in time. Taking this important sartorial example from significant events in Alexandra's life, a close study of the objects offers the opportunity to draw conclusions about the wearer and the occasion at which they were worn that would otherwise have been impossible. The impact of fabric, embellishments and objects hidden from view enables the observer to add considerably to the biographical record. Alexandra's choice of metallic thread in her wedding gown is instructive, indicating her recognition of her central role at this occasion and how she wished to be visible in a most literal sense. Her wish for sartorial visibility during busy public events apparently fascinated her, the firm of Woodhouse and Rawson announcing in their 1888 catalogue that they had supplied Alexandra with their patented electric jewellery: 'a Complete Set, superior, for Ball Room purposes' (Dillon 2001: 77). Mrs Cornelius Vanderbilt had already made the wearing of an electric dress somewhat notorious with her 'Electric Light' ball gown of 1883. There is no recorded occasion at which Alexandra was described as wearing her electric jewellery, however. In the case of a nineteen-year-old bride, the surreptitious addition of fine European lace, hidden from the public gaze but known to the wearer, hints at the more steely side to Alexandra – the side that was prepared to act on her own initiative at the same time as placating the force of a mother-in-law such as Queen Victoria. The alterations most apparent on the wedding gown tell their own tale; a tale of necessity over sentiment and of pragmatism in the face of the social whirlwind that was to follow the royal wedding.

A focused case study of this kind has also prompted an evaluation of Alexandra's 'agency' in appearance. It becomes more apparent that Alexandra did not take a passive role in the preparations for her wedding but quietly negotiated her way through the maze of royal protocol, public expectations, private wishes and the ever-present spectre of her still-grief-stricken mother-in-law to be. The wedding and her appearance at it set the tone for the years that were to follow. The young Alexandra already demonstrated that conspicuous display would be a feature of her public persona, using her appearance to draw admiration from a wider audience in a way that Queen Victoria had long since ceased to do. It was quietly done, however. She was able to achieve her goals discreetly while maintaining amiable relationships with all concerned along the way. She entered St George's Chapel in her sparkling silver and lace gown as a relatively unknown Danish royal. She left as Princess of Wales (Figure 2.5).

3

EVENING AND COURT DRESS

By far the largest grouping of garment type to have survived from Alexandra's wardrobe is that which can be defined as evening or formal court dress, the most conspicuous of sartorial statements (Figure 3.1). Stored in museums around the world they consist of an array of silk, satin, chiffon, sequins, diamante and beadwork. They perhaps occupy a space which is arguably the most queenly in an inventory of her clothing. Certainly it was the clothing in which she was at her most public. Not only was she observed by those in attendance at any given occasion but these were the events that were reported in the court circular and so her appearance was disseminated more widely. Evenings out, whether ceremonial, official or for private entertainment, were a key factor in Edward and Alexandra's annual calendar from the very point of their marriage in 1863 until Edward's death forty-seven years later.

Dress has long been bound by rules that demarcate appropriate garments for different times of day. The observance of these rules and what it meant in practice for those adhering to them has been explored in some detail in exhibitions, highlighting the role of fashionable dress in following these societal dictates.[1] Molly Sorkin, curator of an exhibition at FIT, New York, describes the ever-changing rules governing changes of dress: 'Sometimes they operate as a flexible set of guidelines, at other times as strictly observed etiquette that is continually reinforced in the fashion press' (Sorkin 2009). The second half of the nineteenth century fell within the latter category, bound as it was by a rigid code of dress whose nuances required careful negotiation. A single volume of *The Queen*, bound to contain six months' worth of the weekly periodical dating from 1882, contains regular illustrations of the different degrees of evening dress, that include dinner dress, reception dress, home dinner toilette, evening demi-toilette, concert toilette, evening dress and ball dress.[2] In practical terms the differences were based around sleeve length, neckline and ornamentation and the variations of these determined the type of occasion attended. Contemporary etiquette books advised, down to the last detail, the exact degree of variation expected, although it might be argued that these instructional manuals operated

Figure 3.1 Alexandra, Princess of Wales in full court dress, 1888, taken by Walery, 164 Regent Street, London, Royal Collection Trust/© Her Majesty Queen Elizabeth II 2016.

as an aspirational guide to those unfamiliar with certain social expectations. It is not easy to ascertain who was reading etiquette manuals. They may indeed have been read by the up and coming middle-class women fearful of making a social faux-pas. They were perhaps useful volumes for a lady's maid to ensure that their mistresses were appropriately attired at all times or they were perhaps studied by the upper-class ladies whose every social move they expected to be scrutinized. However, what they do demonstrate is the importance attached to appropriate evening attire for those women whose social position required their attention to such details.

One such manual from the mid-nineteenth century stresses from the outset: 'Let your style of dress always be appropriate to the hour of the day. To dress too finely in the morning, or to be seen in a morning dress in the evening, is equally vulgar and out of place' (Anon 1860: 12). Advice pertaining to evening dress is given with a cautionary word: 'With respect to ball-room toilette, its fashions are so variable that statements which are true of it today may be false a month hence' (Anon 1860: 12). This continued to apply for the decades to follow, causing the popular weekly periodicals to regularly update their illustrations and advice to their readers. Generally, however, an elbow length sleeve and higher neckline denoted the transition from day to evening and was suitable for dinner dress. A reception or home dinner garment was similar but less ornamented; concert dress too was expected to consist of long or elbow length sleeves and higher neckline but might demonstrate a higher degree of ornamentation and full evening and ball dress featured a low décolletage and were either sleeveless or short sleeved. The different degrees of variation between these general expectations were described in publications such as *The Queen* and *The Ladies Realm*, alongside detailed descriptions of the entertainments to which they would be worn. In April 1897, *The Queen* filled one and a half pages with those society happenings worthy of note. A Mrs Tennant gave 'a pleasant dinner followed by an evening party at her house in Richmond Terrace'. The following list of guests present included a description of the female dress in each instance: 'Lady Conway in a yellow brocade gown with Watteau pleat and ivy leaves in her hair; Miss Green in brightest red chiffon over silk with a gold waistband; Mrs and Miss Channing in pink moiré; Lady Seymour in black velvet and diamonds; Mrs Strachey in pale yellow, wearing some pretty old jewels.'[3] This account alone was only one of many in this issue and one of hundreds featured in the periodical over the course of the season each year.

Influences

The summer of 1863 breathed new life into the London Season with the establishment of the new Prince and Princess of Wales at Marlborough House. Alexandra's first grand function took place at the Guildhall. This magnificent ball was held by the London Corporation, the purpose of which was to present the Prince of Wales with the Freedom of London. In truth it was the first time that London society was able to assess the new princess and for the most part they were delighted. They unveiled a vast illuminated picture of her old Danish home in her honour. One contemporary writer summed up the response: 'No wonder that the worthy Aldermen flopped themselves about in an agony of delight and basked in the Princess's smiles like their own turtles in the sun' (cited in Tisdall 1953: 58). Of this early and significant appearance, *The Times* reported:

> The [Princess] wore a rich but simple white dress, with the coronet and brooch of diamonds given her by her Royal husband, but with the superb City necklace of brilliants. Her hair was turned back from her forehead, in the style

with which her portraits have made us all so familiar, setting off her fair young features and fine expressive, intellectual forehead to the utmost advantage. She looked if possible even younger than on her marriage day-quite girlish, in fact, in her simple white attire.[4]

Records of Alexandra's early sartorial decisions at many conspicuous evening events are consistent in one respect. She chose white. Winterhalter's portrait of the Princess of Wales a year after her marriage sits neatly alongside the press assessments of the princess, a splash of blue silk the only colourful concession to the plain white of her evening dress, two curls falling either side of her neck and her pale face and shoulders merging into her décolletage. It is a composition suggestive of purity and obvious youth. Another portrait by Lauchert commissioned by Queen Victoria after the announcement of the couple's engagement is a record of the Queen's vision of her new daughter-in-law. The construction of the dress is that of a contemporary evening gown, but one utterly lacking in adornment of any kind. It is indicative of the Queen's wish that through simple dress and sober ways, Alexandra might prove to be a calming influence upon her wayward son. Certainly during the first London Season, reports of the Princess of Wales' evening attire subscribe to those edicts laid out by her mother-in-law, although the frequency with which the young couple appeared in public worried Victoria. She wrote to her eldest daughter the Princess Royal: 'I fear Bertie and she will soon be nothing but two puppets running about for show all day and night' (Fulford 1968: 236).

It becomes increasingly apparent that during these early appearances she essentially presented herself as a bride in gowns described as 'simple' but accessorized with fantastically costly jewels. She recognized that there was a public appetite for a view of 'the bride' following years of the monarchical 'widow' as represented by Queen Victoria.

There is little existing material culture from the early years of her marriage. Two evening dresses that have survived are not white, but would most certainly have met with the approval of Alexandra's mother-in-law. Both garments bear the label of Mme Elise and both are a vibrant red tartan. The earlier of the two dates to c1863[5] and possibly formed part of Alexandra's trousseau for her first visits to Balmoral. The second is remarkably similar in its detailing – both white skirts trimmed with red silk piping with the overskirt of tartan – but dates to c.1870.[6] The tartan may refer to the Royal Stewart pattern, appropriated by Prince Albert and therefore Queen Victoria's tartan of choice. Since Edward and Alexandra spent part of every year at their Scottish residence, Abergeldie, it is entirely feasible that these gowns were worn to one of the evening entertainments while in the Highlands. In August 1863 the *Glasgow Herald* reported that 'the Princess wore a Victoria tartan dress' to the Braemar Games and so it seems entirely feasible that she would have taken the Scottish sartorial theme into the evening.[7]

Their similarity, spread over almost a decade, is suggestive of a uniform: of a mode of dress that would have been anticipated by either Queen Victoria or the local population during their stay. This in itself is illuminating. It is perhaps illustrative of Alexandra's choices of evening dress determined by specific social factors. Influenced by Queen Victoria whose romanticized relationship with the Highlands was well publicized, Alexandra ensured that her evening attire subscribed to Victoria's partiality, if not her own. Certainly there is no evidence, either through surviving objects or the written record, to suggest that Alexandra continued to subscribe to Highland dress or tartan during her years as Queen.

By the early 1870s, the Princess of Wales had become bolder in her choice of colour in evening dress. Although there are no known surviving gowns of hers dating to this period, it is possible through a careful analysis of court circular reports in publications such as *The Times* and *The Queen – the Lady's Newspaper and Court Chronicle* to make some reasonably comprehensive observations about the Princess of Wales' appearance at evening functions. Descriptions show that she had begun to wear stronger colours, particularly in evening wear, by the late 1860s into the 1870s. On 9 February 1870, Alexandra attended the Honourable Artillery Company's ball, wearing 'a dress of blue tulle covered with rich lace and looped up with white roses and a head-dress and necklet of diamonds on blue satin'.[8] On 22 March of the same year, 'Her Royal Highness the Princess of Wales wore a train of green satin covered with fine Irish lace and a petticoat of rich green silk, trimmed with plaitings of tulle and satin and a flounce of Irish lace looped with bouquets of stephanotis.'[9] C. Willett Cunnington's comprehensive survey of women's dress in the nineteenth century confirms this fashionably eclectic approach to colour during this period: 'It is perhaps in their colours that the dresses of the '70s are most striking to the eye; the monochrome has vanished and the blend of tones now produce the effect of a picture – sometimes even the appearance of stage costumes' (Cunnington 1990: 254).

Throughout the 1870s Alexandra's palette of choice for evening and state dress was comprehensive, including crimson, primrose, brown, rose, ecru, black, blue, green and violet (Table 1.1). Cunnington's research reveals that this broad range of hues was in line with prevailing trends suggesting that the young princess's evening choices were, if not fashion forward, at least in vogue. The 1870s and 1880s were arguably the decades during which Alexandra was at her sartorial peak, her youth and beauty so regularly praised in the press, her tailored suits the subject of much scrutiny and comment. Such a shared awareness of her public figure during this time may explain the broad variety of colour exhibited in her evening dress, offering to those in the role of observer an ever-changing assortment of colour. White or cream remained a firm favourite, appearing in thirty-seven descriptions during the period. Placed into a biographical context, this choice bears some interrogation. By the late 1860s and into the 1870s, Edward had proved to be a far from predictable husband. From his name

Table 1.1 *Colours of evening dress worn by Alexandra, Princess of Wales as reported in* **The Times** *from 1870 to 1890*

Colour	Frequency of wear
Black	24
Blue	22
Brown	10
Gold	12
Green	14
Pink	4
Purple	11
Red	9
Silver/grey	18
White/cream	31
Yellow	10

appearing in a high-profile divorce case and facing criticism for his profligate lifestyle to a colourful host of mistresses in between, Edward's reputation was far from exemplary. In 1871, at the request of Queen Victoria, the Dean of Windsor had a 'serious talk' with the Prince of Wales, whom he reported was 'evidently deeply attached to the Princess, despite all the flattering attractions that beset him in Society: and the Dean hopes and believes that he will be more careful about her in future. We shall see' (cited in Magnus 1964: 112). Alexandra remained untainted by her husband's indiscretions and retained her widespread popularity. Her appearance at these evening functions which would subsequently be described in detail in the press dressed in white may have been a deliberate attempt to demonstrate her purity and innocence in opposition to reports of Edward's private life.

White may have been the most favoured colour during this period according to the evidence gleaned from printed reports but the press and subsequent biographers described her favourite colour as blue. Sarah Tooley, an early biographer wrote: 'Blue is her favourite colour and was much used for her dresses and bonnets at one time' (Tooley 1902: 161). *The Queen* similarly informed its readers that at a state ball in 1875 'the Princess of Wales wore her favourite colour, blue; her dress was a pale shade of blue composed of satin, crepe, lisse and poult de soie arranged with Brussels lace and ivy leaves, silk ruchings and blush roses and red roses; headdress of the same flowers and diamonds, diamond and pearl ornaments.'[10] It is possible that there was some sentimental attachment to her choice of blue. Charlotte Nicklas observes that certain colours were named after popular public figures. While she does not record a colour for Alexandra, there was a Dagmar blue, named after the princess's younger sister (Crosby 2009). There is no surviving evidence that Alexandra herself chose Dagmar blue for garments in her own wardrobe, but a synchronicity of colour choices between the sisters was to be an occasional feature of their relationship. It was perhaps significant for Alexandra to choose a colour also preferred by her sister so that, separated as she was geographically, she could make at least a sartorial connection.

Further evidence of her confident approach to strong colours in evening dress was exhibited by Alexandra in 1874 at the wedding of her brother-in-law Alfred Duke of Edinburgh, held in St Petersburg. Alexandra stood next to her sister in a vibrant red evening gown. The vividness was captured in a sketch made by the artist Nicholas Chevalier for his commission to paint a wedding portrait for Queen Victoria. The wedding was conducted first in the form of a traditional Russian ceremony followed by an English service and was an international state occasion. That Alexandra chose to wear red rather than a paler shade that might have blended into the background is an early example of the penchant for visible evening dress she was to develop later.

A strong feature of Alexandra's reported appearance during the 1870s and 1880s was the abundance of fresh flowers used to trim her evening gowns. This in itself confirms her adherence to contemporary trends at this time. Fashion plates of the period consistently depict evening gowns adorned with both flowers and foliage of many varieties and hues. Anne Buck wrote in her study of Victorian dress that 'trimmings were used with great lavishness in the dress of the 1870s … . Evening dresses were trimmed with sprays of flowers in additions to their flounces of muslin, net or lace' (Buck 1984: 53). Similarly, the descriptions of Alexandra cover all manner of nature's adornment. In May 1875, a typical example in *The Times* ran: 'Her Royal Highness the Princess of Wales wore a dress and train of paille poult de soie richly embroidered in paille and nacre, with draperies of tulle embroidered to correspond; guerlandes of Marguerites, field daisies, buttercups and poppies.'[11] Not confined just to flowers, reports included currants, chestnuts and moss among the chosen trimmings. At this stage in her royal career, far from removing herself from her peers, the Princess of Wales was clearly allying herself with popular developments in fashionable dress. Where Queen Victoria had distanced herself from her subjects through her unremitting mourning attire, her daughter-in-law apparently sought to democratize her dress in a manner that was accessible both to those in attendance at the evening functions and those reading about it afterwards.

A leap forward to the 1890s and five surviving gowns make a significant addition to what is known about how Alexandra approached evening wear in her final years as Princess of Wales. Although these objects are separated physically, stored in the collections of four different museums, studied collectively they make a valuable contribution.

The most immediately apparent difference in Alexandra's dresses of this period, compared to her earlier choices are the colour. The other remarkable feature about the surviving evening garments is that all are French. The princess had bought clothes in Paris from the very beginning of her marriage. A fascinating passage from a letter written by Edward to his mother in 1872 describes their time in Paris: 'You need not be afraid, dear Mama, that Alix will commit any extravagances with regard to dress, etc. I have given her two simple ones, as they make them here better than in London; but if there is anything I dislike it is extravagant or outré dresses – at any rate in my wife' (cited in Magnus 1964: 105). It is unlikely that Queen Victoria gained much reassurance from her son's missive since his own extravagance in dress was well known to her. What is noticeable by this later period, however, is the exclusivity of Parisian manufacture among Alexandra's range of surviving evening dress.

There are four evening dresses that fall within the date range of 1890–1900 with Alexandra, by this time a middle-aged Princess of Wales, but accepting the same social expectations the rigours of the London Season demanded. These dresses, all muted in shades of white or mauve, were fashionably cut, of Parisian design, but not heavily adorned. One example of the relative simplicity that these garments exhibit is a two-piece mauve dress dating to c1893. It forms part of the collections of the Fashion Museum, Bath and is recorded as a 'watered lilac evening dress, poult de soie with toning velvet and cream lace'.[12] It is described as an evening dress, and would certainly have suited a late dinner and dance rather than a state ball. Nevertheless, its most notable attribute lies in the absence of ornamentation. It was felt to be so unadorned in fact, that the accession card adds the information, 'white bead trimming added by museum'[13] for the public display of the dress in the 1960s. It was apparently felt that this gown did not sufficiently portray the evening wear of a princess and so applied a white beaded fringe around the décolletage and sleeves. The muted colours verify Alexandra's predilection for perpetual half-mourning in the wake of her son Albert Edward's death, an event that changed her relationship with dress for the rest of her life, and the plain gored skirt and self-coloured decoration appears to support accounts of her pared down silhouette: 'In an age when fashion and the arts generally were remarkable for a profusion of ornament and detail she relied, as a good architect does, almost entirely upon perfection of line' (Battiscombe 1969: 106) wrote her most noted biographer. A contemporary view was given, again by Sarah Tooley: 'Tall and graceful and invariably dressed in what appears to be just the right thing for the occasion, devoid of exaggerations of style, the Queen has that easy and reposeful demeanour, which perfect dressing gives' (Tooley 1902: 160). As a reflection of Alexandra's personal circumstances, this dress is perhaps indicative of her desire *not* to stand out at this time. Thirty years as consort-in-waiting, coupled with the loss of her eldest child, may have influenced her decision making around evening entertainments and how she wished to dress.

Two further garments, one held in the V&A, London, and the other at the National Museums, Liverpool, support this theory. Both are cream satin, one figured in a floral motif and the other overlaid with lightly spangled net. As suggested with other examples, both are Parisian in manufacture, Maison Laferriere and Henriette Favre, respectively. While they exhibit elements of decoration, both with embellished hems and some applied detailing to the bodices in both cases, the ornamentation is not heavy in stark contrast to those that form the collection dating to after the coronation. Both of these examples fit into the profile of greater simplicity exhibited in Alexandra's evening dress of this period, but the Henriette Favre dress displays elements of the decoration that was to follow during the years of Edward's reign.

These examples are of course only a fraction of the contemporary wardrobe of the princess, and in the absence of other evening gowns of a similar date, it is impossible to make a definitive assessment. However, the evidence presented in these less embellished garments sit in marked contrast to those that were to follow the coronation. Without exception, these dresses shimmer. Constructed from silk and chiffon and richly embellished in beadwork, metal thread embroidery, sequins and spangles they are uniform in their conspicuousness. While the palette of the foundation layers remained the same as those from the 1890s, confined to white, mauve, pale yellow, grey, silver and gold and some black, the embellishment applied to the surface of each garment exceeds anything from her years as Princess of Wales. Almost overnight, it would appear, the new queen (for consort she refused to be called) ensured her prominence at evening events through her sparkling attire.

An obvious distinction, immediately noticeable, is in the nature of the embellishment. The gowns from the 1890s display elements of applied decoration – a lace trim, a décolletage decorated with motifs of pearl or diamante, a figured silk, but largely plain, gored skirts. Where the later garments differ, is in their almost total surface decoration (Figure 3.2). Five of the gowns exhibit trailing floral designs, repeated in motifs across the bodice and covering the garment with gold or silver embroidery, reminiscent of Alexandra's coronation gown. Four others do not feature any discernible motifs, but are covered with spangles and sequins across their entirety.

The most obvious conclusion to draw from Alexandra's later evening dresses is a necessity on her part for visibility. The new queen, who had been subservient to her mother-in-law for forty years, now had the right to outshine every other woman in the room. These garments suggest that she took this right to its most literal expression. As a demonstration of her place at the top of the aristocratic hierarchy, Alexandra covered herself in fabrics that would have glittered under the artificial lights of the ball rooms, state dinners and myriad evening functions she was obliged to attend. Alexandra had decided that 'majesty' should be represented sartorially through a gem-filled display. She wanted to be the image

Figure 3.2 Photograph of Alexandra as Queen in ornate evening/court gown heavily embellished across its surface, complete with diamonds and tiara, 1905 (author's own collection).

of a queen that Victoria, for all her solemnity and strong monarchical sense of duty, had never been for those functions at which she was the most important woman in the room.

The evening gown that dates to the very end of Edward's reign when Alexandra was in her late sixties continues to subscribe to this approach. Dating to c1910, the one-piece purple chiffon garment is a profusion of metal thread embroidery, heavily embellished across almost the entirety of its surface. The motifs are bold, the embroidery lavish. Alexandra's appropriation of Indian gold and silver thread embroidery, or 'zardozi' embroidery, for her Western garments was to be a regular feature of her evening dress commissions. A letter from Charlotte Knollys to Lady Curzon dated 20 May 1902 is illustrative of Alexandra's penchant for the glitter of the Indian embellishment: 'Then the black and silver is already made up and is to be worn at the next Court and the mauve and gold is in the dressmaker's hands and will also be worn to the Coronation Festivities.'[14] The late nineteenth and early twentieth centuries did witness an emerging trade in the technique of zardozi as 'the British ladies accompanying their husbands to India started taking much interest in zardozi craft' (Gupta 2006: 351). It was Lady Curzon who sourced and oversaw the execution of the Indian commissions for Alexandra, and whose own evening garments drew upon the same style of embellishment. The courtly origins of zardozi and its adoption by Lady Curzon whose sartorial taste Alexandra admired, cemented its place in Alexandra's wardrobe as a signifier of her public status.

The dress is constructed with a fashionably high waist, revealing that at 65, Alexandra was yet instructing her couturiers to cut to a pattern that was modish if not cutting edge. The maker's label identifies the gown as a creation of the house of Doeuillet. Georges Doueillet's evening dresses specialized in 'beautiful, all over embroidered dresses of heavy pastel crepes' (Brookes Picken and Loues Miller 1956: 45). According to the wardrobe accounts, Alexandra first began to patronize his establishment in the summer of 1908, making a large order that amounted to the sum of £511.0.9d.[15] Two more payments were made in February and July 1909.[16] The accounts record only one payment made to Doueillet in 1910, reflecting the sharp drop in expenditure to Parisian dressmakers from 1910 onwards.[17] The payment amounted to £134, but it would be speculation only to suggest that this dress is the material embodiment of that order. The relative modernity of this dress and the other orders received by Doueillet would seem to imply that Alexandra, far from becoming staid in her choices of evening wear during this later period of her life, was embracing new designers and incorporating at least a passing reference to contemporary line in her gowns.

The profusion of metal thread embroidery and beadwork that embellishes this garment bears some comparison with design elements from earlier dresses of Alexandra's, most notably the coronation gown and the fancy-dress costume worn to the Devonshire House Ball. All three garments share a large triangular panel of embroidery across the centre front of the skirts in trailing naturalistic designs. The presence of a heavy train cut into the later dress implies that this garment too was to be worn to a particularly grand event, over and above the everyday dinner parties. The dates of these skirts ranging from 1897 to 1902 to 1910 reinforces a sense that Alexandra continued to incorporate her favourite elements into her evening wear, irrespective of prevailing trends. This tendency is illustrative of the agency that Alexandra exerted over her appearance, balancing a line between regal and fashionable. There is a hint of theatricality too, incorporating the shapes which she chose for the dramatic coronation gown and the fantasy of the Marguerite de Valois fancy-dress costume into an evening gown. These influences may allude to Alexandra's sense of assuming a role. At this later stage of her life, when arguably evening functions were becoming more of a trial, her sense of the majestic appropriate to these occasions could best be met in such conspicuous garments.

There was a duality to Alexandra's visibility in such public settings, however. At the same time as displaying her royal body she had also to conceal it, as the evidence from one particular dress reveals. (See Plates 4 and 5.) A serious bout of rheumatic fever Alexandra had suffered in 1867 not only robbed her of her hearing but also caused a more significant impairment. She was left for the rest of her life with a completely stiff and painful knee, still only able to walk with two sticks nine months after the first attack. The stiffness remained and she was to walk with a limp thereafter. Briefly her gait became a social sensation as she developed a way to move that circumvented her disability. The Alexandra limp was copied for a time by society ladies in the ball rooms of London although the Princess of Wales herself was able to maintain her former activity – skating, riding and dancing (Battiscombe 1969: 92). There were to be long-term health implications for this early illness, however, which only came to light after close analysis of another of her garments.

A court gown, now in the collections of the Royal Ontario Museum, Toronto, features a distinctive iris motif across both the bodice and skirt. During photography of the bodice it was noticed that two of these iris motifs at the centre back appeared to sit incorrectly. They did not align symmetrically as it seemed they ought to have done. An email the next day from the American curator, Jean Druesedow, in answer to my enquiry, revealed the reason. Many of Alexandra's surviving evening gowns are now in the Costume Institute at the Metropolitan Museum of Art, New York and while mounting some of these dresses Druesedow made the following observation in her message: 'The dresses belonging to Alexandra at the MMA indicate that she had some curvature of the spine – the center back is not straight or symmetrical, as I recall, and there was much talk about it when we did "La Belle Epoque" Exhibition.'[18] This new information suggests that, rather than demonstrating some failing on the part of the couturier, the iris motifs were cleverly placed so that the flowers sat symmetrically once they were worn by the Queen, thus disguising her deformity. A spinal curvature has not been mentioned by any of Alexandra's biographers, presumably unaware of the possibility of it resulting from her permanent limp. It is only through studying material culture that such a significant aspect of her physicality is revealed although, conversely, the intention was to disguise her physique through clever workmanship. She normalized her silhouette through structural changes to her dress and so avoided unwanted speculation about her health and well-being, a recognizably modern phenomenon which Jean Spence described as 'part of the landscape of every woman's efforts to clothe herself in a manner which reflects her own self-perceptions and desires but which must be ever alert to the ascription of feminine identity in the public world' (Spence 2001: 186).

After Edward's death, Alexandra largely retired from public life preferring to live quietly at Sandringham surrounded by her pets. When she did attend large public events, she did so in a glittering gown, usually bedecked with diamonds in a bid to distract from the realities of her failing physicality. But for almost half a century she had maintained a prominent presence at the heart of London society. Influences upon her choice of evening dress were many, from her early wish to demonstrate her youth and innocence and to please her mother-in-law, to a growing confidence with colour and style. Influenced by her own circumstances as both aggrieved wife and grieving mother and in her later years fulfilling her own perceptions of the majesty and glitter of a 'queenly' role, Alexandra used evening dress with all its publicity to maintain her popular image. But how far did this image deviate from her private self? Why did she wear what she did in the evenings, if her choices during the day were significantly different?

Managing the public persona – Practical evening dress solutions

From her twenties through to her sixties, Alexandra could not venture out for the evening without attracting the public gaze. The knowledge that she was under regular scrutiny would determine how as both princess and queen she would appear at evening entertainments. Even to define evenings out for her was more complex than it would have been for other members of society at that time and the degree of 'eveningness' could vary depending on the occasion, the host and the location. Thus it is important to explore how Alexandra controlled her appearance during evenings which could vary from a dinner with friends at the beginning to a ball at the end, navigating the intricacies of appropriate dress in between. How she dressed during the evening in what could be described as a public setting bears some comparison with the garments she wore during the day which, if not completely private, were at least less observed. Age was to become a determining factor in her evening dress choices as the years passed, but she was no less in demand socially.

Evening entertainments for Alexandra in practical terms meant hard work. Between April and July of 1875, for example, *The Times* recorded forty-four evenings out for the Princess of Wales covering dinners, concerts, dances and state balls. Out of these forty-four, seven consisted of two or more entertainments on the same night in a different location and under the eye of a different host. A dress in the Liverpool collection appears to offer a solution to the multi-venue evening. This example, a creation of the Parisian house of Rouff, brings an altogether different dimension to Alexandra's evening dress, not so far represented in the other gowns. Dating to 1895, it is fragmented having been unpicked at some point before its entry into the museum. However, its constituent parts have survived and reveal a surprising addition. Instead of one, there are two bodices. The practice of constructing two bodices to be worn at different times with the same skirt was not uncommon. Known as 'transformation dress', it was possible with one skirt to create two outfits suitable for different times of day (Arnold 1972: 28–29). Often the transformation took the wearer from day to evening, with a long-sleeved plain bodice for daywear and a low décolletage more decorative example for evening. In this case, the fabric and embellishment of the skirt precludes it being worn during the day. However, a closer study of the bodices allows a greater understanding of the nuances of evening wear and the potential complications of Alexandra's evening wear, in particular, in a garment that was designed to meet a variety of needs.

Evenings in particular demanded careful negotiation. In any one evening she might attend the opera, followed by dinner, rounded off in a different location entirely by a ball. In spite of its fragmented condition, this dress offers a practical solution to an evening such as this, a high bodice with full elbow length sleeves being eminently suitable for early evening, theatre or dinner, while the alternate bodice of the same fabric and embellishment but with a lower décolleté and shorter sleeves would suit the later events such as the many balls attended by Alexandra throughout the London Season. How the Princess of Wales might have navigated these changes of dress is open to interpretation. It may have been the case that private residences would offer a royal visitor the use of a private room during the course of the evening in which case Alexandra might avail herself of such a facility to make the requisite change before donning an evening mantle and venturing out to the next venue. Frieda Arnold, dresser to Queen Victoria, described in letters home just how complex such evenings could become from an organizational perspective. Of a state visit to Paris in 1855 she wrote: 'We had to dress the Queen at the Tuilieries on two evenings, which meant that we had to pack up everything large and small, and that is more than you think – each time and send it there' (Stoney and Weltzien 1990: 100). There are no such corresponding accounts pertaining to Alexandra's experience, but given the degree to which she embraced fashion and its social expectations, it can safely be assumed that her arrangements would have required similarly convoluted solutions during the busiest times of year.

Given the preference for plain tailored wear during the daytime that contrast with the highly embellished evening gowns of the period, it becomes clear that evenings meant something entirely different during the later stages in her life. Alexandra celebrated her sixtieth birthday in 1904. At a period where many of her contemporaries would have rejected some of the demands of the annual season, Alexandra's position as Queen required her attendance at a wide variety of functions. She was profoundly deaf and found her movement hampered by the stiffness of her knee. Arguably evenings out might be considered something of a trial. Where her personal taste appeared to lean towards the more understated garment, it is possible that rather than let her own taste dictate, Alexandra chose the evening wear of her decade as Queen to serve a more practical purpose. Through over-elaboration of dress it seems likely that the Queen intended to exude the requisite aura of 'majesty' while protecting her frailties behind the glitter and long train of her dress.

Popular photographs of Alexandra during this period that depict the Queen in state and evening dress have been retouched in many instances. Her smooth unlined face in the coronation photograph was a widely circulated image in the early years of the twentieth century. However, the same image in its untouched state shows a more realistic and age-appropriate woman. If this was the public image chosen by Alexandra to be disseminated by this period of her life, it is likely that the heavy embellishment of her evening gowns during her decade as Queen *was* part demonstration of majesty, but also in part a deflection from those aspects of her appearance that she preferred not to emphasize in public.

That most of the photographs of Alexandra in evening dress date from the 1880s onwards is illuminating. Out of a survey of 300 images of Alexandra only twenty-eight can be described as depicting evening dress and of these twenty-eight all of them feature Alexandra aged forty or over. Without exception they present an image of Alexandra, while Princess of Wales and then Queen, that is deliberately flawless. From her sculpted, tiny waisted gowns and jewels to her perfectly unlined face, these images are curiously recognizable in a twenty-first century context. (See Twigg 2010 and Slater, Tiggemann, Firth and Hawkins 2012.) The art of photographic retouching was a topic of wide debate in the nineteenth century, the processes subject to unpredictable results: 'The medium used to retouch the print in the early days did not always age consistently with the print itself. As a result after a while the print presented an unpleasant, spotty appearance little calculated to enhance effect' (Linkman 1993: 78). As the practice became more reliable, the vast majority of commercial photographers employed retouchers to enhance the likenesses of the sitter: 'As a matter of course all negatives passed through the hands of the retoucher, often even before the proofs were dispatched to the customer' (Linkman 1993: 81). How far the retouching process was carried out without the sanction of Alexandra herself is impossible to say although as the years passed she presumably approved of those images that were disseminated publicly. Unlike photographs taken during the day or at least of Alexandra in daywear in which photographic settings were outdoors and more spontaneous, the images in evening wear are carefully staged affairs. In an age where state balls and evening functions were not subject to a resident photographer, her evening dress was thus captured in a prearranged setting and as such might be carefully managed. Just as *Vogue* covers today represent an air-brushed, finely crafted version of femininity in which all flaws have been erased, so Alexandra's evening dress portraits present the 'perfect' vision of a princess and a queen complete with silks, jewels and ageless skin (Figure 3.3) .

If the photographic record and the recollections of her peers all support the notion that Alexandra chose simple unfussy styles for her daywear, the contrasting styles of evening wear from 1901 onwards suggest the adoption of a role. With increasing age, deafness and sometime lack of mobility, the public occasions which might have proved to be a trial to Alexandra, and perhaps often were, could be negotiated through the assumption of an overt and highly visible garment. As an actress becomes the character through donning her costume, so Alexandra became Queen within her glittering evening gown both at the event itself and for the subsequent distribution of the persona via the idealized photograph.

Figure 3.3 The widowed queen Alexandra made fewer and fewer public outings but when she did attend ceremonial events she wore glittering garments such as this fully spangled one-piece dress c. 1912, W and D Downey (author's own collection).

Conclusion

It would be unwise to assume a definitive assessment regarding Alexandra's taste in evening dress. The material culture left is only a small proportion of what would have been a much larger grouping. But, covering so many decades as the surviving objects do from the tartan ensembles of the early 1860s to the regal purple embellishments of the latest surviving gown of c.1910, it is possible to measure to some degree how Alexandra's choices and influences changed over time. Her early experiments with colour and style, in a sense democratizing her dress so that it might appeal to her peers and the public was an early feature of her evening attire. Her ability to strike the correct sartorial note was evidenced through the similar tartan ensembles so redolent of a uniform, designed perhaps to flatter Queen Victoria's tastes. A step forward to a more assured approach in her thirties and the muted tones adopted following the death of her son, Alexandra's choice of evening dress was shaped by many factors. Her preference for Parisian design, particularly in evening wear, is demonstrated through both the surviving garments and the wardrobe accounts, marking a clear division between her daywear and evening wear. Each one constructed in tones of half-mourning, grieving at the loss of her eldest son while recognizing that to descend into perennial black would prove deeply unpopular. The lack of adornment which characterized the 1890s gowns suggested that to stand out was not her overarching intention by this date, thirty years into her royal career. In stark contrast, the dresses of the decade during which Alexandra was Queen shimmer with embellishment, a declaration of majesty at her most public functions.

Alexandra managed a complex system of evening engagements, utilizing the technique of transformation dress to convey her from one type of entertainment to another in appropriate attire. The range of evidence that supports her preference for simpler styles during the day might also suggest that the more elaborate evening gowns were an additional method of managing her public persona, creating a queen for evenings only. This theatricality is also suggestive of distraction – diverting the observer from elements of her ailing, ageing body using sequins as a kind of sartorial armour, a carapace to protect her softer, more private self.

4

THE TRAVELLING PRINCESS: THE LOGISTICS OF ROYAL TRAVEL

Describing a particularly arduous journey with Queen Victoria in 1888 to Balmoral, a lady-in-waiting Marie Mallett concluded in a letter: 'Such are the manifold perils and luxuries of Royal travel' (Mallet 1968: 25). Her account captured both the tediousness and potential discomfort of regular long journeys with the monarch which were coupled with elements of extravagance that might be expected of the court in progress. Seemingly endless train journeys to Balmoral, crossing and recrossing the Solent to Osborne House, packing and unpacking. Such was the tenor of daily life for members of the royal household.

While clearly fundamental to a better understanding of how Alexandra maintained her public appearance, this is not a straightforward narrative. The workings of the royal household were rarely recorded in detail and the experiences of the dressers are for the most part never told. Royal travel and its realities was a subject that was referred to circumspectly in the sources. It was a means to an end and as such requires some careful unravelling to build a more coherent picture of how it actually worked. Thus the sources are fragmented, patchy and sometimes peripheral. Collectively, however, they can shine a light upon this fascinating, yet under-researched, element of royal dress.

Nomadic royals – Travel and the royal luggage

For the duration of their married life, Edward and Alexandra were great travellers, both at home and abroad. The civic duties that were the mainstay of Edward's career as Prince of Wales, coupled with the cyclical events on the annual royal calendar, meant that trips around the UK were frequent and varied either between royal residences or to the large country houses of the aristocracy. The pattern of their year varied little during their married life and a study of the court circular over a number of years confirms the consistency of this annual pattern interspersed with their trips abroad. Edward himself had become accustomed to such regularity of travel from his childhood. Queen Victoria's dresser Frieda Arnold recorded in a letter home in 1856 a typical fortnight following a lavish garter ceremony at Windsor: 'After this magnificence followed days full of fatigue and exertion: we had to pack and unpack continuously for fourteen full days' (Stoney and Weltzien 1994: 50). The sartorial logistics for such a nomadic lifestyle are only hinted at rarely and by Alexandra herself not at all. Queen Victoria clearly participated in elements of such planning. She wrote in 1855 on returning from her state visit to Paris: 'Unpacking and distributing presents and now, all the bother of selecting things and packing for Scotland' (cited in Stoney and Weltzien 1994: 111).

Since her reputation for shrewd dress choices followed her for decades, it is fair to assume that Alexandra too would have liaised with her dressers in the garment choices for such trips accounting for particular occasions, evening entertainments and seasonal requirements. Once such decisions had been made it was then left to the dressers to pack and eventually unpack, a duty that was the most tiring according to Frieda: 'To arrive like that at a house where one's only welcome is from endless boxes with still more endless contents to unpack is dreadful beyond description' (Stoney & Weltzien 1994: 179). Alexandra's faithful assistant, the Hon Charlotte Knollys, wrote of the strain of so nomadic a life: 'We had a most restless, busy summer ... never more than, at most, two Sundays in the same place and such endless heaps of letters and people to see.'[1]

From a practical viewpoint, the nature of the luggage itself warrants some reflection, given the complexity and volume of female dress during the second half of the nineteenth century. Alexandra's wardrobe accounts prove to be of little help in this respect and so it is to the warrant holders that information relating to luggage is sourced. Still holding two royal warrants today, the firm of Asprey were the principal suppliers of royal luggage from the 1850s onwards. Their dressing cases had first come to prominence at the Great Exhibition in 1851 where they received an 'honourable mention' for their ladies dressing case. They recognized the changing market heralded by rail travel: 'In the 1850s, the old wooden dressing cases used by the gentry when they travelled about in their private coaches were being superseded by more portable and less cumbersome leather cases, suitable for travel on the fast-spreading railways. The Aspreys set out to capture this market' (Hillier 1981: 34). And capture this market they surely did. In 1862 Aspreys received a royal warrant from both the Queen and the Prince of Wales and regular invoices to the company feature in the wardrobe accounts although sadly no details. Aspreys enjoyed the exclusivity of this royal patronage: 'Trunks for the royal family were made in black leather instead of the normal brown' (Hillier 1981: 48).

More oblique references to at least the maintenance of luggage can be found in the royal accounts. The company of S. Last were charged with the repair of trunks amounting to £41.12s in February 1899 although the nature of the repairs is not described.[2] The exact composition, however, of Alexandra's travel luggage is not known now other than the occasional reference to its volume. A report of Edward and Alexandra's visit to Cragside House in 1884 noted that 'the guests were quickly followed by their servants and attendants accompanied by five tons of luggage'.[3] In her Mediterranean cruise album of 1899 the Princess of Wales wrote simply: 'This is our baggage' underneath a photograph depicting a mountain of cases of varying sizes.[4] Thirty years earlier Mrs Grey, Alexandra's lady-in-waiting wrote in her journal at the beginning of a long visit to Egypt: 'After we had all retired to our cabins, a fearful fire broke out in some of the warehouses close to the Quay. I rather think that all our luggage, sent on before, had been kept in this very house until the morning of this day, when it was put on board the Ariadne. Thus we had a very narrow escape of losing all our property, which, considering where we were going would have been very serious' (Grey 1870: 21). The party numbered forty-two in total and the indication that the luggage had filled a warehouse signifies its great size.

While those items most likely to be required for any journey were kept with the royal party, the bulk of the luggage was sent on ahead accompanied by one of the dressers who undertook these duties on a rota. Frieda Arnold wrote in 1855 of a journey to Balmoral: 'I went with the carriage this time, for we always take turns' (Stoney and Weltzien 1994: 59) That this practice operated as part of a regulated system within the royal household is evidenced through a series of printed vouchers which members of the household completed in order to claim for travel expenses, including their date and purpose of travel, how long the journey took and any additional expenses such as the hire of a carriage or transport of luggage.[5]

Much of Edward and Alexandra's travel abroad took place at sea either in the form of a multi-stop cruise or a more direct journey to a given destination. This was the era of the royal yacht, vessels of immense luxury. For Alexandra they were spaces to escape to and it is worth noting that the most comprehensive selection of her own writing to have survived in the UK comprises a series of travel albums written to commemorate such cruises in the 1890s and 1900s. Living as she did under such regular public observation, her time on board one of the royal yachts offered her privacy and a sense of camaraderie. A community spirit developed which Alexandra cherished and she mourned its loss as the trips reached their conclusion. She recorded with pleasure in 1893 an evening of dancing and singing with the crew on their last night of a Norwegian cruise.[6] She also recalled an incident in which the speed of a carriage she was being driven in caused her hat to work itself awry: 'It was very nice but very cold and blowy which blew my hat all awry of which however I was in blissful ignorance until I got into the boat & the people cheered – I tried to bow with great dignity!! And when I saw Captain Holford and the mess in fits of suppressed laughter on the subject, as the more I bowed the more crooked got the hat until I fear at last I must have looked perfectly cracked.'[7]

These albums were written by hand and filled with her watercolours, postcards, menus and newspaper clippings – travel scrapbooks that memorialized the trip. Sartorial allusions are almost never included, perhaps further evidence that in the more relaxed context of the cruise it was something to which she gave little thought. Only once does she casually remark: 'Friday August 25th I got up at 6 o'clock & began making a sketch out of the window of my cabin. I confess it was very cold work by the open port so I wrapped myself in a shawl & my old sealskin cloak (the very same old thing I wore on my arrival in England 63 when I landed at Gravesend before my marriage).'[8] Without any other comment it is difficult to understand if she had retained this garment out of a sense of nostalgia or for its practical qualities in such a setting but this is the only reference to dress in the album. Her photographs of the cruise, pasted into the album alongside the other ephemera reveal that the tailor-made prevailed as a presumably practical and appropriate garment. All of the women on board including Alexandra, her family members and her ladies-in-waiting dressed as such in these snapshots. Aesthetically too the tailor-made suit complimented the naval attire of officers and crew, reinforcing the sense of shared experience that Alexandra so enjoyed. Without exception in each image in which she appears she wears a navy/black or cream suit with often an oversized cream cap: undoubtedly of superior quality but also utilitarian and understated (Figure 4.1).

Accommodation on board the royal yacht allowed for the variation in dress that was required for those cruises that included official state visits. In 1905, Queen Alexandra recorded in some detail the many weeks of cruising the Mediterranean, including state visits to Portugal and Malta and a family visit to Greece. They travelled on board the *Victoria & Albert*, one of the largest yachts of its day whose accommodation was described by Captain Augustus Agar: 'The reception rooms and dining saloon were on upper deck level, while the cabins and other private suites and rooms were one deck below. ... There were 14 cabins for guests, with a further 7 for their maids and valets' (Agar 1959: 161–66). On the state deck were the private suites for the King and Queen, which included the Queen's bedroom, dressing and bathrooms and the Queen's dresser's cabin (Dalton 2001: 177). As with the earlier Norwegian cruise album, Alexandra herself makes no direct reference to dress but the album itself is full of photographs in which the full range of her cruising wardrobe is displayed. The patterns for dress appear to be dependent upon the space she occupied. On board ship during the day she once more adopted her tailor-made suits in a quasi-naval context, even doing so for more formal presentations. A newspaper clipping pasted into the album records the maritime authorities welcome of the

Figure 4.1 Queen Alexandra on board the royal yacht c.1905, her place of escape and companionship (original postcard, author's own collection).

royal party on board the yacht: 'At the reception of the Spanish authorities the Queen wore a black walking costume with a toque to match.'[9] Unlike her sister, Empress Marie Feodorovna of Russia, Alexandra never wore formal uniforms but it seems plausible here that at sea the tailored suit with its origins linking it to the yachting suits of the 1870s appealed to Alexandra's sense of appropriate attire. On disembarking from the yacht her garments changed and so for a similarly formal presentation in Lisbon two days later the local press recorded that she was 'dressed in a becoming costume of violet & lilac. Her appearance is charming.'[10] So for a public presentation away from the yacht, Alexandra adopted a less utilitarian style, more in keeping with public expectations for a feminine queenly figure. Her garments became more formal again for evening and state receptions. A detailed description of such a dress supposedly worn during this trip survives in the Anderson Galleries catalogue of 1937: 'Embroidered white satin State gown. Of white satin, back and front panels with appliqué borders of rose tissue covered with embroidered tulle bearing floral rinceaux in gold cordonnets and bugles. In one piece with short rose tissue sleeves and square-cut neck. Worn by HM the Queen in Portugal (1905) on a visit to the King & Queen of Portugal; also worn for State visits and at the Grand Opera, Lisbon.'[11] Alexandra did indeed attend the Opera in Lisbon on 24 March after which she wrote: 'They gave me quite an ovation which *touched* me deeply but made me so shy.'[12] The whereabouts of this dress are not currently known but its description fits that of the formal state gown, other examples of which have survived and which clearly formed a part of the wardrobe maintained on board by the dressers.

Accommodation was not always so easily managed in a single space. For the Egyptian tour, the number of vessels required to transport the entire party along the Nile was extensive and varied. Mrs Grey was to share the second steamer of the party with the Prince and Princess and this she deemed excellent: 'The Prince and Princess have a very nice sleeping cabin with a bath-room and dressing-room apiece. There is a large sitting room with a piano and very pretty furniture and then come my two cabins; small, about seven feet square, but very comfortable and outside these a large cabin for the dresser Mrs Jones and my excellent Fins' (Grey 1870: 47). She went on to describe the rest of their convoy consisting of five boats and included the main steamer, the accommodation steamer, the kitchen boat, a boat for donkeys and horses and at the rear a boat for the French washerwoman, indicative of at least part of the maintenance of clothes during the tour.

Travel garments

The act of travelling itself had its own vocabulary of clothing with which Alexandra would have been familiar and which would have formed part of her ensemble. Few outer garments relating to Alexandra as Princess or Queen have survived. Of the five that remain, four of them are of a quality and design that indicates they were worn for public and formal engagements – decorative dolmans certainly not suited to rail travel but outerwear nonetheless and so part of her travel between a variety of locations. (See Plate 6.) It is probable that Alexandra would have possessed coats such as those frequently depicted in the pages of women's periodicals. In these, garments such as the 'travelling ulster' were illustrated against the backdrop of a railway ticket office, locomotive steaming into the station behind, advertising its suitability as an overcoat robust enough to withstand the rigours and grime of the railway. These ulsters or dust cloaks were described as being fabricated from 'tussore, double alpaca, waterproof tweed or checked camel's hair'.[13] Documentary evidence suggests that Alexandra did order some of her travelling clothes from her favourite tailors. Though the objects have not survived, a record of their purchase has. Susan North's research into the couture House of Redfern includes an appendix in which she identifies Redfern clothes made for royal and aristocratic patrons as recorded in *The Queen*. According to this the Princess of Wales purchased from Redfern one ulster in October 1881, a travelling costume in July 1883, a walking cloak in December 1883 and a travelling cloak in May 1884 (North 2008: 165–66).

While there are no specialist outerwear suppliers that feature within the wardrobe accounts such as Aquascutum or Burberry, there are many outfitters whose wares would have included such protective items. Included on a single folio of the accounts from 1898 are four such establishments – Swan & Edgar, Graham & Son, Woolland Bros and Howell & James – all of whom may have supplied Alexandra with additional travelling coats.[14]

Often these garments inhabit a shadowy place in the sartorial record. From a royal perspective they were not necessarily designed for public display, performing at a practical level rather than a stylish one. Certainly there are no images of Alexandra wearing such a garment, even as she stood at the railway platform, a garment that might be dispensed with swiftly as welcoming parties gathered. Duster coats now in the collections of the Royal Ontario Museum reveal the plain and pared down construction of such garments consisting of pale unadorned cotton or silk, deep collars and cuffs and centre front buttons. They are protective and functional and not at all decorative.

There is a single coat now in the collections of the Metropolitan Museum in New York which dates to c1863 and may have formed part of the young Princess of Wales' trousseau. This has been recorded as a driving coat. Made from white wool with deep lapels and cuffs of lambswool it appears functional yet the gold braid frog trimming makes it decorative also. (See Plate 7.) In the light of this sole surviving coat, it is perhaps too large a leap to suppose that Alexandra applied such decorative elements to all of her practical coats thereafter but it is a possibility to consider. Knowing from an early point in her career that there were few opportunities for her to enter into the public domain unobserved it is feasible to suggest that her travel clothes might reflect this.

Receiving royal visitors

In addition to their habitual visits to royal residences outside London, Edward and Alexandra were regular visitors at private residences around the UK. Often these stays formed part of a civic appointment and the country estates of the aristocracy substituted as a hotel for the royal couple. To many houses they were frequent guests, such as the estate of the Duke and Duchess of Manchester at Kimbolton Castle. Edward first visited the estate in 1861, at which point, compared to other large country estates, 'Kimbolton must have seemed small and inconvenient, with insufficient accommodation for the valets and lady's maids who would accompany important guests' (Butler 2007: 8). It was in the 1860s that the architect William Burn was given the task of extending parts of the servants' accommodation, to include more rooms for visiting maids but also a 'Wardrobe Room'. The description of this space as a wardrobe room and its position on the plans showing it directly next door to the dressers' accommodation suggests that rather than storing luggage, this was an area where the extensive travelling wardrobe of a woman such as Alexandra could be unpacked and maintained for the duration of the stay.[15]

Even for the owners of the largest estates in the country, the prospect of a royal visit and the logistics it entailed could be the cause of some anxiety. In 1872 the Duke of Devonshire wrote to his son in anticipation of a visit by the Prince and Princess of Wales: 'Glad you are staying at Sandringham, for you will be able to get answers to several things I want to know. How long do they stay? How many servants do they bring? How many maids for the Princess? Do you think you could bring any horses? Am so afraid that our own may not stand the cheering' (cited in Vane 2004: 95). Consuelo Vanderbilt, the American heiress married to the Duke of Marlborough, recorded similar concerns when Edward suggested he would like to visit Blenheim: 'We at once began the rather onerous preparations such a visit entailed. Our proposed list of guests having been submitted and approved, we became engrossed in plans to make the visit agreeable and memorable' (Vanderbilt Balsan 1973: 91). There follows her slightly anarchic description of the sartorial expectations of such a visit, an account laden with the bewilderment she still felt towards the British aristocracy and what she perceived to be their absurdities:

> The number of changes of costume was in itself a waste of precious time. To begin with, even breakfast, which was served at 9.30 in the dining room, demanded an elegant costume of velvet or silk. Having seen the men off to their sport, the ladies spent the morning round the fire reading the papers and gossiping. We next changed into tweeds to join the guns for luncheon, which was served in the High Lodge or in a tent. Afterwards we usually accompanied the guns and watched a drive or two before returning home. An elaborate tea gown was donned for tea, after which we played cards or listened to a Viennese band or to the organ until time to dress for dinner, when again we adorned ourselves in satin, or brocade, with a great display of jewels. All these changes necessitated a tremendous outlay, since one was not supposed to wear the same gown twice. That meant sixteen dresses for four days. (Vanderbilt Balsan 1973: 93)

Sixteen dresses over a four-day period, with the addition of travelling garments, footwear, nightwear, underwear and accessories, amount to a sizeable volume for what was a relatively short period.

Cragside – A case study

It was not exclusively to the large homes of 'old' money that Edward and Alexandra stayed. Edward famously supported and befriended successful nouveau-riche entrepreneurs and was fascinated by new technologies. In 1884, driven by his curiosity for electrical innovations, Edward secured an invitation to Cragside in Northumberland the home of the industrialist William Armstrong whose home was the first in the world to be powered by hydroelectricity. This particular visit is worthy of note, owing to the detailed record of it. For Edward and Alexandra this three-day stay was one among dozens of similar trips around the country every year. For William Armstrong, however, it was a great occasion and he ensured that it was suitably memorialized. His preparations were extensive and on 18 August, two days before their arrival, *The Newcastle Daily Chronicle* noted: 'The work of preparation has been pushed forward most vigorously during the past week. An army of workmen has swarmed all over the establishment.'[16] The house had been built in the 1860s to Armstrong's particular vision which included the unique approach to its lighting. It had taken some time to finish completely, the drawing room only just ready in time for the Prince and Princess of Wales' stay. The couple were to stay in the 'owl suite' a series of three rooms which had been specially refurbished and included a plumbed-in washstand and central heating.

Local artist Henry Hetherington Emmerson was commissioned to capture the royal visit through a series of watercolours and so a record of Edward and Alexandra's visit to the house from the moment of their arrival at Rothbury station now exists. Armstrong collated these illustrations into a tooled leather album and it is in the pages of this album that certain elements of Alexandra's wardrobe during this visit were chronicled. The album contains a variety of images that feature Edward and their children in different parts of the house and garden. In five of these watercolours, Alexandra features most prominently and the representation of her dress is instructive. In one she is depicted being welcomed to the house by Armstrong's wife in which image she wears a sober black tailored day dress and bonnet. In another she wears a less structured white embroidered morning or afternoon dress seated in the drawing room at Cragside with her daughters and Armstrong himself. The informality of the composition and the suggestion of sartorial comfort it displays were perhaps for Armstrong a means of illustrating his elevated social position in which he was clearly 'at home' in all respects with royalty. The persona of the Princess of Wales as depicted here though was of a princess off duty. She might have been staying in a house with people whom she presumably hardly knew, but in this domestic setting she dressed in unceremonious fashion.

This white embroidered garment features again in a full-length portrait, only this time accessorized with a woollen shawl crossed over her chest in a pastoral setting and informal pose, a bunch of heather in the crook of one arm and a sun bonnet slung across the other. Whether this was a sitting drawn from life or whether the artist took a degree of licence it is impossible to know. Certainly it is the same dress as painted before. However, the addition of the casually crossed shawl and the unstructured blue sun bonnet creates a picture that is anything but regal. Rather than fill his album with a vision of the Princess of Wales glittering in jewels and silks, he chose to highlight how ordinary her attire was in a familial context.

Two other images, however, perhaps more clearly demonstrate the princess 'at work'. These more formal garments set against the more casual portrayal of Emmerson's other watercolours imply that Alexandra had to pack suitable clothes not only for the different times of day but also for the different versions of herself that she would be obliged to present to the world: on the one hand, the opportunity to relax with her family in a small country house, dressed accordingly in a soft and unstructured garment, while, on the other hand, the formal receptions and dinner parties at which she must present herself as the princess. In one, Alexandra is being introduced to the guests of Sir William and Lady Armstrong at an evening entertainment given by their hosts. Here Alexandra has chosen a white evening dress embellished with lace and pink roses and adorned with jewels and tiara. In this she is unmistakably the Princess of Wales. Finally taking up her public duties in a civic setting, she is illustrated in a more formal day dress of pink silk and white lace, greeted by the worthy gentlemen of Rothbury at the train station. It is a striking garment in juxtaposition to the sober suits of the men surrounding her, suitably feminized through her colour choice. She might presumably have worn a tailor-made, which she so often wore during the day, but for this particular setting such a masculinized garment was perhaps not suited to the occasion at which she needed to be visible from among the uniformity of the men.

Foreign travel – The preparation

Travelling abroad formed a significant part of Edward and Alexandra's annual calendar. Their motives varied from trip to trip. Sometimes they were simply on holidays abroad conducted away from the public eye. Sometimes their travels took place as official tours of state. Often they were a combination of the two, connecting with family members from among the European monarchies at the same time as demonstrating an informal diplomatic mission to strengthen ties between nations. Trips abroad generally took place twice a year and were timed to fall either side of the London Season. Moreover, the records show that, either together or separately, Edward and Alexandra were often out of the country from August to November and from January to May either for extended periods of time or shorter trips within those months. For example, in 1874 the royal couple attended the wedding of the Duke of Edinburgh in St Petersburg before an extended stay in the country arriving back in Dover on 6 March. Later that year Alexandra spent a number of weeks in Copenhagen visiting her parents from the end of August until October. In 1885 the Prince and Princess of Wales made a state visit to Ireland in April, followed by a trip to Greece and a number of other European cities in August and September. This pattern of international voyaging remained fixed until the death of Edward in 1910.

The extent to which Edward and Alexandra travelled abroad had little historical precedent. David Duff points to the previously limited experience of travel by preceding British monarchs when describing Queen Victoria's continental holidays: 'In this area of travel the Queen made a clean break with tradition. Of her three immediate predecessors only one, George IV, had left British shores, and he only to visit his own principality of Hanover' (Duff 1970: 13). In venturing as far as Egypt, Constantinople, Russia and in the case of Edward, India, Edward and Alexandra set new standards of royal travel, standards that were to become commonplace by the mid-twentieth century. While preparations for foreign travel were presumably extensive, evidence of the preparations themselves is not. References to such logistical arrangements are sparse and sit at the periphery of other narratives. Thus pasted among the pages of Oliver Montagu's record of the royal visit to Russia in 1874 is an unattributed newspaper clipping charting their passage: 'The whole of the arrangements for the trip from London to Russia are under the control of M. Kanne, her Majesty's director of Continental journeys who attends their royal highnesses throughout their visit to the Russian capital and during their return to England.'[17] Any other reference to the role of M Kanne, the nature of his employment more generally or the duties he performed are regrettably absent. His intriguing job title 'Her Majesty's Director of Continental Journeys' hints at the place he occupied and suggests overall supervision of the travellers and their baggage from departure to arrival. For some trips independent experts were hired to plan and accompany the royal travellers. In 1869 Edward had engaged the explorer Sir Samuel Baker to make the arrangements for their trip to Egypt. 'Baker of the Nile' as he was popularly known proved a wise choice, all of the logistics overseen by him: 'And very well he has succeeded' Edward was to surmise (cited in Battiscombe 1972: 104).

The planning and preparation of Alexandra's wardrobe for such extended stays undoubtedly required her attention alongside that of her dressers. The nature of her contribution to these arrangements has not been recorded but evidence from some of her contemporaries has. In 1905 Alexandra's daughter-in-law Mary undertook the planning of her wardrobe for a trip to India. She travelled to London on 27 September, three weeks before their scheduled departure to arrange her trousseau for the trip. An acerbic note from Queen Alexandra to her son revealed her own rather jaundiced view of the situation: 'So my poor Georgie has lost his May, who has fled to London to look in her glass!! What a bore and a nuisance, but I cannot understand why she should have gone so soon, as the dresses for India cannot take quite such a long time to do or try on either.'[18] Criticism aside, this remark appears to suggest that Alexandra herself disliked spending too much time over such advance strategies. It may have been simply that by this stage in her royal career her dressers and suppliers were familiar enough with both her physical requirements and her taste to construct a travelling wardrobe with little input from their mistress. For Mary such time spent was a trial. She wrote to her husband of the self-same preparations of 'a hard day's work at tiresome clothes' (cited in Battiscombe 1972: 259). It was not an occupation she enjoyed. Her husband replied: 'I am delighted to hear that you have now finished trying on all yr dresses & I hope they fit well. In all the papers I see long accounts of them' (cited in Pope-Hennessy 1959: 396). That the descriptions of the dresses were featured in the press prior to their departure hints at the public appetite for such preparations. One of the only images of Alexandra in a periodical which is accompanied by descriptive text does in fact relate to a garment ordered and purchased specifically for an extended European tour. Underneath a sketch of the princess wearing a simple double-breasted suit trimmed with braid and worn over a high-necked blouse is the note: 'A gown made for the Princess of Wales By W. Gent and Son, 28 South Audley St, Grosvenor Sq & of Birmingham. This dress was composed of the very finest dress suiting in a tropical weight, the whole gown lined throughout with silk cord, had smart slashed pockets to correspond, and the skirt was trimmed in a similar manner.'[19] That it was described as being of 'tropical weight' suggests to the reader that this garment had been ordered for foreign travel, advertising both Gent's wares as suppliers of travel garments and also their royal patronage. From Alexandra's perspective it is further evidence of the kinds of preparations taken for hotter climates.

When Mary Curzon's husband George, Lord Curzon, was made viceroy of India in 1898, her thoughts quickly turned to the sartorial requirements of her new life. Lady Curzon wrote long letters to her family outlining her intentions: 'She detailed her plans for her wardrobe noting that she would employ a seamstress for two months to make her "thin" day clothes, while for her evening dress no expense would be spared: "I shall go over to Paris in the Autumn and get my evening dresses of Worth (a queen's!)"' (Thomas 2007: 374). Such descriptions are rare, however. Other notable aristocratic women of the period forgo descriptions of plans for foreign travel. Consuelo Vanderbilt and Jenny Randolph Churchill, for example, both travelled extensively during their lives and wrote detailed memoirs but neither chose to illuminate their readers with details of dress during their travels (Cornwallis-West 1973 & Vanderbilt Balsan 1973). There was certainly no shortage of advice relating to appropriate attire for would-be travellers. Volumes such as *Travelling and its Requirements – Addressed to Ladies By A Lady* offered guidance on topics as varied as fabric choice, most convenient style of footwear and colour of dress depending on destination: 'A serge costume is much to be preferred to homespun for train and boat use; as no amount of water or mud can impair a really good one of the former material' the anonymous author observed in the 1878 publication (Anon 1878: 16). Given that there was no royal precedent for foreign travel, especially to countries beyond the continent, it seems fair to assume that the dressers would have conducted a degree of research relating to climate and landscape when preparing for overseas travel, and advice books of this nature may have provided at least a framework for those preparations.

Once the wardrobe was complete, the art of packing the items logically must be undertaken. Packing was a skill that upper-class women were prepared to pay for. An exhibition featuring the designers Louis Vuitton and Marc Jacobs explored Vuitton's early career in Paris: 'Louis Vuitton gained his experience in the art of packing by travelling to the homes of wealthy ladies where he was employed to pack their clothes before they embarked on long journeys. Within ten years he had become such a master in the art of packing that he would regularly accompany his master Romain Maréchal to the Tuileries Palace where they worked as exclusive packers to the Empress Eugenie and her ladies-in-waiting' (Anon 2012: 3). There are no references in either Queen Alexandra's wardrobe accounts or any surviving documentary material to suggest that she paid for her clothes to be packed for long journeys, but the length of the voyages and the separation of baggage and traveller meant that logistically this had to be carefully managed. The dressers had to be clear that they retained enough clothing for the days or weeks of travel while the bulk of the luggage was transported. The care of clothes in transit was addressed in instructional manuals in the nineteenth century, allowing the reader some idea of the range of garments that needed to be packed and the way to achieve it. The *Workwoman's Guide* of 1840 offered this suggestion of the layering of a trunk:

> First, divide the light things from the heavy ones; lay boxes, shoes and all hard flat things at the bottom of your trunk, taking great care to fit them together, so as to be perfectly even at the top, putting paper or any small soft things in the crevices; then put in a packing cloth, and on this lay flannels, linen, &c, &c: these things should be opened to their full extent and laid quite flat; in the corners stockings, rolls of ribbon &c may be put: silk or any thick dresses,

folded as described above, may be laid at the top and the whole carefully covered with the packing sheet tightly pinned down, and strong brown paper to prevent the possibility of rain getting in. Bonnets, caps, muslin, or gauze dresses and collars should be put in a box by themselves: tapes may be nailed across the box and the bonnets or caps pinned to them to keep them steady. (Anon 1840: 121)

Different country, different climate

The diary kept by the Hon Teresa Grey of the royal tour in 1869 offers a detailed record of this first extensive trip embarked upon by the young Prince and Princess of Wales. It was to be a full schedule carefully described by Mrs Grey who was not always comfortable with the 'otherness' of the East and its customs but which the Princess of Wales apparently embraced enthusiastically. While sartorial descriptions are not plentiful, she does occasionally refer to changes of dress and choice of clothing in such a way as to demonstrate the practicalities of climate and geography. On 10 February she notes that thus far they were pleasantly surprised at the lack of bugs: 'All our precautions against them such as insect powder etc have as yet been unnecessary; our special night-dresses have not even been unpacked and we are as clean and comfortable as in our own home' (Grey 1870: 54). As they ventured along the Nile and made daily stops to explore the countryside she briefly described their expeditionary garb: 'The Princess and I again changed our dresses and put on the not very graceful, but very comfortable and sensible costumes made of flannel which we always wear upon these riding expeditions' (Grey 1870: 63–4). These appear to be the dresses which she later more nostalgically calls 'the old Nile Costume' (Grey 1870: 122) when the entire party were photographed in Cairo for posterity. A visual interpretation of these 'Nile costumes' can be made from William Howard Russell's published diary of the royal tour (Russell 1869). Although Mrs Grey's journal describes the journey with Alexandra from a more personal viewpoint, Russell illustrated his publication with colour plates and a number of these feature the young princess. The frontispiece of the first volume entitled 'Ships of the Desert' depicts Alexandra on the back of a camel. She is dressed in an unstructured striped gown, without crinoline or petticoats (the Nile costume?) holding aloft a parasol. Interestingly her headgear consists of an Arab-like headdress wound around her head and hanging around the back of her neck. It has a distinctively Eastern character, revealing that Alexandra was happy to adopt such sensible indigenous garments to protect herself from the desert heat (Figure 4.2). On 22 March Russell described the princess's forays into the Egyptian bazaars: 'Once again the Princess, attended by Mrs Grey, mounted on donkey back set out on a ramble through the never-failing delightful

Figure 4.2 Alexandra during her trip to Egypt in 1869 wearing what might be the 'Nile costume' described by Mrs Grey in her diary, Royal Collection Trust/© Her Majesty Queen Elizabeth II 2016.

labyrinth' (Russell 1869: 419). His description was accompanied by a sketch of the princess in a loose-fitting dark garment with the same striped and fringed headdress, exploring the markets on a donkey. It is an image that demonstrates the fusion in dress between East and West. The Western dress itself is not the domed and wired gown of high fashion, however, but an altogether softer garment more akin perhaps to the robes of the native Egyptians.

Negotiating cultural aesthetics or not was a necessary part of being British and abroad during this period. Some women chose to retain as much of British etiquette and sartorial custom as possible in spite of climatic differences whereas others were less rigid in their clothing choices. Emma Tarlo points out that in India, expectations of dress were not so prescriptive: 'Indian reactions to "the other" were neither as rigid nor as stereotyped as British ones' (Tarlo 1996: 42). However, cultural differences did shape the choices in dress made by European women travelling for long periods or living in the region: 'Selections of

European women's white dresses were available by mail order from Bombay in 1911. Virginal white was popular among British women but not with many Indian women, being associated with widowhood' (Tarlo 1996: 31). Recent research by Dianne Lawrence considers the tensions around dress which might arise for women occupying colonial spaces: 'Their dress, that most intimate expression of subjectivity was critical in helping them to negotiate their new and often alien surroundings, for without such items their very sense of self was threatened' (Lawrence 2010). It is of course difficult to quantify individual responses to dressing in such circumstances. It is possible that as a relatively short-term traveller Alexandra felt more prepared to experiment with 'otherness' in dress for the novelty it offered. However, Western aristocratic customs prevailed in certain situations such as dressing for dinner in the evenings.

Additional to the practical costumes worn among the ruins of ancient Egypt were the evening dresses of modern Europe. Maintaining standards of etiquette in the most unlikely of settings, Mrs Grey noted that they changed for dinner each evening, even when she felt ravaged by the day's exertions: 'I dressed and, in spite of kind advice to go to bed instead, I went to dinner, which had been laid out in some tents pitched before we arrived on the edge of the bank' (Grey 1870: 79). Suitable desert dress and evening wear aside, there were entirely different conditions to accommodate later in the trip during their time in Constantinople. Mrs Grey wrote then: 'The weather has become dull, damp, cold and showery, and we have been obliged to return to our warm clothes and furs' (Grey 1870: 175). These fleeting allusions to dress demonstrate two key elements relating to dress and international travel. First, that measures were taken for what were perceived to be unusual conditions such as the 'special' nightdresses that were apparently supposed to ward off native bugs. Second, that a comprehensive range of garments were packed to suit all possible occasions and conditions; hence the ability to ride in the desert, dress for dinner, appear suitably attired to meet local dignitaries and wrap up in furs and warm clothes when the temperature dropped.

Such careful planning prevailed too in 1874 when the Prince and Princess of Wales took an extended trip to Russia for the wedding of Edward's brother Alfred, Duke of Edinburgh and the Grand Duchess Marie Alexandrovna. As with the earlier tour of the Near East, this trip was also recorded in great detail in the diary kept by a member of the royal household and great favourite of Alexandra, Oliver Montagu. Unlike Mrs Grey's diary, which dwelt more upon aesthetics and her feelings as well as the terrain they encountered, Montagu's diary is an efficient day-to-day account of events. Clothing does not feature beyond noting those occasions for which he was obliged to wear a uniform. What becomes apparent in each entry he makes between their departure from Charing Cross on 10 January and their return on 5 March are the rigours of the schedule they followed during their stay. Montagu records on 29 January:

At 11 Prince inspected the Pompiers; after we all went to the Manage where the Princess & Czarevna joined us to see the Cossack regiment go through their riding. At 2 to skating, a lovely day. Pss, Czzarewitz (*sic*), Czarevna, Duke & Dss of Edinburgh & several of the Grand Dukes there. Dinner at home and at 8.30 to the Winter Palace ball. 2000 people a fearful crowd & not much dancing to be done. Supper for everyone sitting down.[20]

Three days later on 2 February his brief notes concerning the day's activities ran thus: 'To the Anitchkoff at 12.30 at 2.30 to skating dinner at home & at 10.30 to a ball at the British Embassy. Home at 3.45.'[21] The next day was even longer: 'Skating at 2.30. Dinner at home & at 10 to Grand Duke Nicholas' ball. Very fine house & beautiful staircase. Home at 4 and then dressed in undress uniform & started for the station where we got into the Imperial train waiting there, went to bed and at *4th* 6am left for Moscow. The Emperor & the Imp. & Royal persons in another train that left at 8am & travelled through very uninteresting country. At 1 we stopped for luncheon, at 6 for dinner & arrived at Moscow at 9pm. We all drove to the Sclavonsky Bazaar [*sic*]. The Imperial party arrived at 11.'[22] These descriptions of civic functions, cultural visits, skating parties, dinner and a ball are not unusual on this trip or indeed any other foreign visit made by Alexandra. What each detail reveals, however, is the number of changes that were required at each point. On 3 February it can be assumed that Alexandra wore a morning gown when she rose, a skating outfit for the afternoon, possibly an afternoon dress before changing for dinner, then potentially a further change into a ball gown. Finally after the conclusion of the ball, a final change and journey to the railway station in the early hours of the morning to make the trip to Moscow: six changes of outfit in a single day to be negotiated before further packing for their time in Moscow.

On 26 February, Oliver Montagu recorded that the Princess of Wales and czarevna were photographed prior to their departure and it is this surviving image which exposes yet another facet of the trip. In the photograph, both sisters wear identical double-breasted fur-trimmed coats, fur hats and muffs in a display of like-dressing practised occasionally by the sisters. So, in addition to the usual arrangements to ensure that an appropriate number and selection of garments were accounted for, at some point advance preparations were made in order for the sisters to appear in public dressed alike.

Diplomatic dressing

Alexandra's reputation for shrewd sartorial choices extended to her appearance abroad and there is evidence to suggest deliberate and carefully chosen garments that were intended to flatter the host nation. One such trip that was covered in some detail was a state visit to Ireland in 1885. *The Times* described

Alexandra's chosen attire for a number of functions, the garments for which were all presumably intended to compliment the Irish people. On 9 April at a Drawing Room and Levee in Dublin: 'The Princess of Wales wore a dress of bronze velvet draped in gold embroidery embossed with shamrocks. Her head-dress and tiara were of diamonds.'[23] Three days later at a state ball in Dublin: 'The Princess of Wales wore a dress of cream satin duchesse trimmed with gold and silver embroidery, veiled in lisse embroidered with gold and silver shamrocks; her headdress was a tiara of diamond ornaments.'[24] Finally on 22 April the newspaper described the Princess of Wales' dress for the Citizen's Ball in Dublin: 'Her Royal Highness the Princess of Wales wore a dress of green velvet over a jupe of pale green satin and silver gauze, draped with Irish lace, fastened with bouquets of shamrock and lilies of the valley.'[25] These accents consisting of national symbols while not dominating the ensemble, were nonetheless an obvious and therefore easily reportable means of paying a monarchical tribute.

Edward and Alexandra had first visited Ireland together in April 1868 less than twelve months after heightened activity by the Irish Fenian activists had caused some governmental anxiety. Queen Victoria had her reservations about the possible dangers of such a trip in the face of Irish hostility, although she herself had sailed across the Irish sea on a similar visit in 1849. On 8 August at a state dinner in Dublin Castle, she had demonstrated her own recognition that the display of dress could be a platform from which to send conciliatory messages: 'That evening Victoria wore a dress of green Irish poplin lavishly embroidered with gold shamrocks and adorned by the blue ribbon and star of St Patrick. By then she could do no wrong in the eyes of Dubliners' (Arnstein: 80–81). In spite of Victoria's reservations, it was Disraeli who entreated with her to allow Alexandra to accompany her husband. Perhaps he recalled the success of the young queen's visit twenty years earlier and recognized the power of a beautiful young princess. He wrote to the Queen: 'Is it not worth Your Majesty's gracious consideration whether the good might not be doubled if His Royal Highness were accompanied by the Princess? Would it not add to the grace and even the gaiety of the event?' (cited in Battiscombe 1972: 92–3). Queen Victoria consented and the trip was to be a wild success, in no small part owing to the appearance of Alexandra. There was even some talk of an official residence in Ireland for the couple, such was their delight with the country – but this Victoria firmly vetoed. Nevertheless, Alexandra silently expressed her fondness for the Irish on her return to England: 'All that the Princess could do to show the friendly Irish populace that she had not forgotten them was to appear at Ascot in the same outfit that she had worn at Punchestown Races, a green dress of Irish poplin trimmed with Irish lace, with Irish shamrocks in her white bonnet' (Battiscombe 1972: 96).

Similarly, following the Irish visit of 1885 Alexandra was to appear at an afternoon drawing room in Buckingham Palace in 'a dress of rich yellow satin and silver brocade, draped with silver lace; corsage to correspond, made by

Mrs Sims, of Dublin'.[26] This is one of the only instances during this period that a newspaper or periodical mentioned a dressmaker by name, surely intended to pay homage to her visit there a month earlier. Such implicit communication with the gaze of the masses that gathered to see Alexandra continued in an Irish context. During a state visit to the country in 1904 Alexandra was in mourning according to the etiquette which still prevailed at this date. In recognition of her role during the visit, however, she waived such protocol as *The Queen* reported on 7 May: 'Queen Alexandra, who doffed her mourning for the occasion, a compliment thoroughly appreciated, appeared in black velvet, covered with a beautiful paletot of bright green cloth adorned with velvet appliqué and sable, and a toque of green chiffon to match.'[27] The relatively simple gesture of donning an emerald green outer garment in public was enough to secure both press editorial and local popularity.

In 1871 the Prince and Princess of Wales made a special trip to see the Passion Play at Oberammergau in Austria. Although this was a low-key visit owing to the spiritual nature of the occasion, Alexandra recognized the cultural aesthetics. An observer, Lady Constance Battersea, recalled of that day: 'I remember how attractive the Princess of Wales looked in a green Tyrolese hat' (Battersea 1923: 91). It was a small detail but to the local population would have been a recognizable one. Indeed, Alexandra expressed a willingness not only to make these small sartorial allusions but to experiment more widely in a different cultural setting. Her visit to the harem of the Khedive of Egypt during the 1869 trip reached a surprising conclusion: 'The Princess paid a farewell visit to the ladies of the harem, who amused themselves by painting her eyes and eyebrows in oriental fashion and sending her back in yashmak and burnous to mystify her husband' (Battiscombe 1969: 105). That the princess showed no reticence in clothing her Western royal body in Eastern dress is perhaps reflective of her popularity abroad more generally. Although she was arguably the embodiment of imperial power given her status, her eagerness to appear as 'other' must have enhanced her standing among local populations.

Conclusion

The scope of travel undertaken over a forty-year period by Edward and Alexandra was a reflection of their modernity. Their willingness to adopt new modes of transport and their mutual desire to visit far-flung countries were to become a substantial part of their married lives. The often-nomadic lifestyle they adopted both at home and abroad was not unheard of in royal circles. Henry VIII's famous progresses around the British Isles set an early precedent for the British monarch to decamp from the capital and explore the country either in a royal residence or the residences of loyal subjects. Arguably Edward's own restlessness was driven by his lack of formal occupation in his role as Prince of Wales, his mother repeatedly refusing to cede any of her responsibilities in favour of her eldest son. (See Arnstein: 135 and Magnus 1964: 116–118.) So through civic commitments, visits to friends and the cyclical trips to other royal homes as prince and princess, King and Queen, Edward and Alexandra travelled the UK aboard the well-appointed royal train.

The planning and execution of these travels from a logistical perspective has taken some uncovering. Dressers and valets are rarely heard of in the historical record and so such narratives sit at the periphery of the royal story. The arrangements of the royal travelling wardrobe similarly merited little documentary evidence. The trunks and timetables have in the past been incidental to a wider discussion of monarchy. Certainly within traditional biographies of Queen Alexandra such details feature not at all. And yet such careful planning and packing that these trips undoubtedly required were instrumental in the building of the public persona that Alexandra needed to adopt when away from home.

The clothing itself remains invisible, either from having not survived at all or from not being photographed. Travel garments were utilitarian and the public expectation of Alexandra when princess and as queen consort was more decorative. Travelling ulster coats would be dispensed with as the welcoming committee approached at the platform and certainly by the time she was revealed to a wider public gaze she was the beautifully attired princess they anticipated. She navigated the public and private spaces and her fashioned body within those spaces. Private spaces were rare for Alexandra and so vehicles such as the royal train or yacht could offer a singular experience for her that went beyond merely travelling from A to B.

Similarly travel abroad might offer the extremes of public and private with long stretches at sea among a small trusted community of people followed by large state occasions: from private family visits in Greece to throngs of people in Lisbon. Alexandra's wardrobe accommodated these public and private occasions. Her garments met the full range of requirements, including that of climate, society, temperature, occasion and activity, and her dressers ensured that regardless of where and when, Alexandra was dressed as per these requirements.

For trips abroad where cultural considerations had to be made, Alexandra demonstrated a willingness to engage with 'otherness' in dress while conversely dressing for dinner on the banks of the Nile. As with other elements of her sartorial career such juxtapositions did not present a contradiction, but rather her chameleon-like ability to alter her appearance as the situation and her own personal whim dictated. Thus there was no tension in such choices. She clothed her royal, imperial body in dress that was sometimes sympathetic to, and on occasion at odds with, a colonial setting, reinforcing the stereotype of the British abroad. Alexandra herself was not British of course and so perhaps it was her identity which allowed her to tread carefully around regional and national sensitivities. Adorning herself with recognizable accents in dress to deliberately appeal to the local population was not new but in her hands was successfully achieved. Indeed it has now become commonplace for a prominent female member of the royal family to adopt such strategies when 'officially' abroad (de Guitaut 2009).

If travel for Alexandra was about both escape from and display of her public persona, it was something she managed successfully all of her married life. She might lounge aboard the royal yacht in her old sealskin wrap one day and dazzle the assembled population of a European city the next. She was a seasoned and comfortable traveller who relished new places and so it is Alexandra herself who sums up her delight during such journeys. From Norway she wrote:

> The descent from our Hotel was too steep for words – so we all had to walk and the ponies slid down. We were so delighted with our excursion in this beautiful spot that we settled to stay here another day – our drive home in the setting sun with the shades of evening was simply lovely.[28]

5
FANCY DRESS

Introduction

A young, pensive-looking Mary Queen of Scots dressed in an elaborate gown of velvet studded with gems and trimmed with gold lace offers a different version of Alexandra Princess of Wales – one in which she is performing a role very differently to her usual public outings. In a second image a more regal and stately 'Marguerite de Valois' is captured by the society photographer James Lafayette for the Devonshire House Ball in a similarly ornate garment. One woman, two glittering costume balls, a twenty-six year gap and two surviving dresses.[1]

Considering these two garments, as well as a range of other material, this chapter explores some of the wider themes surrounding nineteenth-century fancy-dress balls. Although there are only the two surviving dresses that relate directly to Alexandra's choices relating to fancy dress, there is a wealth of written sources that help to round out the narrative of this chapter.

Given the different 'roles' that Alexandra was called upon to play throughout her life in the public eye, the chapter will examine the manifestation of more specific role playing in terms of dressing up. However, in spite of its more concentrated subject matter, the themes that emerge and demand investigation here cover a broader canvas. As a mark of the strength of object-led history, holding a spotlight over these garments serves to highlight a range of themes.

Closely allied to Alexandra's choices of and feelings towards fancy-dress balls is her apparent interest in folk and national dress. Through the pages of her travel journals and contemporary accounts, a picture emerges of her fascination with both the textiles and costumes of other cultures. This section will ask why her surviving fancy-dress costumes, or indeed any other of the recorded costumes that she wore, never displayed this interest in a material sense. Earlier in the reign of Queen Victoria, the choice of the exotic character at a costume ball was considered vulgar: 'The emphasis continued to be on historical characters, which were considered to be in better taste than exotic or humorous ones' (Jarvis and Raine 1984: 14). During the last-third of the nineteenth century, the styling of characters from 'other' cultures was more acceptable, giving rise to a flurry of Cleopatras, Persian princesses and Japanese ladies.[2]

Before considering in any detail the surviving costumes it is important to establish their context within the cultural phenomenon that was the nineteenth-century costume ball. There is a wealth of contemporary material recording such events. Some take the form of comprehensive photographic archives[3]. Other original sources consist of instruction manuals that gave advice and suggested themes for those attending a costume ball. (See Holt 1894 and Bayard 1888.) The most notable publication remains Stevenson and Bennett's *Van Dyck in Check Trousers* (Stevenson and Bennett 1978), which studies the historical pattern of the costume ball and its antecedents from an art history perspective. Subsequent research into the nature of fancy balls is surprisingly thin.

In attempting to evaluate how royalty approached the social conventions of the fancy-dress ball it is possible to examine other notable examples, principally the imperial Russian balls of 1903 and the three occasions organized by Queen Victoria. The conspicuous nature of these events as social platforms, in which guests could display both the ingenuity of design and their wealth, makes the role of the royal guest potentially problematic. Would other guests expect members of the royal family to attend in garments that would outshine their own, complete with jewels in abundance? Did tensions arise between members of the wealthy elite bidding to outdo all in a show of outrageous consumption? Invitations for the largest and most anticipated events were highly coveted and the social competitiveness that arose forms a large part of this narrative.

This is also the story of Alexandra's costume choices through close attention to the objects and to the characters they intended to represent. This prompts an examination of some key themes: disguise and display, fantasy and 'otherness' and authenticity. One of the recurring themes is the degree of agency Alexandra was able to exert over her appearance. In the context of fancy dress it is possible to interrogate how this remains the same as other garments or if the nature of the event affected her ability to choose what she could wear. Were her choices part of a wider narrative that concerned the construction and maintenance of her public image through dress?

Set within a different social environment to that which would be considered 'everyday', even against other balls and special occasions, the culture of the costume ball offers a differently angled insight towards Alexandra's clothed body.

Folk and national dress in the life of Alexandra

The tale of Alexandra's encounter with the Khedive's harem, related in the previous chapter, reveals the then unusual interest on the part of a Western royal female in the clothing traditions of a culture that was so aesthetically different.

It seems probable that an opportunity to disguise herself was an exciting diversion for the princess. Indeed, the tour as a whole had tried to cloak itself in an element of hidden identity, as Alexandra and Edward went under the assumed names of Mr and Mrs Williams; a bid to lessen the interest in their progress. The presence of Russell, correspondent to *The Times*, implies that this concealment was for immediate purpose only and not to eliminate the wider interest of the British public. From Lady Grey's detailed recounting of this episode it becomes apparent that the young princess Alexandra relished the opportunity to play a role that was 'other', adopting a form of dress that was not only culturally different in style but also disguising in its form.

However, Alexandra's private experience of disguise was recreated in her public life on occasion in London. A report in *The Queen* 25 July 1878 described a Bal Masque attended by the princess and held by Lord Carlingford and Frances Countess Waldegrave at Strawberry Hill: 'The princess appeared in two different dominoes and did not discard the use of one until the evening was far advanced. She wore a lovely dress of dark crimson tulle sprinkled over with diamonds and diamond ornaments ensuite.'[4] Lord Esher noted of the same event, that a friend of the Prince and Princess of Wales, Helen Standish, and the princess took advantage of their similar appearance: 'The Princess and Mrs Standish, dominoed alike, led the baffled dancers into endless confusion' (Esher 1927:163). The dominoe, an all-enveloping garment that disguised the identity of the wearer, perhaps offered Alexandra an evening of relative anonymity where fancy dress could not; an example of the merits of disguise versus display and an alternate experience from her more usual one of public visibility.

This desire to occasionally go 'incognito' features within the pages of Alexandra's biographies and she took advantage of the opportunities to do so as they arose. Tisdall records in his biography: 'When King Edward was away from Marlborough House she used to send out a lady in waiting to borrow a car from one of her friends' thus bowling about the capital in relative privacy (1953:200). Impromptu decisions such as this allowed Alexandra some anonymous moments in an otherwise public life, her support of the London Hospital a case in point: 'Alexandra would arrive at "the London" without warning. She knew all the nurses and she liked to make tea in the matron's room' (Duff 1980: 149). Edward's friend Richard Haldane recorded his own experience of royal subterfuge while motoring around the Austrian countryside:

> He proposed to me one day that we should go in plain clothes as though we were Austrians … . As we were passing a little roadside inn with a wooden table in front of it, the King stopped and said, 'Here I will stand treat.' He ordered coffee for two and then he said, 'Now I am going to pay. I shall take care to give only a small tip to the woman in case she suspects who I am.' (Cited in Hough 1992: 228–9)

As King and Queen, Edward and Alexandra valued these moments of relative normality. Alexandra was to become skilled at playing different parts in her life – that of princess, mother, hostess, nurse and regal queen, thus those opportunities that allowed her briefly to be none of those things appear to have been eagerly enjoyed.

The nineteenth-century fancy-dress ball

'Masking' or masquerading had been popular in Britain since the eighteenth century, inspired by the tradition of the Italian carnivals. This form of social disguise retained some popularity into the nineteenth century, although there were the beginnings of anxieties from some quarters about the propriety of such occasions: 'Because of the anonymity the masks gave, manners could be informal, behaviour free and flirtations and assignations not only possible but probable' (Jarvis and Raine 1984: 5). By the time the Princess Victoria had ascended the throne, the rise of the costume ball as a more popular entertainment was underway: 'Unlike the masquerades, where the participants were masked and incognito, at a fancy ball, masks were not usually worn and the emphasis was on the attractiveness and inventiveness of the costume chosen' (Jarvis and Raine 1984: 5).

The contemporary publication *Fancy Dress Described or What to Wear at Fancy Balls,* by Ardern Holt, illustrates in its 170 pages just how popular these events had become by the mid-nineteenth century. The volume covered detailed descriptions, fabric and accessory suggestions and illustrations of the full cast of popular fancy-dress costumes with instructions for the reader to follow through to construction. Published by Debenham and Freebody, the book ran to six editions between 1879 and 1896 comprising an alphabetized list of suggested attire covering popular historical figures and allegorical characters. Mrs Holt's advice tended towards the prescriptive in tone, but was nothing if not thorough. Her suggestion for a costume based on 'Fire' ran as follows:

> Black tulle evening dress over red silk, with tongues of flames formed of red tinsel at the hem, fringed bodice and skirt covered with red sequins, as also the veil; coronet of tinsel to resemble flames; ornaments, garnets. Torch

carried in hand. It may also be carried out with black and crimson velvet embroidered with flames, or in flame colored and orange lisse. (Holt 1894: 87)

Naturally, Debenham and Freebody could supply any of the costumes described to order, as well as the component parts for those who preferred to make up the garments themselves.

As Mrs Holt demonstrated, the list of available and socially acceptable costumes was vast, although there were those that were more popular and could be relied upon to make an appearance at the balls given during this period. The romanticism of Sir Walter Scott's novels captured the public imagination to the extent that a Rowena, an Amy Robsart, a Di Vernon or a Lucy Ashton was almost certain to materialize at the majority of costumed events. Scott's heroines 'seemed to embody all the attributes which the young Victorian woman would have most liked to emulate but which the dictates of society made her unlikely to achieve' (Jarvis and Raine 1984: 7). They were beautiful and brave, exhibiting qualities of courageousness and daring in a romanticized past, in the form of the historical novel for which Sir Walter Scott was renowned.

The social context of the fancy-dress ball was well established by the time of the Princess Alexandra's arrival in the UK. It was available as a form of entertainment to most levels of society throughout the second half of the nineteenth century, excepting the poorest: 'In one issue of *The Queen* alone, 14 January 1893, there are accounts of the Lord Mayor of London's Fancy-dress Ball at the Mansion House, 'A Pretty Fancy Ball for Children' held at the Assembly Rooms, Southsea, in aid of the Portsmouth and South Hants Eye and Ear Infirmary, of the Annual Fancy Dress Ball at the Drill Hall, Merthyr Tydfil, in aid of the General Hospital, and of several private balls, of which a 'successful Fancy Ball was given at Maple Heyes [sic] near Lichfield, in honour of the coming of age of Mr W Worthington, son of Mr A. O. Worthington JP on the 10th inst [instance]' is a typical example' (Jarvis 1982: 41).

Fancy dress was appropriate for civic occasions, such as the tercentenary celebrations of Shakespeare's birth, at which a fancy-dress ball was central to the evening's entertainment. They were frequently associated with charitable benefits, to mark the opening of a new building, to celebrate a birthday or to welcome persons of note to a city, as in the case of the Mayor's Grand Fancy Dress Ball given in Liverpool in 1863 to honour the arrival of the Channel Fleet. Two thousand invitations were sent and from this one ball it is possible to assess in some measure, the industry that surrounded fancy dress. Within days of the announcement, there was a rash of advertisements to tempt those invited. J&W Jeffery & Co had the pleasure of announcing a large variety of fancy dress which could be viewed: 'Show rooms lighted with gas will be appointed for their display of which notice will be given.'[5] In the same issue J. A Bioletti announced his intention of hiring special assistants from Paris for the dressing of hair, and of providing costume ball moustaches guaranteed not to fall off. Nathans of London opened showrooms in Liverpool, making costumes to order and Charles Powell & Co held a book of costumes to assist clients with cosmetics, taking on six extra male coiffeurs from Manchester for the occasion.[6] That a single occasion such as this generated so much local and, in the case of Nathans, national income is an indication of the scale of the fashion for fancy dress by this period.

More examples of contemporary advertisements imply that women at the higher end of society would expect to attend at least one, if not more, fancy-dress balls annually as an anticipated part of the social calendar. Nathans, one of the biggest and oldest establishments specializing in theatrical and fancy dress, advertised regularly in the national press, promoting their new ranges of costumes 'suitable for the approaching Season'.[7] Implicit in this line is the expectation that clients would pre-order a fancy-dress garment as part of their wardrobe for the months ahead. The short notice given by the announcements of some of these balls certainly suggests that for the most part, those invited would already have a suitable costume. For many families at the upper end of the social scale, ancestral garments formed the basis for fancy-dress costumes, lending a distinctly eighteenth-century flavour to many gatherings.

Determining Alexandra's place in the midst of this popular phenomenon is problematic. That she took part in fancy dress at certain times during her royal career is a given, having two surviving garments from which to work. The extent to which she was a regular participant in such occasions is more difficult to ascertain. References to her attendance at any fancy-dress balls are non-existent. Besides the three well-documented occasions in 1871, 1874 and 1897 to which the two surviving garments belong, reported instances of Alexandra in fancy dress do not appear in the contemporary press. Given that Alexandra's appearance was an often-reported feature of daily news, this omission would appear to infer that she only took part in such entertainments rarely.

Fancy dress and royalty

The attendance of royalty at grand occasions of masquerade and fancy dress was not exceptional in the nineteenth century. It was in May 1842 that Queen Victoria and Prince Albert held the first of their *bal costumés* in a bid to bolster the declining British silk industry, 'by requesting the two thousand invited guests to wear accurate historical costume of any period or country, or national dress, made of Spitalfields silk' (Staniland 1997: 134). The royal couple drafted in the expertise of the costume historian James Robinson Planché to advise upon the styling of their costumes. While their guests might choose from any number of eras and types of fancy costume, Victoria and Albert decided upon the medieval figures of Queen Philippa and Edward III, accompanied by members of the royal household in the garb of fourteenth-century courtiers. Landseer's portrait of the Queen and prince consort is illustrative of the brocades, velvets and furs of which the costumes were made, no remnant of either now surviving. In spite of the call for historical accuracy, both Victoria and Albert 'improved' somewhat upon the clothing as depicted upon the tomb effigies of their medieval predecessors in Westminster Abbey, a customization that gave her gown a modern silhouette. In reality she digressed hardly at all from her customary shape. Public interest in their young queen's costume was demonstrated the day before the ball, permission having been granted to the dressmaker Vouillon & Laure to exhibit the dress at their premises: '250 carriages of the élite of the aristocracy and *beau monde* crowded to see it' (Miller 1985: 1024–26).

Victoria's call for historical accuracy, her adherence to a 'safe' characterization and the subsequent publication of her own image and that of some of the other prominent guests, both in the daily press and in the form of an album, set the precedent for those that followed. Alexandra's consistency in following a similar pattern of female royal participation may suggest that she took, in part at least, some inspiration from her mother-in-law.

Where Victoria's balls were based on supporting domestic industries, those of other contemporary monarchies demonstrated the political bias that such entertainments could display. In 1903, Emperor Nicholas II of Russia gave two Winter Costume Balls to mark the bicentennial of the founding of the city of Petersburg. The invitations specified the dress code: 'Ladies and gentlemen to come in costumes from the time of Tsar Alexey Mikhailovich' (Amelekhina and Levykin 2008: 100). Nicholas revelled in the finer points of militaristic display, attending the many and varied presentations of troops that were a regular part of his duties as emperor: 'The tedium of such occasions was reduced for Nicholas by the fact that, unlike his father, he loved military display' (Lieven 1993: 60). The choice of the seventeenth-century Russian nobility appealed to Nicholas's autocratic views and his self-perception as military leader in a feudal hierarchy.

The result of Nicholas's endeavours in 1903 was an occasion remarkable for its paradox. The costumes themselves were not the authentic garments, uncontaminated by Western European influence that Nicholas imagined they were: 'Petersburg high society hired Russia's premier tailors and dressmakers, all trained in European design, to create their costumes' (Ruane 2009: 168). Although the fabrics used to make the costumes were sourced from Russian textile manufacturers, the irony, in their bid for an authentic display, was that the Muscovite aristocracy of the seventeenth century was more cosmopolitan in its acquisitions: 'In the seventeenth century the imperial couple's clothing was undoubtedly made from brocades and silks imported from China, Persia and Italy, since the Muscovite court ordered only the finest fabrics for court dress' (Ruane 2009: 168). Much anticipation preempted the ball in Russia: '"No one is capable of talking about anything but the ball in Saint Petersburg" wrote Count P.S. Sheremet'ev in his diary. "Tailors and dressmakers are arriving every minute." Moreover, "everyone kept their costume a secret, in order to surprise other guests on the night"' (cited in Amelekhine and Levykin 2008: 100). Lady Randolph Churchill described similar scenes in London prior to the 1897 Devonshire House Ball: 'With bated breath and solemn mien a fair dame would whisper to some few dozen or more that she was going to represent the Queen of Cyprus or Aspasia, Fredegonde or Petrarch's Laura; but the secret *must* be kept' (Cornwallis-West 1973: 301).

The empress Alexandra chose to attend as the wife of Czar Alexey Mikhailovich Romanov, the ancestor that Nicholas II himself portrayed for the occasion. It was an unsurprising choice for the imperial couple, devoted as they were. While the emperor had given orders for an appropriate costume, 'something full length and not too garish', the empress desired 'that His Majesty's attire should resemble hers' (Amelekhina and Levykin 2008: 101). Her costume was based upon an ancient icon that the imperial family worshipped, lending her appearance a religious as well as a royal significance. The official photograph of the empress shows a sombre and serious countenance in spite of the magnificence of the robe she is wearing (Amelekhina & Levykin 2008: 102).

The empress embodied a former ruler of her adopted country. She represented a loyal wife, revered in Russian iconography, the gown made by the celebrated wardrobe mistress of the imperial theatres, A. F. Ivashchenko, with adornments by Fabergé, constructed in the form of a traditionally styled sarafan. The empress had never been popular with the Russian people and was less well versed in the art of dress as a political or diplomatic tool, a point illustrated in the young empress's participation in a waltz during the ball: 'The idea of the Empress waltzing in her Muscovite robes was precisely the social gaffe that Nikolai Grech had warned Russian women against fifty years earlier. One guest even commented that many of the women had difficulty in waltzing in Muscovite clothing' (Ruane 2009: 169).

If the underlying principle of the Russian balls was highly politicized, there were still elements of the spectacle which resonated with those of the British aristocracy. What these comparative examples demonstrate is that the monarchies in question used fancy dress to reinforce issues of their own identity. Where other social groups used the opportunity to dress up as a means to either disguise or blur their usual identity, prominent royal figures used costume balls to underline their status, dressing as their predecessors to underpin their place in the monarchical hierarchy.

The surviving garments

It was as one of Sir Walter Scott's most famous literary heroines that Alexandra chose to appear at the Waverley Ball in 1871. The dress now resides in the Royal Ceremonial Dress Collection at Kensington Palace in a somewhat altered condition, since it was subsequently remodelled as a costume for the

Marlborough House Ball of 1874. It is still, however, easily recognizable from its first incarnation (Figure 5.1). The dressmaker's label identifies Mme Elise as responsible for the dress as it is now, although whether she was commissioned with the remodelling only of the garment for its later outing in 1874 is not known. The dress as described in *The Times* for the Marlborough House Ball of 1874 matches the existing appearance of the garment now: 'Her Royal Highness wore a ruby coloured Venetian dress, with a blue front to the skirt, sewn with jewels and gold embroidery. The close sleeves were of ruby velvet with blue satin puffings, gold embroidered; the small ruff was edged with gold, and the body of the dress covered with strings of pearls; but the most charming and becoming part of this magnificent costume, was the small, close velvet cap, laced and covered with jewels of marvelous splendour.'[8]

A closer study of the style and execution of the surviving garments, even in the absence of an accompanying historical record, may yet reveal some of the tensions that existed for so prominent a guest at these events. (See Plate 8.)

Figure 5.1 Alexandra Princess of Wales dressed as Mary Queen of Scots for the Waverley Ball in 1871. The dress is now in the collections of Historic Royal Palaces, Royal Collection Trust/© Her Majesty Queen Elizabeth II 2016.

A number of photographic portraits were taken of the Princess of Wales in her ruby velvet gown representing Mary Queen of Scots for the eagerly anticipated Waverley Ball of 1871. *The Court Journal* reported that 'the demand for tickets reached to such a fever heat, that for nearly a week past the committee have found it necessary to resort to the expedient of doubling the price of the tickets to lessen in some measure the pressure put upon them'. Of the Princess of Wales, the report continued: 'No less fair than the hapless original, but born to a purer life and a happier fate, the Princess of Wales as Marie Stuart moved with a quiet, pensive grace that, while it was all her own was nonetheless true to the character she had assumed.'[9]

This assessment of Alexandra's appearance and the easy comparison with her chosen character hints at the relationship that contemporary Victorian society had formed with the 'story' of Mary Queen of Scots. Jane Elizabeth Lewis has examined the phenomena of Mary Stuart's 'legend' as it has been shaped across generations, and in her introductory paragraphs, stresses that 'the reader will understand that by 'Mary Queen of Scots, I refer as much to an image or an idea as to a historical woman' (Lewis 1998: 2). In Lewis's estimation, Mary Queen of Scots had become part of what she calls the 'fiction of Britain', the construction of an imagined past based on certain historical figures, through art, poetry, plays and novels. The political propaganda that blew up around Mary in her lifetime and for the centuries after her death, clouded most of the facts of her life. In Victorian Britain there were two Marys. One was the rather saccharine portraiture of martyred Mary: 'Many canvases captured a lady of ethereal loveliness, one who – when not occupied with her needle or the feeding of her doves – was usually to be found enduring some distress with every flounce, rosette and sausage curl in place' (Lewis 1998: 173). The 'other' Mary was, 'the more demanding (and more psychologically convincing) Stuart Queen of Walter Scott' (Lewis 1998: 173). The Victorian appropriation of Mary was the more sentimental, where Scott's character was tempered with political machination and scheming. These two 'fictions' create some complexity to Alexandra's choice – she was a Victorian woman dressing as a martyred Catholic queen for the memorial of a male author whose character was both beautiful and charming but manipulative and scheming.

The actuality of the Princess of Wale's decision to dress as Mary Queen of Scots may of course be far simpler. The volume of image making relating to Mary Stuart in the nineteenth century may have been a contributory factor: 'Between 1820 and 1892 the Royal Academy alone displayed fifty six new scenes from Mary's life' (Lewis 1998: 173). The seeming popularity of the iconography of Mary at this time may have offered some correlation to Alexandra as a popular royal female herself. Given that the Waverley Ball was a fundraiser and a celebration of Sir Walter Scott, it is thus fair to suggest that Alexandra was attending as an image of Mary and not as the historical figure, a supposition supported by Sara Stevenson: 'It is notable that in several of the major balls, Mary Queen of Scots

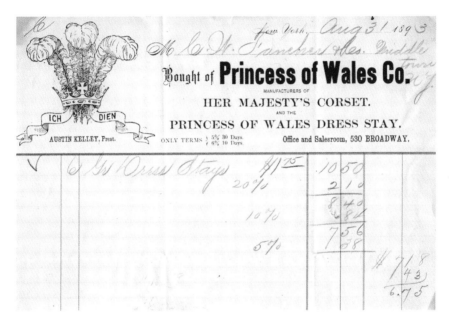

Plate 1 Even if a company did not officially hold a royal warrant, the chosen product names could still reflect royalty, demonstrated here with the advertisement for the Princess of Wales Corset Co, courtesy of the FIDM Museum at the Fashion Institute of Design and Merchandising, Los Angeles, Photo: FIDM Museum & Library Inc.

Plate 2 Marianne Skerrett was principal dresser to Queen Victoria for many years. It is unusual for a dresser to be recorded in this way. Chalk sketch by Rosa Koberwein, 1880, Royal Collection Trust/© Her Majesty Queen Elizabeth II 2016.

Plate 3 The hand-stitched cipher specific to Alexandra's garments that was both decorative and functional in terms of royal laundry, detail from one of her surviving nightgowns © Historic Royal Palaces.

Plates 4 & 5 Court gown dating to c. 1904 and detail of bodice illustrating the seemingly mismatched floral motifs at centre back, with permission of the Royal Ontario Museum, Toronto © ROM.

Plate 6 Decorative dolman, one of the rare pieces of outerwear from Alexandra's wardrobe to have survived, made by Dieulefait & E. Bouclier c. 1870, courtesy of FIDM Museum at the Fashion Institute of Design and Merchandising, Los Angeles. Photo credit: Brian Sanderson.

Plate 7 Lambswool coat, described as a driving coat, possibly from Alexandra's trousseau in 1863. One of the most functional pieces to have survived, The Metropolitan Museum of Art, Gift of Miss Irene Lewisohn 1937, www.metmuseum.org.

Plate 8 A watercolour sketch of Alexandra in her costume for the Waverley Ball taken by Princess Louise, Royal Collection Trust/© Her Majesty Queen Elizabeth II 2016.

Plate 9 Engraving showing Alexandra relaxing in her trademark tailor-made at Marlborough House in 1882, original drawing by Chartran (copied engraving in author's own collection).

Plate 10 One of the few surviving pieces of tailoring from Alexandra's wardrobe, a cream serge yachting jacket by Vernon. By the early twentieth century Vernon had become her tailor of choice © Fashion Museum, Bath and North East Somerset Council.

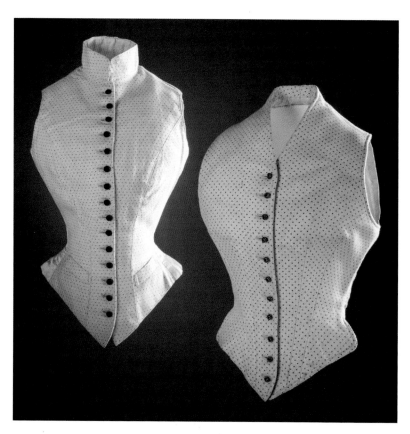

Plate 11 Spotted hopsack waistcoats made for Alexandra by the tailor Busvine who appeared with greater frequency in her wardrobe accounts from the late 1890s onwards, courtesy of FIDM Museum at the Fashion Institute of Design and Merchandising, Los Angeles. Photo credit: Brian Sanderson.

Plate 12 Cream silk and lace mantle made by the mourning warehouse Jay's of London, c. 1863 and so possibly made for Alexandra's trousseau, The Metropolitan Museum of Art, Gift of Miss Irene Lewisohn 1937, www.metmuseum.org.

Plate 13 The half-mourning bodice from a dress worn by Alexandra to the christening of her grandson David in 1894, spotted lilac and black moiré silk made by Madame Fromont © Historic Royal Palaces.

Plate 14 Portrait of Queen Alexandra by Luke Fildes. The garment has never been mounted or photographed as it has become increasingly fragile and so this is one of the only colour images of the garment, 1902, oil on canvas, Royal Collection Trust/© Her Majesty Queen Elizabeth II 2016.

Dress worn by
Queen Alexandra, it was
given me in 1912 by her
dressmaker's sister

Plate 15 A piece of figured silk kept as a souvenir by the sister of one of Alexandra's dressmakers as the label attached to the fabric explains (author's own collection). Photograph: Matt Mulcrone.

Plate 16 A photograph of the label of one of the surviving Busvine waistcoats, demonstrating how this kind of provenance is so valuable when trying to piece together the now separate pieces of one woman's wardrobe © Fashion Museum, Bath and North East Somerset Council.

Plate 17 Cream and pink jacket only re-attributed to Alexandra in 2016 after being catalogued originally as a garment belonging to Queen Mary. An identical jacket, but in blue, is in the Museum at FIDM, Los Angeles © Fashion Museum, Bath and North East Somerset Council.

turns up as a character out of Scott's novel rather than an historical individual' (Stevenson and Bennett 1978: 8).

There is more evidence suggesting that choosing to dress up as Mary Queen of Scots was in fact rather commonplace. As early as 1742, Horace Walpole wrote in a letter to Horace Mann of a costume ball that he had attended where there were 'dozens of ugly Queens of Scots' (Toynbee 1903: 181) while over 140 years later, the satirist George du Maurier illustrated the continuing over abundance of 'Marys' in a Punch cartoon of 1885, in which rather ironically under the title of 'Who'd Have Thought It?' a rather ageing Queen of Scots is chatting over tea with a Horace Walpole.[10]

The reality of life behind the serene photograph marking the occasion and the contemporary journalistic hyperbole that accompanied her appearance may have been quite different. In 1871 Alexandra was a very different princess to the young girl who had arrived in England eight years earlier. Although Mary Queen of Scots was a popular choice for Alexandra to make for the occasion of a Scott-inspired event, here was a princess living with a number of newly realized realities in terms of a not unproblematic marriage, motherhood including loss of a young child and life as a prominent royal figure.[11]

It is possible that in opting to dress as Mary Queen of Scots, the Princess of Wales was able to appear both to conform in a populist choice of garment and transgress with the complex character that Mary was in the nineteenth century. It may be an example of the duality in dress that Alexandra was to show on other occasions, that she struck a positive note with her audience at the same time as telling an alternate but largely private story.

Three years later, Alexandra reinvented her look and her gown closer to home, for the Marlborough House Ball in 1874. It is an interesting facet to this garment that it was not worn for a single event but was reinvented for a second public occasion. It might be supposed that Alexandra simply disliked the fuss that accompanied the planning of a fancy-dress ball and its costumes. However, Lady Constance Battersea records in her memoirs a conversation she had with the then widowed queen Alexandra in 1912: 'When later I ventured to mention fancy dress parties to Queen Alexandra, Her Majesty quite warmed to the subject and said "Oh it is a capital entertainment; it means three weeks of amusing preparation, and as long after the event in talking it over, and then in being photographed in costume"' (Battersea 1922: 358). The memory of her enthusiasm for the occasions suggests that her approach to the creation of a fancy-dress garment was a positive and active one.

Across London, closeted in another collection, is the second of Alexandra's surviving fancy-dress gowns, worn to the glittering Devonshire House Ball of 1897 (Figure 5.2). Hosted by the indomitable 'Double' Duchess of Devonshire, the ball was inspired by the diamond jubilee of Queen Victoria and was intended to be the most glittering event of the season. Invitations were fiercely sought

Figure 5.2 Alexandra Princess of Wales dressed as Marguerite de Valois for the Devonshire House Ball of 1897, held in celebration of Queen Victoria's diamond jubilee (original *carte de visite*, author's own collection).

and preparations by the guests meticulous. Lady Randolph Churchill recalled: 'Historical books were ransacked for inspirations, old pictures and engravings were studied and people became quite learned in respect to past celebrities of whom they had never before heard' (Cornwallis-West 1973: 301). Each of the splendid costumes was captured by the photographer James Lafayette 'in a special photographic studio tent erected in the grounds in which Lafayette labored until 4.00am the following morning' (Pepper 1998: 20).

The dress exists now in some fragility at the Museum of London. Made from white satin and richly decorated with an applied polychromatic scheme of sequins and spangles, Alexandra dazzled as Marguerite de Valois of France. Unlike its earlier counterpart, this garment is not identified by a maker's label.

Unlike a large number of other couture houses and theatrical costumiers who swiftly advertised their clients for the event, none appear to have claimed responsibility for Alexandra's dress for this event. A clue may lie, however, in a closer study of Alexandra's daughter Princess Maud's gown. Maud's dress remained intact and was featured in the exhibition *Style and Splendour; The Wardrobe of Queen Maud of Norway* at the Victoria and Albert Museum. It was made by the firm Morin Blossier.

A closer study of the image of Alexandra at the ball, next to the photograph of Maud's dress, reveals that the sleeves appear to be of the same design: strips of satin running lengthways down the arm revealing puffs of white chiffon in between. The satin is decorated with small diamante rosettes which are just discernible along the sleeves of Alexandra's dress. Morin Blossier was certainly Alexandra's favourite couture house in the 1890s, evidenced in the accounts ledgers that record the sums paid to her many suppliers. The Parisian establishment's probable commission is supported in an entry recorded in the wardrobe accounts of 1898. A large retrospective sum of £501/0/8d was paid to Morin Blossier for an order from 1897, the payment for which appears on the first page of the accounts.[12]

The Princess of Wales' choice of characterization is once again an interesting one. Marguerite de Valois, born in 1553, was the daughter of Henry II of France and Catherine de Medici. Her life was a tumultuous one of an arranged, unhappy marriage, a failed coup d'etat against her brother, imprisonment and divorce, culminating in the publication of her memoirs, prompting widespread scandal at the time. As with Mary however, there was an alternate Marguerite, a fictional construct of greater familiarity perhaps to readers and opera officianadoes of the nineteenth century. *La Reine Margot* is a fictionalized and indeed romanticized account by Alexandre Dumas of the events surrounding Marguerite's marriage while Shakespeare's *Love's Labour's Lost* is based upon an attempt at reconciliation with her husband. The character of Marguerite has a central and heroic role in Meyerbeer's opera *Les Huguenots* first shown in 1836. As an opera lover, it may have been this last depiction of the French queen that Alexandra 'knew'. It was too, according to Ardern Holt, a more generally popular fancy-dress choice, appearing as the first colour plate in *Fancy Dresses Described* (Holt 1894: 10).

The Devonshire House Ball aspired, through its costumes, to a high point of historical accuracy. Certain commentators stressed the extent to which guests went to achieve such sartorial precision: 'The Costumes, most of them archaeologically correct, and copied from old pictures, permitted every licence in point of expense and magnificence, and ladies and gentlemen both freely availed themselves of the opportunity' (Greville 1897: 78–9). In the London papers, Alexandra's Marguerite was lavishly complimented as was her youth and beauty.[13] However, the reporter for the *Freeman's Journal and Daily Commercial*

Advertiser in Dublin, took a slightly different view of the princess's costume, noting of her appearance only: 'The Princess, too modern and too like herself in a Paris dress.'[14] The photographic record of Alexandra at the ball certainly supports this assessment, as aside from the wired collar, excess of jewellery and slashed sleeves, the cut and construction is that of a contemporary evening dress. There was a long precedent for this approach towards historical characters. Queen Victoria's costume for her *bal costumé* of 1851 saw her dressed in supposedly sixteenth-century style: 'The neck and sleeves were trimmed with antique lace but, even so, the composition and the narrow waisted, full skirted silhouette are unmistakably those of 1851' (Stevenson and Bennett 1978: 70). Holt explains at the earliest opportunity in the introduction to her volume of costumes that 'it does not purport to be an authority in the matter of costumes for, as a rule, the historical dresses worn on such occasions are lamentably incorrect' (Holt 1894: 1).

To strive towards greater historical accuracy at costume balls was a rationale much admired in certain quarters during the nineteenth century. To copy portraits of the old masters or to recreate the look of the ancestors lent a degree of gravitas to the frivolity of the costume ball. While some certainly tried to adopt a liberated approach to historical representations of dress, as Lafayette's images from the Devonshire House Ball demonstrate, for many the influence and the underpinnings of contemporary dress were too difficult to abandon.

A useful comparison might be drawn from the experience of Mary, Lady Curzon, vicereine of India from 1899 to 1905. She attended costume balls annually during her years in India, often creating her costumes from elements of garments in her wardrobe: 'She maintained her viceregal authority even on these occasions, however her fancy dress does give an important signal of her subjectivity beyond her viceregal persona' (Thomas 2007: 382). A photograph that Mary sent to her father in 1903 shows her dressed as a former vicereine of the early 1800s. The dress itself makes one or two stylistic references to the early nineteenth century, but is in essence a contemporary evening dress, signalling a reluctance shared by the Princess of Wales to make a grand historical statement. Mary Curzon prided herself on her ability to make the correct assessment of expectations in terms of her appearance. She was not averse, however, to indulging in a degree of fantasy in her dress choices at costume balls which both reinforced her actual position but also represented her subverted desires: 'For an evening in October 1905 Mary became Berengaria of Navarre, wife of Richard the Lionheart, with her daughters Irene and Cynthia dressed as her pages alongside fully costumed male attendants who were members of the Viceroy's household staff. Her choice of costume for her last fancy dress ball in India reveals the enduring strength of her own subjectivity as a Queen within a viceregal court' (Thomas 2007: 384).

If the historical precision of the costumes worn by both Alexandra and Mary Curzon was lacking, it is perhaps through the characterization itself that both women were making their points. By dressing as queens, they expressed their hierarchical positions and their desires to be perceived at the pinnacle of their respective hierarchies. If fancy dress is indeed an opportunity to subvert the social norm, then it could be argued that in certain respects this is what Alexandra was doing. The norm for all of her adult life had been as Princess of Wales, the queen-in-waiting. To appear as a queen at occasions such as these allowed her to maintain her place of precedence in society, but also to fantasize in the role of queen. As Mary Queen of Scots and as Marguerite de Valois, an accurate transformation would perhaps have been too problematic for Alexandra, and perhaps too daunting a departure feted as she was for her general good taste in dress. She appeared at both the Waverley Ball and at the Devonshire House Ball, as herself but also as the self she was waiting to become.

This may once more indicate a sense of public versus private. In public Alexandra chose fancy-dress costumes that were, to a large degree, safely styled with a contemporary silhouette. At her more informal moments away from public occasion, her dress became simplified while in public she maintained the sartorial expectations of the stately, elegant princess.

Events such as the fancy balls, at which the Princess of Wales was such a prominent figure and whose costumes underwent a high degree of scrutiny, meant that personal preference in the choice of costume was less important than maintaining the status quo. At each of these three highly visible entertainments, Alexandra attended, in almost all respects, as herself; three balls, two garments, three queens. Unlike so many of the other guests whose costumes permitted them to reveal another facet of themselves, Alexandra's choices were ultimately safe. Perhaps the establishment could not allow the future queen consort of England to appear as a Greek peasant or an Egyptian princess. The social hierarchy and the concept of a rigid class structure that was such a large part of Victorian society could only tolerate a certain degree of deviation. The Princess of Wales, at the very top of this social structure, had to represent the wealthy, privileged aristocracy even at such light-hearted displays as these.

Like-dressing – Alexandra and Dagmar

In June 1873, Alexandra's younger sister, the czarevna of Russia, Maria Feodorovna, and her husband Alexander, heir to the Russian throne, planned a state visit to the UK. The two sisters were close and corresponded regularly following Alexandra's marriage. Perhaps as a tribute to the playful atmosphere of their shared upbringing, the two sisters determined on a sartorial display which deserves some consideration here for its performative qualities and the desire to dress in a way that was in many ways 'other' in a public context and therefore intended to provoke comment. In a biography of the Russian czarevna, Corynne Hall explains: 'She and Alix determined to make it the highlight of the Season and soon hit on a novel idea – they would dress exactly alike, day and evening. Soon their letters were full of dress patterns, materials, hats and trimmings' (Hall 1999: 58). How this was achieved given the great distance between them is testament not only to their organization but also to their familiarity with the workings of the couture houses. Worth claimed that his atelier facilitated the plans of the sisters, the Russian czarevna already a loyal customer of the Parisian maison. De Marly writes: 'It was this empress's fervent admiration for Worth's confections which persuaded her sister Alexandra, Princess of Wales, to visit the house, for the two liked to dress alike even though they lived far apart. When a meeting was likely letters flew between them secretly arranging to arrive in identical clothes and sometimes Worth was involved in the conspiracy' (De Marley 1980: 131). It may have been that their physical presence was not in fact required. Wealthy clients of many leading couturiers had their measurements kept on file, or even a dress form dedicated to them.

Such a phenomenon was not uncommon in the nineteenth century (Kirk 2013). Teenage sisters were often photographed in matching garments – Alexandra's own daughters were similarly attired on occasion. The significance of Alexandra and Dagmar's decision, however, lay in the very public nature of the visit and their mutual positions as consorts-in-waiting of two of the world's largest empires (Figure 5.3). No longer teenagers, they were both wives and mothers. In creating matching wardrobes for a prolonged state visit and appearing in matching gowns, they planned and participated in the performance of dressing up for an audience. The spectacle was timed to commence from the minute of the Russian imperial couple's arrival: 'In June the Imperial yacht sailed into Woolwich, where it was met by the Prince and Princess of Wales. The Princess and the Tsarevna were dressed identically, each in a white dress and a straw bonnet with cherries on it. Such a sight had never been seen before on a royal occasion' (Hall 1999: 58).

The performance was not reserved only for formal occasions: 'Dagmar and Alix were determined to enjoy every moment. Crowds gathered as they took a morning drive in Hyde Park wearing blue and white foulard dresses: in the evening they caused a further sensation when they attended the great balls given by the leading Society hostesses' (Hall 1999: 60). Louisa, Lady Antrim, wrote of one of these occasions: 'The sisters set each other off and became the centre of a glittering crowd wherever they went' (Antrim 1937: 20). Dagmar's married life had quickly followed a path at variance to Alexandra's. Marrying into the imperial Russian family, she was not only obliged to change her faith, becoming a member of the Russian Orthodox Church, but also changed her name in line with royal tradition. She married a man more comfortable when at home with his children than out in society and she married into a country that was beset with divisions. She became empress at a much younger age than her sister, but like Alexandra was aware from a young age, just how much her appearance, and the correct choice of dress given her position, mattered to those who observed her.

Figure 5.3 Alexandra and her sister Dagmar, the Russian czarevna Maria Feodorovna, in 1876 during the state visit and their synchronized appearances, Royal Collection Trust/© Her Majesty Queen Elizabeth II 2016.

For the duration of the visit periodicals recorded the like-dressing of the two women, including occasions where it had been executed with a variation as described on 2 August 1873: 'HRH the Princess of Wales wore at the last garden party at Chiswick, pale blue silk trimmed with velvet of a darker shade and a bonnet ensuite. The Czarevna was in pink silk made in the same style and a bonnet to correspond.'[15] A number of photographs captured the visit and the sisters in matching gowns, including perhaps the most famous image of the two women together in spotted silk day dresses. It is likely that Maria Feodorovna was referring to this dress two years later in a letter to her sister dated 5 April 1875: 'I just realised that I brute (sic) never paid you for all the dresses, and I have lost the bill; I'm sending you a little dress by opportunity, which every day shall take the place of our poor dear old spotted one. It's a lovely present! Hopefully you will like it!' (cited in Klausen 2001:56). While this missive suggests a degree of reminiscence for their visit in 1873 and the device of dressing alike in public it is also indicative of a continued flow of acquisition between the sisters taking the form of gifts or the placing of orders. Official photographs originating from Russia attest to a similar correspondence of dress six months later when Alexandra and Edward travelled to St Petersburg for the wedding of the Duke of Edinburgh to the Grand Duchess Maria Alexandrovna. The extent to which this took place is less well documented. However, as young women still in their youthful twenties their ability to bring off such a sartorial performance at such great distance offers a compelling insight into another facet of Alexandra as consumer but also as performer.

Conclusion

Glenn Adamson recommended in his paper considering the absent object that 'the best thing to do when faced with an unexpected "hole" in the historical record is to look at the edges of the perceived gap, in the hope of delineating its precise contours' (Adamson 2009: 196). Queen Alexandra's surviving examples of fancy-dress costume arguably represent the reverse of this conundrum. Two garments of similar sartorial function in the royal wardrobe represent a distortion in the wider picture of random survival so that it is in fact the much larger 'holes' around the fancy dress that require caution. There is barely any mention of Alexandra appearing in fancy dress in contemporary descriptions outside of the occasions recorded here for which both garments are extant. Presumably it was the very novelty of these items that ensured their survival.

Alexandra's participation in such entertainments was entirely in keeping with social norms of the period, not just in the echelons of the upper classes but as a form of entertainment that was enjoyed across a wider social spectrum. The regularity with which Ardern Holt's instructional manual was reprinted and the many contemporary newspaper reports detailing fancy-dress balls in both urban and more provincial settings places her clothing strategies for fancy dress into a context that would have been familiar to many more people than perhaps her usual choices of state or public dressing would have been. From a royal perspective, Alexandra was following the precedent set by Queen Victoria and her successful *bal costumes,* while at the imperial Russian balls held in 1903, confirmed the longevity of such masquerades and the supposed benefits that such events brought to home trade. As confirmed elsewhere, Alexandra did not necessarily subscribe to such edicts concerning patriotic patronage, her Devonshire House Ball gown almost certainly having been fashioned by Morin Blossier.

It is perhaps Alexandra's chosen characterization and the evidence of the surviving pieces themselves that reveal the most about the Princess of Wales, for at each occasion it seems clear that she essentially dressed as versions of herself or at least the self she was waiting to become. Where other guests were prepared to appear in costumes that were to a greater or lesser degree 'other' than their normal selves, Alexandra either could not or would not take that step. More than at any other public occasion, the wrong costume at a fancy-dress ball might speak volumes and colour a reputation thereafter. Alexandra never made such mistakes but reinforced her status through conservative regal costumes.

This does not mean, however, that her garments were entirely without meaning on her part. As the guest who might be expected to receive the greatest scrutiny at these fancy-dress balls, Alexandra's sartorial message trod a more subtle path. Helen Hackett in her paper considering the image making of monarchs acknowledges the tensions bound up with the monarch on public display: 'On the one hand the monarch is the incumbent of an institution which claims to be timeless and sacred, a symbol of national values; on the other, he or she is a human being with a life story of birth, love, death, mistakes and triumphs' (Hackett 2001: 811). While not the monarch in these cases, Alexandra was in effect the female public face of the monarchy in the absence of Queen Victoria. As the fictionalized Mary Queen of Scots and the similarly invented Marguerite de Valois, Alexandra managed to present herself as queenly but could also hint at some of her life story as well – the loves, deaths, mistakes and triumphs that shaped her life.

6

TAILOR-MADE FOR
A QUEEN

Introduction

Of the many hundreds of photographs taken of Alexandra during her royal career, the images that have been most often reproduced in secondary sources and therefore have arguably generated the most widely disseminated sense of her style are those in which she appears in a tailored costume. (See Plate 9.) As the broadsheets and contemporary periodicals were describing in detail her highly embellished court and evening wear, descriptions often released through the court circular, Alexandra herself was generating a style of garment that was to become synonymous with her personal choice of daywear. In complete contrast to those bejewelled garments worn to the drawing rooms and state balls of the mid-to-late nineteenth century, Alexandra's appropriation of the simple tailored style was, I would maintain, her most individually distinctive contribution to fashion among her peers.

At a time when women only wore tailored garments for very specific sporting occasions as either participant or observer, the young Princess of Wales took the unprecedented step of taking these functional, pared down garments into a different sphere. Alexandra took to wearing the 'tailormade' every day, removing it from its original context. This chapter will examine the development of this transition, considering first the British tradition of bespoke tailoring and how the female consumer first forged links with the tailoring establishment through the design of the eighteenth-century riding jacket. Riding habits more generally were the earliest and most common form of sporting attire for aristocratic women and were the only time that women forged sartorial relationships with male designers. Alexandra's own relationship with the Savile Row tailor Henry Poole, maker of her own riding habits from the earliest days of her marriage, was perhaps her first experience of any kind of tailoring and so warrants consideration here.

The growth of the sporting aesthetic among the middle and upper classes in the second half of the nineteenth century was the catalyst for the more regular choices Alexandra made by the late 1870s and 1880s. With their annual attendance at Cowes Week for the regatta, trips to Scotland for the field sports and an array of country house parties in between, the opportunity to dress in sporting fashion was much increased and resulted in a more coherent approach by manufacturers to cater for the female client. The feminization, even democratization of formerly male, lower-class fabrics such as tweed and serge, is intrinsic to the shaping of the woman's tailor-made and needs to be examined in the context of Alexandra's consumption. Unlike other royal contemporaries, she never wore uniform but there were certain militaristic and naval elements inherent in the styling of suits she wore which warrant further analysis.

Given the ubiquitous nature of the tailored suit in Alexandra's wardrobe for the majority of her public life, the surviving material culture fails to reflect such riches. The tailored elements of her wardrobe as it exists now comprise three waistcoats, three jackets with the skirts no longer extant and a decorative riding jacket. The vast majority then of the tailoring in which she is pictured on countless occasions no longer exist. Those pieces that have survived, however, offer at least a sense of how such garments were fashioned for her, and alongside other robust sources such as the wardrobe accounts, business archives and the images themselves, a more rounded picture begins to emerge. Thus the names of Henry Poole, Redfern, Busvine and Vernon will be subject to some scrutiny for their long-held and well-documented royal patronage.

The overarching question that Alexandra's relationship with the tailored costume poses is this: Why did the Princess of Wales take such a sartorially daring step? With her reputation thus far having been one of appropriate conservatism in dress – feted certainly but not for styles that were at the cutting edge of the fashion system – why did she engage so strongly with this aesthetic? In many ways the close-fitting nature of the tailored garment only served to highlight her unfashionably slender frame. A sense of the fashioned Victorian body requires some thought here, the work of Jennifer Entwistle and Diana Crane offering some useful boundaries to such a discussion (Entwistle 2006 and Crane 2000). Clothing herself in a form-fitting garment might have been a deliberate choice and if so may be indicative of a growing sense of her own agency relating to clothing strategies that flew in the face of prevailing style. Of course it was a divergence that paid off. Alexandra's choice was widely admired and it was perhaps the only instance in her career where it might be said that the popular royal actually precipitated a style rather than followed it.

Traditions of royal uniform

Strongly associated with the heritage of British tailoring, military uniforms as appropriated by the monarchy need some consideration. Perhaps the monarch most famous for his propensity to both dress in and design uniforms for himself and others was King George IV. Christopher Hibbert records: 'One of his first acts on being made Prince Regent was to promote himself Field Marshall and when he wore the uniform people noticed that even the seams of the coat were heavily embroidered' (Hibbert 1964: 143–4). This tradition of donning a military uniform placed the monarch at the head of the armed forces, signalling their status but it was a practice that was adopted to a greater or lesser degree dependant on the monarch in question. King George III's chief innovation in dress was to be the Windsor uniform which was first worn in the late 1770s. The blue coat with scarlet facings was to serve as a generic uniformed option for the royal family that might be worn in place of court dress or to survey troops and according to research by the dress historian Sacha Llewellyn it 'was inspired by the hunting livery designed for his father, Frederick Prince of Wales in 1729' (Llewellyn 1996: 12). This was certainly its purpose when a version of it was made for Queen Victoria, a description of which was recorded by Lady Lyttelton in 1839. She noted that the young queen wore 'a smart shako, with plenty of gold about it, and the Windsor Uniform riding habit and the beautiful blue ribbon and (I believe) the Star of the Garter over all' (Mansfield 1980: 169). Parts of the Queen's Windsor uniform have survived and are testament to the tailor's art, it being credited to her habit maker Peter Thompson (Staniland 1997: 103–105). She wrote in her diary of her delight at being saluted by the regiments: 'I saluted them by putting my hand to my cap like the officers do and was much admired for my manner of doing so. The whole went off beautifully and I felt for the first time like a man, as if I could fight myself at the head of my Troops' (cited in Staniland 1997: 103). The Windsor uniform also signified a rejection of the more elaborate military and dress uniforms, providing a soberer alternative for the monarch and their family: 'In contrast to the increasingly extravagant dress uniforms, which mirrored the rich court costumes worn throughout George III's reign, the Windsor Uniform appeared unsuitably plain' (Llewellyn 1996: 13). Such plainness clearly suited George III and his desire for a simpler life, but it suited the wishes of the young queen Victoria too.

For the young queen to revel in feeling as powerful as a man is an interesting observation and highlights some of the possible tensions arising from women wearing garments more traditionally associated with men. From its inception the female uniform was a masculinized garment, constructed by a male tailor and with all of the trappings of male insignia. The Queen's elevated social position may well have placed her outside such social anxieties, but during the second half of the nineteenth century other upper-class women adopted military uniform for particular occasions. Elizabeth Ewing notes in one of the only publications to consider the history of women in uniform: 'The feminine regimental uniform usually consisted of the correct male-style tunic with high neck and epaulettes but with left hand buttoning and a woman's skirt, riding style' (Ewing 1975: 63). Upper-class women were thus aping their husbands and brothers in a form of dress that was recognizably male, acceptable apparently within a certain social context.

Queen Victoria abandoned the wearing of uniform during and after her pregnancies, but the tradition was enthusiastically sustained by her son Edward. Much like his great uncle George IV, Edward regularly wore the uniforms of a range of European monarchies throughout his life. His interest in such sartorial trappings was reflected during his trip to India in 1875–6: 'Bertie had been shocked to discover that the Indian Civil Service had no official uniform to wear in order to receive him and he was disappointed when his proposal for a brass-buttoned blue coat was rejected' (Ridley 2012: 175). His attention to detail was noted by an incredulous Daisy Warwick who 'noticed that he would turn from discussing European politics to consider the buttons and tabs on a regimental uniform "with a gravity that seemed quite out of proportion to the matter in hand"' (Ridley 2012: 350). It was into this climate of monarchical military splendour that Alexandra found herself from the very day of her marriage to which the groom wore the scarlet tunic of a British general. And yet Alexandra herself never wore a uniform in the sixty years of her royal career. There were those among her peers and indeed family who did so. Many of Queen Victoria's daughters and granddaughters as well as other European royal women had uniforms made for them as honorary chiefs of various regiments. Alexandra's own sister Maria Feodorovna of Russia was colonel-in chief of two guard regiments, the uniform for which survives in a Russian collection today. The precedent was set but Alexandra resolutely rejected uniform in any context.

There may have been a number of reasons why she did so, although I would argue that it was not an issue with masculinity in dress since she wore tailored garments so much. Was it therefore a dislike of martial ambition? Alexandra's childhood was punctuated by Denmark's vulnerability at the hands of larger states such as Germany. To appear in public in the uniform of a German colonel would have been to sanction their past misdemeanours perhaps. It is possible too that Alexandra identified something of the ridiculous in the appropriation of such nominal roles. Edward's interest in such matters and his insistence upon wearing all manner of different uniforms despite his increasing girth with age may have served to reinforce a sense of impotence in such role playing. Evidence suggests that in the correct context, Alexandra showed great interest in the importance of uniform. In 1902 she became the first president of the Queen Alexandra Imperial Military Nursing Service a cause to which she dedicated a great deal of time in the last decades of her life. The appearance of the nurses was of interest from the outset, 'approving its uniform and being consulted on all suggested changes or adaptation. The grey dresses, white veils and caps and the sisters' scarlet capes were given her approval and are still worn, with of course much updating. The Dannebrog Cross of the Royal Arms of Denmark, her native country, surmounted by the imperial crown, is also still part of today's uniform' (Ewing 1975: 48). Her active input here is indicative of a keen recognition that in the appropriate setting uniform, and more specifically female uniform, was a significant part of such an organization's public and professional face.

The development of the riding habit

Though Alexandra may have disliked the political aesthetic of the military uniform, she embraced the lines upon which it was based – the riding habit, arguably her first experience of the tailor-made for which she would become famous. Alison Matthews David's assessment of these so-called 'Elegant Amazons' concludes: 'In the same way that punks and motorcycle gangs wear black leather to display their rebellion against the dominant culture, wearing a riding habit conferred a power that was not normally accorded to women in Victorian society, marking them as both potentially dangerous and capable of physical activity, if in a restrained sense' (Matthews David 2002: 184). Riding habits had become a feature of an aristocratic woman's wardrobe from at least the eighteenth century as Cally Blackman emphasized in her paper 'Walking Amazons': 'Riding habits are alluded to in many memoirs and letters throughout the period, and though their utility perhaps prevents them from being described in great detail, these allusions do show the variety of activities for which they were worn' (Blackman 2001: 57). It seems that far from being worn only for the hunt or more general horse riding, the habit served a more ubiquitous purpose as an outdoor garment. In 1754 Horace Walpole wrote to Horace Mann of his shock at the attire of Princess Emily: 'Coming to Chapel last Sunday in riding clothes, with a dog under her arm' (cited in Blackman 2001: 49). In spite of certain quarters of male censure the riding habit retained its place in the female wardrobe.

There is too the suggestion of the body beneath the riding habit. The very nature of its cut and the lack of ornamentation meant that it might be seen as a sensualized garment in spite of its mannish associations: 'Though masculinized in many ways, the tightly-molded habit displayed the horsewoman's form to advantage. Her elevated position on horseback made her visually accessible' (Matthews David 2002: 193). Catherine 'Skittles' Walters, courtesan and one of the 'pretty horsebreakers' who daily frequented Rotten Row in Hyde Park, 'was rumoured to wear nothing beneath her close-fitting riding habit, which was expertly tailored by Henry Poole of Saville Row' (Breward, Ehrman and Evans 2004: 42). For the Princess of Wales to display the outline of her body so markedly in both the riding habit and later the tailor-made might indicate a degree of agency that flew in the face of some contemporary criticism regarding her slenderness (Figure 6.1). It could be argued that, unlike her husband, Alexandra maintained a 'sporting' body all of her life. She enjoyed a range of physical activities and the masculinized habit and tailored gown might both facilitate such activity and display the figure that participated in it. Charges of extreme slenderness had been levelled at Alexandra from the early years of her marriage, Queen Victoria regularly commenting on Alix's thin frame (see Fulford 1968: 226 and Fulford 1971: 105) but the waist measurements for her clothing from her wedding dress to her coronation gown and indeed the ledgers at

Figure 6.1 Photograph of Princess Maud, Alexandra's daughter, in her riding habit on horseback and Queen Alexandra in a black tailored suit, c.1905 (original postcard, author's own collection).

Henry Poole serve to illustrate that Alexandra's shape changed barely at all, six pregnancies and a serious illness notwithstanding. In choosing daywear that largely accentuated her slender form, I would argue that Alexandra was demonstrating a degree of agency that moved beyond her mother-in-law's approval. Jennifer Entwistle maintains: 'When we get dressed we do so within the bounds of a culture and its particular norms, expectations about the body and about what constitutes a 'dressed' body' (Entwistle 2000: 11). Alexandra's dressed body had to accommodate a number of public and social expectations relating to status and her role as the most visible of female royals after her marriage. Clothing her body in a feminized version of a male garment may indeed have been a form of non-verbal resistance as considered by Diana Crane (Crane 2000: 99), although not necessarily against men in particular as Jennifer Craik has asserted: 'It is possible to distinguish techniques associated with the occupancy of a female body (being female) from techniques that employ gender as a social strategy (being feminine)' (Craik 1994: 44). Alexandra's choices both embraced her femininity and asserted her slim and pared down fashioned body in certain social contexts.

Recently discovered records show that from the very start of her marriage Alexandra ensured that an English tailored riding habit formed part of her new wardrobe. Ledgers in the archive of Henry Poole & Co (see Sherwood 2007: 63–68) (frequented also by Skittles Walters), Edward's favourite tailor for many years, indicate that Alexandra's measurements were taken on 18 March 1863, a week to the day after their marriage in St George's Chapel.[1] The contemporary tailor's shorthand attests to Alexandra's slender figure, her waist measuring 18." A single line of measurements seemed to suffice for the duration of her patronage at Poole's, no amendments having been made to their records, in stark contrast to Edward's columns of figures written and rewritten, crossed out and increased as his jackets and trousers expanded with his waistline.

The measurements having been taken, Alexandra's first order at Poole's was placed on 25 March 1863 and comprises what is presumably her first tailored garment as Princess of Wales. The Livery Ledger describes: 'A fine black habit lined silk bound braid - £12/12. A pair of black elastic trousers lined silk. 2 sets collars and cuffs.'[2] It was probably logical that Alexandra order her first habit from Poole's given her husband's preference for the firm. While no complete riding habit is listed again in the ledgers between 1864 and 1872, there are enough elements to suggest a regular association with the firm. She ordered new cloth skirts, habit skirts, overcoats and cloaks from the company during this period and in December 1870 she placed an order for 'making and trimming a green fancy checked angola small riding jacket. D/B lined silk, trimmed velvet, silk velvet collar and cuffs and facings'.[3] Clearly Alexandra appreciated both the cloth and cut that a gentleman's tailor such as Poole could offer, heralding her masculinized approach to daywear later in the 1870s.

These were of course the years during which Alexandra spent much of her time in the various stages of pregnancy. Certainly there are entries that suggest the changing shape of the princess at this time: evidence that is not forthcoming from any other source. In October 1863 when the princess would have been seven months pregnant with her first child Albert Victor, the ledger records: 'Altering and pressing overcoat – 10/6d. Altering and pressing another overcoat. Altering and pressing a habit body.'[4] Such alterations at such a time can only lead to the conclusion not only that Alexandra's figure had changed enough at this point to warrant the change to her garments but also that she was still participating to some degree in outdoor activities.

The feminization of fabric

An analysis of some of Alexandra's orders placed at Henry Poole points to a growing feature of the second half of the nineteenth century – the feminization of certain fabrics which had previously been confined to masculine garments only. On five separate occasions between 1864 and 1872, the Princess of Wales ordered a jacket or cape of grey barathea.[5] According to the definition given by Turnbull & Asser, barathea is a weave most commonly associated with men's garments: 'Barathea generally uses a worsted "yarn" woven with a twill hopsack or broken rib weave. The resulting cloth has a fine texture with a slightly pebbled effect and faint regular twill lines running in opposite directions ... has a matt finish and is used in many forms of formal wear including bow ties and cummerbunds.'[6]

Alexandra's appropriation of a 'male' fabric was part of a contemporary trend being played out among other traditionally masculine cloths also. Chief among these was tweed, a fabric Alexandra was to wear regularly in the form of the tailor-made throughout the 1870s and 1880s. Fiona Anderson's research into the gender coding of tweed considers 'the deceptively simple notion of the crossing of a gender divide through the adoption by women of what was principally a menswear textile, which was in broad terms the change in sartorial practices that began to take place in Britain from the late 1860s onwards' (Anderson 2006: 166). The Scottish sporting heritage of tweed was traditionally bound up with the male experience: 'Sport and sporting dress were coded very powerfully as masculine in the late nineteenth century and these associations were pivotal to the identification of tweed as a masculine cloth' (Anderson 2006: 180). However, the new emerging market of women's sport and leisure which grew out of the 'teachings of Social Darwinism' (Anderson 2006: 180–81) began to acknowledge the importance of a healthy and fit female body. Manufacturers too recognized the potential of this emerging market and changed their cloth accordingly. Where Scotch tweed was still arguably the home of the traditional masculine tweed, so the mills of Yorkshire produced tweeds that catered to the female consumer. The difference lay in the aesthetics of the cloth itself as Lou Taylor has considered: 'Whereas a big bold check might look handsome made up into a large and loose informal overcoat for a man, on a woman the results could be less than beautiful' (Taylor 1999: 39). Reducing both the size and colour of the check enabled the tailor to fit the cloth to the fashionable female silhouette. Princess Alexandra certainly embraced this development, photographed in a garment of small checked tweed on numerous occasions, and her wardrobe accounts as Queen indicate that she was still purchasing tweed in 1908, the sum of £10/17/6d paid for tweed cloth to Field, Hawkins & Co.[7] For the upper classes tweed inhabited a rural space and certainly the images of Alexandra in which she is wearing tweed are all taken in the Highlands or at country house weekends, a common trend observed by Lou Taylor once more in a paper examining three different garments of woollen cloth: 'Rapidly commodified into fashionable necessities, these new garments were quickly accepted as Society's correct, outdoor rural wear' (Taylor 2007: 98).

What then of serge which was formerly identified with the male working class or soldier class but appropriated by women of the leisure classes by the 1870s and Alexandra in particular whose own particular choice of daywear became synonymous with the fabric? Defined by Edward Miller as 'a firm, compact, twill-weave worsted (wool) fabric with a clear face finish' (Miller 1992: 191), serge was associated most commonly with naval and army uniforms. Its weight and smooth surface lent itself well to the needs of the military uniform and for the same reasons it was adopted by the tailor John Redfern.

Redfern

The name of Redfern has become synonymous with Alexandra both contemporarily and in subsequent volumes of biography. In 1876, the firm of Redfern were advertising themselves as being royal warrant holders, with HRH the Princess of Wales as one of their esteemed patrons.[8] Although appearing less frequently in the surviving wardrobe accounts the firm nevertheless held a royal warrant for Alexandra as both Princess of Wales and Queen from 1876 until her death, one of the longest and perhaps most significant of her associations. In fact, a handwritten bill, discovered among many hundreds in Queen Victoria's ledgers of ordinary and extraordinary bills, reveals most probably her first encounter with the firm from Alexandra's earliest visit to the Isle of Wight; her honeymoon.[9] Near the bottom of a bill largely consisting of orders of wadding, webbing, braid, tape, ribbon and silk cord, there are three entries of particular significance, given that the date, noted at the head of the page covers 'the quarter ending 31st March 1863'.[10] Following the marriage of the Prince of Wales to his Danish princess, the couple honeymooned at Osborne House for the latter half of the month of March. A direct reference to the purchase of 'a cushion for HRH the Princess of Wales' for the sum of 2.2d confirms Princess Alexandra's early association with Redfern during the period before his rise to fame as a dressmaker.

Indeed, the content of the bill as a whole and its inclusion in this particular series of ledgers reveal that he was still a local draper at this stage, supplying household goods and other dressmaking sundries to Queen Victoria although he is mentioned frequently in the office of robes accounts for the Queen even at this early date in his career.[11] This in itself is significant. In Queen Victoria's office of robes account books, the firm of John Redfern makes a regular appearance, alongside other more well-known names, as early as 1860, where he is described as a silk mercer. Clearly he enjoyed royal favour three years before the marriage of Edward and Alexandra, so it is entirely feasible that the Queen may have recommended him to the young couple when on their honeymoon. This throws a different light onto Alexandra's future relationship with the company; one which has traditionally been documented as new and daring in the 1870s but which was apparently forged on the suggestion of her mother-in-law ten years earlier. Interestingly, the bill also describes 'making and fitting a muslin and silk toilette. Coral. Complete', followed in the next entry by 'making a muslin and silk linen toilette complete to pattern'. These two were charged at 14.5.0d and 13.13.0d, respectively, by far the costliest items on the bill. Given the date, the description and the order of a cushion specifically for the princess, this would suggest that Alexandra ordered two garments from John Redfern at a time when he was not a known dressmaker. That the order is complete from pattern perhaps suggests that the Princess of Wales asked for a particular model and presented a pattern from which the establishment was only too happy to make a gown. John Redfern must surely have seen a glimpse into his future, supplying toilettes to the feted new bride.

The subsequent success of John Redfern's tailoring establishment was in no small part thanks to Alexandra herself. The small port of Cowes on the Isle of Wight had participated in the sport of yachting from the early years of the nineteenth century, the Yacht Club having been founded in 1815. It was not until the 1870s, however, that yachting, and more specifically the Cowes Regatta attained immense social cache as a favourite event of the young Prince and Princess of Wales (North 2008: 145–46). Suddenly the 'upper ten thousand' and the leading lights of European royalty descended upon the little port every August (Figure 6.2). John Redfern's future was assured. He had begun his career as a woollen draper, and it was this early knowledge of cloth which has been widely credited as one of the central factors of his success as a tailor and as a probable creator of the 'tailor-made'. Historically, male tailors had made garments for women only within the specific remit of the riding habit. In the 1870s Redfern and another of his contemporaries, John Morgan, expanded upon this narrow participation in women's wear, and began to produce women's garments for yachting. Susan North's thesis explored the growth of Redfern's business, charting the rise in popularity of this innovative form of daywear:

> The development of the tailor-made of the nineteenth century was dependent on three factors; the application of the tailoring methods used for the female riding habit to the loose protective outerwear worn by women for outdoor activities, the increased popularity of a range of outdoor sports for women, and the participation of the Princess of Wales, the leader of women's fashion in England, in these activities and her adoption of the new fitted, tailored outfits. (North MA 1993: 22)

The very nature of the tailor-made appears to have suited the Princess of Wales' favoured simplicity in daywear and a number of contemporary accounts support this. Lady Battersea recalled a brief visit to Sandringham, when the

Figure 6.2 Alexandra relaxing at the Cowes Regatta in what may well be a Redfern suit and had become her trademark by this time, Royal Collection Trust/© Her Majesty Queen Elizabeth II 2016.

Queen came out to meet her, 'my chauffeur and his companion on the box never surmising that the active lady in a plain walking suit who sprang lightly into the car could be Queen Alexandra herself' (Battersea 1923: 357). Consuelo, Duchess of Marlborough, found that 'life at Sandringham was simple and informal' (Vanderbilt Balsan 1973: 89), and Lady Randolph Churchill, in a lengthy description recording the homely atmosphere of Sandringham remarked: 'The Princess of Wales, looking in her neat dress and small felt hat as young as her own daughters, would drive a pair of ponies' (Cornwallis-West 1973: 145). These numerous descriptions of Alexandra dressing privately away from the season and during the day are illustrative of her lack of ostentation in these situations. Arthur Beavan, invited to write about life at Marlborough House in 1896, made his own observations: 'When the Princess calls at York House [the London residence of her son George] she almost always goes on foot and dresses so unpretentiously that even the sentries have been known not to observe her and have failed to present arms' (Beavan 1896: 121).

Yachting costumes were limited to a narrow fabric choice, predominantly serge, which could withstand the ravages of salt water and remain intact and retain its elegance of line. Colours too were confined to a palette of blue, black, cream, purple and red. Where Redfern excelled was in his ability to reinvent each year, new and exciting looks within the remit of cloth and colour. Certainly Princess Alexandra's look during this period is synonymous with the Redfern phenomenon – simple, beautifully cut, tailor-made suits. Photograph after photograph illustrate her preference for the finely made serge costumes. From the earliest years of her marriage, Alexandra was showing in official photographs her preference for the tailored line. An early *carte de visite*, c. 1865–70 by Hills and Saunders, shows the couple in riding costume, the prince leaning nonchalantly in a doorway, the princess next to him in a two-piece riding habit. The bodice is buttoned through centre front, with a fullness at the sleeves, while the skirt falls in a long bell shape. The high collar and top hat mirror her husband's attire; indeed with the hat on she appears taller than the prince.

A slightly later image could portray an early Redfern suit. The princess wears a dark wool/serge one-piece dress ruched a la polonaise and decorated with white braid appliquéd in a naval fashion at the cuffs, belt, neck and centre front, the outfit completed with decorative buttons. The fashionable line of the early 1880s allowed Alexandra to play with the naval theme again in a striking set of images taken on the Royal Yacht Osborne. The princess is wearing a white two-piece outfit exhibiting all the details of a contemporary sailor suit of the kind so often worn by children during this period. The double-breasted effect of applied buttons, the braidwork and the navy boater create an elegance of line effective for her height and figure and demonstrating further her awareness of how best to utilize this style.

Her slender figure, which she retained throughout her life, was accentuated to its fullest in the tailor-made. While her slightness was not fashionable there was no doubt that the pared down, elegant lines of the yachting suits could have no better advertisement than to be seen modelled by the ever-popular Princess of Wales. A photograph of 1876 taken at the annual Cowes Regatta emphasizes Alexandra's figure and how she took the new vogue for the tailor-made and literally made it her own. 'She wears a tailored cloth jacket-bodice, drawn in tight to the waist with a matching belt, and worn with a matching skirt. Alexandra's ensemble is completed by a matching, functional, round cloth hat with narrow brim, reminiscent of a man's bowler' (Lambert 1991: 45). It is a striking image, almost androgynous in tone.

Furthermore, Alexandra took the tailor-made beyond the confines of the yachting world: 'She wore them as morning gowns, inspiring the rage for the tailor-made of the 1880s. The Queen noted in 1883 that at recent festivities at Sandringham, "The Princess of Wales in the daytime wore nothing but exquisitely fitting tailor-made costumes"' (North 1993: 26). Unfortunately, and perhaps surprisingly, given their ubiquitous status thanks to so prominent a customer, hardly any of Redfern's tailor-mades have survived today, and certainly none of the early examples so favoured by Alexandra. This tailored elegance, however, was to remain the preserve of craftsmen in the UK. Proust made a sharp observation of Madame Standish, a Frenchwoman who also happened to be a mistress of Edward's, noting that she wore suits that 'moulded her figure with a precision that was positively British' (cited in Painter 1969: 162). His choice of words – of precision moulding – captures the skill of the British tailor and the style that originated with Alexandra.

There was another innovation credited to Redfern and once more popularized by Princess Alexandra and that was the jersey costume. Originally made for the princess in 1879, Redfern advertised themselves in the October as 'Inventors and makers of the celebrated Jersey gowns worn by H.R.H. the Princess of Wales'. In November, *The Queen* noted the new style as modelled by the princess: 'At the first shooting party at Sandringham this season, H.R.H. the Princess of Wales appeared in a costume admirably adapted for the occasion. It was designed by Messrs. Redfern of London and Cowes, the originators of the now popular Jersey Costume, and in some special points this shooting dress resembled its predecessor.'[12] In the wake of reports such as this, the jersey costume was soon copied by tailors and department stores alike, so that by 1880 jerseys were available in popular stores such as Debenham & Freebody and Dickins & Jones.[13] In the mid-1880s, the period of the sheath-like bodice and fitted drapery, Alexandra and her daughters were photographed in these jersey bodices that were at once both apparently comfortable and stretchy, well suited for the active Princess of Wales, but fitted tautly over the structured under garments and emphasized as no other garment could have, the extreme slenderness of the Princess. Once again, she appears boyish in the tweed, buttoned jersey and soft cloth cap, especially alongside her now portly husband (Levitt 1991: 56). Redfern reinvented the jersey over fifteen years later, with the addition of the voluminous sleeves of the 1890s.

However, by the later years of the nineteenth century, Alexandra's patronage of her once favoured firm appeared to be on the wane. Between 1897 and 1903, there are only four purchases made from Redfern, the largest of which amounted to £48/1/6d, a relatively small sum placed alongside the many hundreds of pounds that were being paid to other couture houses in the same period.[14] Ironically, it is probable that the fame and widespread patronage that the House of Redfern had achieved by the end of the nineteenth century, due in no small part to Alexandra herself, were the very reasons that she had largely ceased to buy from the firm by this time. In the 1890s, Redfern's popularity rivalled and eventually overtook that of the great House of Worth. With branches all over Europe and in the United States, Redfern was no longer the edgy young establishment it once used to be. Anyone who could afford to shop at Redfern did so; and Alexandra moved on, her former exclusivity no longer possible.

The establishment of John Redfern remained a warrant holder of the Queen until the end of her life, one of the longest to have enjoyed her custom, and although the payments received from Alexandra as Queen are far less significant than those as Princess of Wales, her loyalty held true to the end. This is entirely in keeping with Alexandra's well-known philanthropy which these later smaller payments appear to indicate. Regular purchases, however small in value, meant that Redfern could retain the Queen's royal warrant even though the bulk of her tailored wear was no longer purchased from the establishment. But from that first costume made to pattern on Cowes, the meteoric rise of the Isle of Wight tailor and the new stylish princess had taken place hand in hand.

Vernon and Busvine

Alexandra's reduced patronage of Redfern at some point in the 1890s heralded the arrival of the tailor that was to produce what appears to be the majority of her suits for the rest of her public career. The name of Vernon appears with regularity in the pages of the wardrobe accounts between the years 1898 and 1910 and three of the surviving tailored garments bear the Vernon label (see Plate 10). However, the establishment itself faded into obscurity after a relatively brief period of prominence and now has left barely a trace of its former influence. In the Post Office London Directory of 1895, Vernon & Co appear under the tailoring section based at 191 Sloane St (Anon 1895: 2177). Four years later the star of Vernon must have risen steadily as the firm were now styling themselves as Vernon et Cie in the same directory with the accompanying symbols indicating that they were ladies' tailors and habit makers and had expanded into 191 & 192 Sloane St (Anon 1899: 2420). By 1910 Vernon & Co were 'ladies tailors, habit makers, court dressmakers & artistic milliners (by Royal Warrant to HM The Queen)' (Anon 1910: 1269) and now occupied 190, 191 & 192 Sloane St: the steady expansion of both premises and services offered to clients a clear indication of their place in the tailoring hierarchy. Alexandra's daughter Maud ordered a number of garments from Vernon for her trousseau in 1896 and the company also assisted with the creation of her coronation dress when she became Queen Maud of Norway in 1906. An advertisement in 1911, described in the V&A catalogue of Maud's clothing, hints at one of the services offered by the establishment: 'A special mention is made of its ability to cater for orders from abroad or out of town. Such orders were probably supplied by fitting on a bust made to a customer's measurements. This is probably how Vernon made clothes for Queen Maud as one of her preserved dressmaker's mannequins is marked "Vernon"' (Kjellberg and North 2005: 94). This was perhaps a feature that appealed to Alexandra also, given the peripatetic nature of her life. Since the evidence has shown Alexandra's measurements changed very little during the course of her public life, Vernon's expertise at fitting suits without the presence of the customer was perhaps a particularly attractive feature of the establishment for her.

A suggestion in the December 1911 issue of the *Ladies Field* implied that Vernon had a reputation for being the preserve of only the most privileged: 'A journalist ... recommended that readers visit Vernon and reassured them that it was untrue that only the very rich could purchase clothing there' (cited in Kjellberg and North 2005: 94). The surviving garments support the very high quality of the tailoring that Vernon produced. Unembellished as they are, the construction is testament to the tailor's art. Interestingly, all of the garments, including a fourth suit not related to Alexandra but dating to the same period, are made from cream serge. What embellishment there is, is mostly self-coloured with the occasional accent of black, such as the complete two-piece suit now in the collections of the Royal Ontario Museum, Toronto.[15] A trim of silk-plaited braid features on three of the four garments, echoing the braided decoration of men at sea. Many of the photographs taken of Alexandra on board the royal yachts in the 1890s and 1900s show her in either navy or cream serge suits and so presumably appealed to her sense of appropriate dress on board ship with connotations of naval dress. If not the explicit copy of a uniform, she chose at least to echo those contextual elements that reflected their life at sea and abroad.

The two tailored jackets recently acquired by the Museum at the Fashion Institute of Design and Merchandising, both by Vernon, appear to have been worn by Queen Alexandra during a Mediterranean cruise in 1905 and can be identified from photographs pasted into her travel album for that year. A snapshot taken of Alexandra riding a donkey during a tour of Gibraltar on 28 March 1905 depicts a jacket identical to that now in Los Angeles,[16] while another cream suit with distinctive black trim appears to match the second jacket now in the LA collection.[17] This rare opportunity to match garments with an occasion for which they were worn allows the tailor-made to be considered within a very precise worn context. It may be that Alexandra ordered suits from Vernon that were specifically intended for European travel, cream being well suited both to the aesthetics of the naval tradition and the climates of those countries they visited en route. The provenance of all three garments originates from Miss Giltrap, Alexandra's dresser, who was certainly present during the 1905 cruise since she is mentioned on more than one occasion in Alexandra's travel journal. Without a specific reference to the manner of her acquisition it is impossible to surmise further. It may indeed have been the case that Harriet Giltrap was given these suits by Alexandra by way of souvenir, recalling happy times on board ship, such gestures being entirely characteristic. Although only the jackets survive now, a letter written by one of Miss Giltrap's descendants explains the loss of the skirts: 'The Skirts and other parts of the costumes were made into dresses by Mrs

Cook who was Mrs Giltrap's niece.'[18] Their appearance so prominently within the pages of the 1905 journal does suggest that Vernon was the luxury tailor of choice for Alexandra during her years as Queen. Worn when touring in public around Europe, she advertised the best of British tailoring on an international platform in her crisp cream and navy suits.

If Vernon were the luxury tailor of choice by this date, worn by the Queen while abroad and in public daytime settings, Busvine appeared to inhabit a more utilitarian place in her wardrobe. The firm of Busvine were already holders of Alexandra's royal warrant when she became queen consort in 1901. Their place in the late nineteenth century was bound up with the continued dominance of the riding habit in the upper-class woman's annual calendar. The Duchess of Marlborough wrote of her first ride out with the hounds in 1899: 'I shall always remember the first meet with the Quorn hounds when, perfectly fitted in a Busvine habit, a tall hat and veil, I mounted 'Greyling' inwardly trembling with excitement and fear … a host of others were eyeing me critically and so far, thanks to my tailor and a good seat, had found nothing amiss' (Vanderbilt Balsan 1973: 99). Busvine were known for their technical approach to the art of cutting and tailoring. They patented a number of safety skirts for riding side-saddle and had already been awarded a royal warrant for the making of Alexandra's riding habits as far back as 1883 (Kjellberg and North 2005: 66). Two waistcoats made by Busvine for Alexandra are the only examples of their patronage that have survived both dating to the 1890s; both of a hopsack weave with a spot repeat pattern. (See Plate 11.) Also spotted was a third waistcoat of very similar fabric, which may be associated with Busvine although it does not bear their label.[19] Perhaps more than any other surviving garment, these waistcoats highlight just how slender Alexandra still was in her forties, the unembellished line creating the silhouette of her famous figure. The cut of these waistcoats underscores Alexandra's continued desire to display her unchanged shape almost thirty years after her initial adoption of the tailor-made suit. The context of these pieces is now unknown. It may be that these were worn for riding, although their cream background and spotted pattern may suggest otherwise. They are striking for all their simplicity and paradoxical too: their simple line, high collar and demure spot pattern might be lifted from the male equivalent and yet they are unequivocally female, placing Alexandra at the very heart of nineteenth-century gendered etiquette. Buckley and Fawcett's reading of this period is one of heightened femininity, of an extravagant female body: 'A hyper-femininity similar to that found in the exaggerated artifice of male transvestitism' (Buckley and Fawcett 2002: 16). They discuss the iconography of the actress and the rounding of the fashionable female figure from the 1880s onwards: 'There is a sense that the female body itself had become a site of ostentatious consumption in its ampleness' (Buckley and Fawcett 2002: 35). Yet the images of Alexandra from this period and the style and dimensions of her daywear attest to a very different aesthetic. If in its form it was not un-feminine, it was perhaps more allied to the male approach to plain dressing than to the overt 'frou-frou' extolled by authors such as Mrs Eric Pritchard in her book *The Cult of Chiffon*, published in 1902 (Pritchard 1902). While she adorned herself in suitably embellished attire for evening functions, the iconography and the material culture confirm the different approach afforded by tailoring.

Conclusion

The fate of the vast majority of Alexandra's tailored wardrobe conforms to Glenn Adamson's assessment of material culture more generally: 'When it comes to the material past, disappearance is the norm, and preservation is the exception' (Adamson 2009: 192). Six pieces of tailoring are now all that survive from among what was by far Alexandra's most unique contribution to nineteenth and early-twentieth-century fashion. From her first experiences with the masculine environment of Henry Poole & Co to her more individual relationship with the emerging firm of John Redfern Alexandra as Princess of Wales was to exhibit a sense of style that was far more daring than her customary daywear. Appropriating sporting dress into the everyday suited both her lifestyle and her body shape and is one of the most defining elements of her appearance. The accounts and the garments themselves demonstrate that she was not afraid to deviate from favoured establishments, a number of tailors featuring in ledgers and warrant holders' records over the decades of her public life. While the style may have been updated year on year, the basic elements remained fixed – the plain unembellished skirt, the form-fitting jacket – through her years as Princess of Wales and Queen Consort.

While she rejected the literal concept of uniform, Alexandra nonetheless embraced elements of it in certain contexts. Her cream Vernon suits worn on board the royal yachts were an echo of those early yachting suits that Redfern had designed for her decades earlier. The hints of naval tradition that were bound up in the designs were recurring details.

At the same time, it was not Alexandra's intention to appear masculinized. Indeed the accentuation of her figure within her tailored suit must surely have emphasized her femininity, especially alongside the ever-increasing girth of her husband – hers was the silhouette of restraint and control where his was one of excess and greed. She wore formerly masculine garments in a feminine fashion and formerly masculine fabrics in newly feminized patterns to fashion her own female sporting body. While elements of her tailored garments thus hinted towards the male, her clothed body was undoubtedly female. As Entwistle has observed: 'Practices of dress evoke the sexed body, drawing attention to bodily differences between men and women that might otherwise be obscured' (Entwistle 2006: 141). Alexandra did not want to obscure her body or confuse the observer with her tailored dress.

John Redfern proved to be central to this royal sporting body, and his association with the Princess of Wales was perhaps his most significant client relationship. Alexandra's loyalty prevailed so that she continued to order smaller items from the establishment even when the majority of her tailored suits were being sourced elsewhere by the 1890s. But why did she move on when Redfern's popularity was still assured by this date? I would suggest that it was his continued success that prompted Alexandra to take her patronage elsewhere. Other sources have already hinted at Alexandra's desire to appear in clothing that was different to that worn by the 'London Ladies' as she called them. This may well have been the same determination that saw the young Princess of Wales in appropriate sporting dress for the everyday; another example of placing some distance between herself and her peers through a variation of sartorial norms. Thus as Redfern's star reached its zenith so Alexandra quietly began to order from the lesser known firm of Vernon whose fine serge suit jackets are now the sole survivors of Alexandra's tailored wardrobe. Within the confines and the codified, strictly gendered etiquette of the British upper classes, Alexandra's approach to the art of tailoring is then a display of her own agency arguably more apparent here than in any other aspect of her dress.

7
MOURNING DRESS

The cult of mourning

From among Queen Mary's papers, catalogued by the Royal Archive after her death, two sheets of paper reveal some of the details pertaining to her mother-in-law's wardrobe. When Queen Alexandra died in 1925, her dresser Mrs Giltrap provided Queen Mary with an inventory of those garments still in her care. In her list, Mrs Giltrap records: '3 Good Black Spangled Court Gowns; One High Blk & Steel Gown worn at functions; Many other good black dresses left in the wardrobe.'[1] The other gowns all fall into the category of half-mourning: greys, lilacs and creams, rejecting the brighter colours of her youth. In 1863, however, Alexandra had married into a monarchy that was consumed by the etiquette of mourning. While Queen Victoria's own grief was to become the stuff of legend, suggestions that her response to the death of Prince Albert was the cause for a greatly inflated public adoption of mourning have been refuted by historians. Professor James Curl asserts that 'the widely held belief that her influence on mourning customs was immense is simply not borne out by the facts' (Curl 2000: 230). While Victoria's mourning was certainly intense, what might be described as the 'cult' of mourning that typified a greater part of the nineteenth century had evolved out of complex social and industrial patterns, driven by the British class system: 'In the super-elaborated etiquette of mourning, the Victorians found a superb device in the recognition or non-recognition of kin or friends for placing themselves in the social hierarchy' (Davidoff 1986: 54).

The custom of wearing black to signify grief and loss was certainly nothing new and had been reported as early as the seventeenth century and beyond, but industrialized Britain was able to quantify grief in material goods. The first mourning warehouse in London, Jay's, opened on Regent Street in 1841 and was an emporium in which every possible object associated with the expression of loss might be acquired. Henry Mayhew wrote in his *The Shops and Companies of London*: 'In the present day our ashes must be properly selected, our garments must be rent to pattern, our sack cloth must be of the finest quality and that our grief goes for nothing if not fashionable' (Mayhew 1865: 67). The importance of their wares was reinforced in 1848 by the publication of Richard Daveys' *A*

History of Mourning. Commissioned by Jay's it was a short volume that sought to position the traditions of mourning practised in the nineteenth century, with historical antecedents almost lost in the mists of time. He wrote in his introduction: 'Although tradition has not informed us whether our first parents made any marked change in their scanty garments on the death of their near relatives, it is certain that the fashion of wearing mourning and the institution of funeral ceremonies and rites are of the utmost antiquity' (Davey 1848: 3). It was a clever publication from Jay's perspective, underscoring the importance of tradition in the context of grief. Offering a scholarly treatise within a mercantile environment was intended to lend gravitas to the consumption of their goods: to persuade the customer that this was money spent in the pursuit of deep-seated tradition and respectability.

However, Jay's did not have the monopoly on such wares: 'Pugh's Mourning Warehouse opened at 173 Regent Street in 1849; and Peter Robinson opened a Court and General Mourning House at 256, 258, 260 & 262 Regent Street which became affectionately known as Black Peter Robinson's' (Adburgham 1989: 67).

As with other instances of Victorian aesthetic respectability, the rules of etiquette that had evolved by the second half of the nineteenth century were complex, much more so for women: 'Women were bound by the labyrinth of mourning dress etiquette for a much longer period than their menfolk' (Taylor 1983: 134). In fact, as early as 1848 when women's mourning was still in the process of developing ever more complicated sartorial rules, Richard Davey wrote in his volume *A History of Mourning*: 'Men no longer make a point of wearing full black for a fixed number of months after the decease of a near relation, and even content themselves with a black hat-band and dark-coloured garments' (Davey 1848: 96). It was a very different picture for the widow. At the height of the 'cult' of mourning she was expected to mourn her husband for two-and-a-half years and during this time changed her garments as time elapsed to denote how far along the path of grief she had processed. The first and deepest period of mourning lasted for one year and a day, expressed through the wearing of black that was total and unadorned, with plain linen and a matt finish to the cloth: 'After one year and a day, a widow could move onto the second stage of mourning. She was advised, however, not to do so on the very day she was entitled to, but, for the sake of good taste, to prolong the change for some time' (Taylor 1983: 141). This second stage allowed the wearing of less crape but still demanded that the widow wear unremitting black for a further nine months although jet trimmings might be added after the first six months of second mourning. Twenty-one months after the loss of her husband a widow might enter the third stage or 'ordinary' stage of mourning and while the palette was still overwhelmingly black, it could be relived with silk, lace and jewellery. Finally after two years of monochromatic attire, a widow could go into half-mourning: 'Half-mourning consisted of the fashions of the day but made up in special half-mourning colours' (Taylor 1983: 146). These included shades of mauve and lilac, greys and whites.

The first stage of mourning, which required the wearing of black crape, had created a boom in the associated textile industries. Companies such as Courtaulds thrived: 'From 1835 to 1885 capital [at Courtaulds] rose from £40,000 to over £450,000. The boom years of 1850–1885 coincided exactly with the peak of the Victorian obsession for mourning etiquette' (Taylor 1983: 219). The first mention of crape in a British royal context was in 1694 at the funeral of Queen Mary II and so as a textile that represented mourning status, it had a long precedent. Certainly it is the fabric that today is most synonymous with the aesthetic and material culture of Victorian mourning attire. Crape was lightweight and semi-transparent and was crimped into a textured completely mattified pattern through a complex industrial method: 'Every hint of the beautiful sheen and softness of silk was carefully removed by an elaborate process giving an extraordinarily lugubrious and hard finish' (Taylor 1983: 204).

The complexities of mourning dress operated as a signifier of association: 'The social importance of the deceased was indicated by the degree of mourning: the length of time mourning was worn (and thus restricted social intercourse), the kind of clothing and accessories and the numbers and station of members of the household who went into mourning' (Davidoff 1986: 54). For royalty this was compounded by the number of dynastic associations across the continent that might plunge the court into mourning with great frequency. It was a necessity that brought with it great frustration for those in the immediate court circle. Queen Victoria's lady-in-waiting, Marie Mallet, wrote to her husband from Balmoral in 1889:

I am in despair about my clothes, no sooner have I rigged myself out with good tweeds than we are plunged into the deepest mourning for the King of Portugal, jet ornaments for six weeks! And he was only a first cousin once removed. So I only possess one warm black dress: the Sunday one is far from thick. It is a lesson never, never to buy anything but black! (Mallett 1968: 32)

Alexandra's keen eye to appropriate attire guaranteed her conformity as far as mourning etiquette was concerned in the early years of her marriage. Such was its significance at this date that to do otherwise would have been unthinkable: 'During the 1850–1890 period mourning became such a cult that hardly anyone dared defy it. It was like the story of 'The Emperor's New Clothes' – few were bold enough to speak openly against it. Mourning wear was considered so essential a part of a lady's wardrobe that upper-class women were never without it' (Taylor 1983: 122). As late as 1904, Mary Spencer Warren was advising women about packing for the aristocratic country house visit in *The Ladie's Realm*: 'They should not at the same time omit to take both mourning and half mourning. King Edward and Queen Alexandra are so closely allied to so many foreign courts rendering occasions for mourning frequent and often sudden' (cited in Taylor 1983: 123).

From the very outset of her life in Britain, Alexandra was to show a deference for these practices that were so important to Queen Victoria. Her arrival in Gravesend wearing the half-mourning cloak specially commissioned from Frys in Dublin indicated that she was mindful of the sensibilities of the Queen. Her thoughtful choice was noted by the Queen as the couple arrived in Windsor Castle that night to be greeted enthusiastically by Edward's younger brothers and sisters: 'The Queen lingered behind but as her son led his bride forward, 'looking like a rose' and beautiful in her half-mourning dress of grey frock, white bonnet and violet mantle, on an impulse of affection she came forward and kissed the girl warmly' (Battiscombe 1969: 47).

Alexandra was sensitive to unhappiness. During one of her stays in Windsor with the Queen in the months leading up to her wedding, Alexandra sat with her future mother-in-law and listened to her stories of Prince Albert and her former happiness: 'One evening when they had been speaking of his last illness, she was so moved that she suddenly burst into tears and wept bitterly upon the Queen's shoulder' (Battiscombe 1969: 41).

Mourning jewellery

An important aesthetic that accompanied the requirements of mourning dress in the nineteenth century was the popularity of memorial and mourning jewellery. The Whitby jet industry flourished as demand rose for the polished black stone that could be fashioned into all manner of decorative objects, including jewellery: 'The Whitby jet industry grew from two shops employing twenty-five people in 1832 to two hundred shops employing fifteen-hundred men, women and children in 1872' (Muller 1980: 14). Jet could be faceted and made into brooches, bracelets, necklaces and other small decorative objects that could be gifted in memorium of the deceased. The evidence of surviving objects and contemporary accounts demonstrate that Alexandra recognized the emotional potency of such pieces. Suzy Menkes asserts that 'as Princess and Queen, Alexandra was thoughtful rather than lavish with presents. To her mother-in-law Queen Victoria, she gave in 1878 an onyx locket which had originally been intended for Princess Alice of Hesse, Queen Victoria's second daughter who had died of diphtheria in December 1878 on the seventeenth anniversary of her father's death' (Menkes 1985: 47). In the royal collection, two pieces stand out as particularly notable – the first a small oblong gold, jewelled and enamelled brooch containing a lock of hair from Queen Louise of Denmark, Alexandra's mother. It is dated 1898, the year that Louise died and inscribed on the reverse the words 'From Alexandra Princess of Wales 1898'.[2] The second is a black enamel locket dating to 1874 with six applied diamond stars and inside the locks of hair belonging to the six children of Edward and Alexandra.[3] Most poignant is that Alexandra's youngest son died after only twenty-four hours in 1871 and the gift of this locket to her husband was not only a celebration of their five surviving children but also a memorial to the loss of their baby. Although hair jewellery had been popular since the seventeenth century, it reached new heights of sentimentality in the nineteenth. Rachel Harmeyer, in her thesis examining the historic context of hairwork, notes: 'Hairwork provided its owners with the means to access and reiterate treasured memories' (Harmeyer 2012: np). The appeal of such objects was also the duality of their construction. So much of Alexandra's life was lived in the public eye and much of the narrative connecting the threads of her wardrobe is a tale of the tension between public and private – of her clothed public body and her choices made in private. Mourning jewellery was inherently both public and private – it offered a 'seen' outward aesthetic but invariably contained a secret, usually with the inclusion of the loved one's lock of hair. This kind of secondary relic was deeply personal and hidden from view, inhabiting a private, hidden space.

Alexandra and mourning dress

As with so much of her sartorial life, there is little or no written evidence about what Alexandra herself felt about the expectations of mourning dress. Occasional glimpses of her adherence to etiquette come from other voices than hers – following the death of Edward and Alexandra's eldest son Eddy in 1892, Queen Victoria attended the funeral and recorded in her journal: 'Dear Alix looked lovelier than ever in her deep mourning' (cited in Battiscombe 1969: 192). Alexandra certainly seems to have conformed to the standard of mourning in its earliest stages but her actions suggest that pragmatism was also an important feature of their monarchical position. Victoria's tenacious approach to mourning dress following Albert's death became deeply unpopular and both Edward and Alexandra acknowledged the problems inherent in Victoria's position and her public face, anxieties that were echoed by leading politicians. Plunkett's research into Queen Victoria's role as arguably Britain's first 'media monarch' concludes: 'With the growing dissent in the 1860s over Victoria's continued seclusion, Disraeli and Gladstone both emphasised the importance of monarchy continuing to have a public face' (Plunkett 2003: 55). Her widow's weeds, while deemed acceptable in the first stages of her mourning, were perceived as casting a pall over the monarchy. In later years it was to be Alexandra, ever mindful of public perceptions, who tried to influence her mother-in-law's sartorial decisions on those occasions when she was most under scrutiny. For Victoria's Golden Jubilee in 1887, an open carriage was to convey the Queen around the city of London ending in a service of thanksgiving in St Paul's Cathedral. The Queen decided not to wear either crown or robes of state for the occasion: 'Distressed by this decision the Royal Family sent the Princess of Wales, whom they knew to be a special favourite, to persuade the Queen out of a bonnet and into a crown' (Battiscombe 1969: 174). Her entreaties failed and the bonnet was worn. It makes for a nice story, but at the heart of the anecdote is a more serious recognition, that which both Disraeli and Gladstone had attempted to convey over twenty years earlier, that the tide of Republicanism could turn and that the people needed a visible, appealing monarchy.

Alexandra was to provide that appeal and it could be argued that were it not for her enduring popularity, especially in the 1860s when the widowed Queen had almost completely retreated from public view, the monarchy may have had a much more difficult ride through the nineteenth century. Alexandra brought colour, sparkle and glamour to a monochromatic court. She wore strong colours throughout the 1860s, 1870s and 1880s evidenced through descriptions in the *Court Chronicle* of her court gowns and their varied hues. One garment, now in the collections of the Metropolitan Museum of Art, New York, does originate from one of the large mourning warehouses in London – Jay's of Regent Street. Dating to the mid-1860s it is a cream silk and machine lace mantle bearing the label of the mourning emporium. (See Plate 12.) Given the date, it might have been a convenient purchase for Alexandra's trousseau to ensure that she had items suitable for half-mourning directly after her marriage. There are no other examples now extant from mourning specialists, and the wardrobe accounts are similarly devoid of regular purchases in such establishments. It may be that Alexandra followed the lead of Queen Victoria in this respect. Following Albert's death, Victoria's office of robes volumes reveal that 'considerable purchases were made at Caley's in Windsor whenever the Queen was in residence at the Castle and the payment to them of £155 at the end of this particular quarter must surely reflect acquisition of mourning for the Queen and her family' (Staniland 1997: 154). Alexandra made regular payments to Caley's and other drapers and general department stores, all of whom could cater for mourning requirements. Adburgham points out that 'services to the bereaved and the deceased were the great standby of most Victorian drapers' (Adburgham 1989: 58).

Many of the leading department stores feature in the pages of Alexandra's wardrobe accounts – Howell & James, Lewis & Allenby, Woolland Bros, all of whom may have provided the princess and later queen with the necessary ephemera that went beyond simply the garments themselves – in the royal collection are now a number of black-edged handkerchiefs, identified by Alexandra's royal cipher. Black-bordered writing paper, mourning souvenirs, black stockings and shoes, black gloves, hats and veils – all might be acquired within the department store. It is possible that the absence of orders placed within the large mourning establishments signifies Alexandra's own feelings about such acquisitions – she knew just how influential such patronage was for retailers who often 'stressed the royal origins of their trade and exploited their royal and aristocratic patrons in advertising campaigns' (Taylor 1983: 188). In keeping with her patterns of consumption relating to other garments, Alexandra rarely chose the most obvious retailers. Her evening gowns never came from Worth, but from smaller, although no less exclusive, couture houses; when Redfern became too popular as a tailor she moved her patronage to the less well-known Vernon and so with her mourning dress she perhaps similarly rejected the largest mourning emporiums in favour of a more discreet establishment.

The death of Eddy in 1892, however, was to change the tone of her garments for the rest of her life. In January 1892, Edward and Alexandra's eldest son died shortly after his engagement to Princess May of Teck. Alexandra was heartbroken, writing to her mother in Denmark: 'I have buried my angel today and with him my happiness' (cited in Fisher 1974: 143). Biographers acknowledged the princess's rejection of strong colours from 1892: 'She began a period of mourning that was to last for years. Never again did she dress in the old, bright colours which had for so long been her hallmark' (Fisher 1974: 143). The contemporary biographer Sarah Tooley published her book *The Life of Queen Alexandra* in 1902, only a decade after Eddy's death. She too records: 'Of late years she has preferred silver, gray and pale shades of heliotrope' (Tooley 1902: 161). As Queen Victoria had mourned her beloved Albert for thirty years, so Alexandra's grief manifested itself through her choice of dress. Unlike Victoria though, Alexandra recognized that descent into unrelenting black would be an unpopular decision and wisely opted for the muted shades of half-mourning. The randomly surviving evening gowns from this date forward, all, without exception, adhere to this palette. It was an astute decision on Alexandra's part. She was able to communicate the continuing effect the loss of her son made on her life without materially altering the public's view of her glamorous public self. She was able to articulate this loss through dress but she wore her grief with a lighter hand than Queen Victoria.

An anecdote revealed in the memoirs of one of Alexandra's ladies-in-waiting, Louisa Lady Antrim, suggests that Alexandra was not averse to bending the rules of mourning etiquette after periods of bereavement. In this particular instance she clearly desired distance between herself and the 'London Ladies' as she had been known to call the other women in court circles. Approaching the end of the formal period of mourning for Queen Victoria in 1901, Louisa Antrim wrote: 'The Queen's showmanship became conspicuous the moment she was asked when full mourning had to stop. Could her court drop the black dresses and jet beads for a grand function that happened to coincide with the last official day? Refusing to give a ruling ('such questions bore me intensely') Alexandra guessed that her ladies would stick cautiously to black, as indeed they did, while she herself appeared in stunning white, gleaming with jewels, like a solitary star in the night sky' (Longford 1979: 79). It was a cannily playful move, if no doubt frustrating for the black-clad ladies. Not only was Alexandra asserting herself in her new role as Queen but she was ensuring that she was the most visible woman in the room. White was still officially a colour that could also represent mourning and so she did not deviate in any way that might be deemed inappropriate. Entirely in keeping with her life in dress more generally, Alexandra was able sartorially to conform at the same time as dissenting, to be both conventional and discreetly rebellious. Certainly after Queen Victoria's death there were early signs that Edward and Alexandra intended to offer some sartorial reform, albeit small steps. Recognizing that prolonged official mourning for his mother in 1901 would have serious repercussions for the entertainment and industry that underpinned the London Season, Edward 'did step in and decree that there should be no mourning after April' (Davidoff 1986: 56).

It was at Eddy's funeral that a further unwitting glimpse of her own opinions relating to the wearing of the deepest degree of mourning is revealed. Lou Taylor writes in her seminal volume on mourning dress about the decline of the crape industry from the 1880s onwards, linking royal patronage, or lack thereof, to its changing fortunes: 'First Princess Alexandra of Wales refused to wear it at the funeral of the Duke of Clarence [Eddy] and then at Queen Victoria's funeral in 1901' (Taylor 1986: 222). It is impossible to know whether Alexandra was predicting a change in taste when she chose not to wear crape or if it represented a more deep-seated dislike for the matt black, lustreless fabric that had dominated so much of the aesthetic of the royal household for so long. It would be entirely in keeping with Alexandra's occasional acts of sartorial rebellion if this were the case and it may be that for the funeral of her eldest child she was in a powerful enough position to dress as she saw fit. Certainly none of the surviving garments of Alexandra's that fall into the category of either mourning or half-mourning bears any traces of crape, the closest comparison being bands of black moiré silk trimming two of her dresses now in museum collections. Both are striking examples of the third stage of mourning, garments in which the symbolism of mourning traditions are still clearly in evidence – one a lilac silk spotted with woven black spots and trimmed liberally with pleated bands of black moiré (see Plate 13) and the other later dress of black and white twilled striped silk trimmed with black lace and velvet.[4]

As with so many other occasions in her life, Alexandra knew when to perform the role expected of her and to ensure that her appearance matched the expectations of the observer. This was realized particularly effectively for the first State Opening of Parliament after Queen Victoria's death and was to be Alexandra's first official duty as queen consort. It was planned to the last detail and the appearance of the new king and queen was central to the impression made on that day. Jane Ridley, a recent biographer of Edward's describes accounts of the entrance: 'Bertie walked in procession, wearing a flowing crimson robe and the Imperial State Crown, unused since 1861. Alix, clasping his left hand, wore a black mourning dress and the Koh-i-noor beneath her scarlet robes and Queen Victoria's small diamond crown with a flowing crepe veil' (Ridley 2012: 351). Alexandra herself chose to wear the diamond crown, its colourless hue deemed appropriate for mourning and yet providing sufficient glitter to impress (Figure 7.1). Lady Monkswell was present for the occasion and recorded the day in her diary:

> The Queen was in black and covered with diamonds [she] had a perfect little crown on the top of her head and looked a perfect picture sitting in her chair of state. It was all so perfect and beautiful and unlike common life that, if it had not been for the strong sense of reality that never left one, we must have thought we were at the play. (Collier 1944: 83)

Figure 7.1 Queen Alexandra in the robes worn to the first State Opening of Parliament of the new reign in 1901, worn over black crape dress and with the black veil to denote mourning for Queen Victoria (original postcard, author's own collection).

The performative impression was no accident and like so many of Alexandra's public ceremonial appearances, it was designed to create an aesthetic impact. This is not to diminish her grief – she had a genuine fondness for her mother-in-law and felt her loss keenly – but this was an occasion at which Edward could make his first impression as king. Expectations of Edward were low, such was his reputation as the playboy prince, so a ceremony of this calibre allowed him the opportunity to make his mark. He read the speech himself, something Victoria had ceased to do in 1861 and so the tone was set in their flowing robes of state and Alexandra's sombre yet sparkling attire, a sober yet splendid occasion for the crowd: 'What they were witnessing was the reinvention of monarchy as spectacle' (Ridley 2012: 352).

With this idea of the performative possibilities of dress in mind, there is a striking image of Alexandra in which she wears a dress, the bodice of which is made entirely from pleated crape. In addition she wears a Mary Stuart-style mourning cap denoting that she is indeed in the first stage of deepest mourning as a widow. Taken in 1911 less than a year after her husband's death, in this widely distributed postcard Alexandra conforms completely at a point when crape was already in sharp decline as a mourning fabric (Figure 7.2). The Queen Mother (as she self-styled her new title) appears to be ever youthful in the photographic portrait and yet she was sixty-seven when it was taken. The lines of her face have been erased with the retouching processes that were much in use in Victorian and Edwardian photographic studios so that the impression is of a much younger widow, her face smooth between the wrinkled pleats of the crape and the net cap. Unusually there are words of Alexandra's own that were disseminated publicly following the death of her husband – in her 'Letter to the Nation' she writes of King Edward VII's death: 'Not alone have I lost everything in him, my beloved husband, but the nation too has suffered an irreparable loss by their best friend, father and Sovereign thus suddenly called away.'[5] It is hyperbole on a Victorian scale (Edward was hardly the paragon of virtue thus described), but perhaps the photograph mirrors the degree to which her public mourning was to be articulated in its most traditional and thus recognizable aesthetic. Her almost half century of public life enabled her to make astute decisions about expectations of her appearance. Certainly in this photograph she is every inch the widow, to the point that it might almost be deemed a costume of sorts, a performance of dowager queen that could be widely disseminated and understood. With lashings of crape and a widow's cap surrounding the popularly youthful face, observers young and old alike might easily decode this dress and the message it conveyed. She judged that at this particular time and in this specific context, convention and conformity were a necessary part of her response.

Figure 7.2 Her Majesty the Queen Mother Alexandra in widow's cap and high-necked crape dress juxtaposed against her curiously unlined face, smoothed by the retoucher's tools, 1910 (original postcard, author's own collection).

Conclusion

Throughout her married life Alexandra approached the adoption of mourning dress with the same shrewdness and careful judgement as she did other sartorial requirements. She knew when a thoughtful choice of half-mourning might bring comfort but similarly recognized when full mourning brought unrest. She knew that to convey loss through dress was intrinsic to the British class system and that in a sense the complex degrees of mourning dress mirrored the hierarchies of the British people. That said, she was also prepared to diverge from the rigidity of etiquette and forge her own sartorial path, rejecting the wearing of crape at her own son's funeral, a signal of intent at a point in her life when grief dominated. She did not feel the pressure to conform in garments purchased from the principal mourning emporiums but appears to have sourced her clothing from more discreet, generic stores, this too very much in keeping with her lifelong desire to tread a different path to that of the other 'London Ladies'.

The minutiae of mourning seem a complete anachronism to the twenty-first-century relationship with death and outward manifestations of grief, perhaps more so than other classifications of dress. Alexandra negotiated her own experience of mourning with her place within the framework of time and place in society skilfully ensuring that her popularity remained as ever intact.

8
THE CORONATION GOWN

Introduction

In 1902, Sir Arthur Ellis, equerry to the King, recorded one of his encounters with the new queen as preparations for the coronation of Edward VII gathered pace. The matter of Alexandra's dress for the ceremony had thrown courtiers into a quandary as issues of protocol and precedent swirled around court. Alexandra, however, felt no such pressures, when she wrote to the King's equerry: 'I know better than all the milliners and antiquaries, I shall wear exactly what I like and so will all my ladies' (Esher 1934: 318). After thirty-eight years as queen-in-waiting, Alexandra's time had arrived and she revelled in her new position. The change from Princess of Wales to Queen was notable enough to have been remarked upon by Lord Esher in his journal, when he wrote: 'It is queer, her determination to have her own way. As Princess of Wales she was never, so she says, allowed to do as she chose. "Now I do as I like" is the sort of attitude' (Esher 1934: 373). The unwritten intimation in this entry is that Alexandra was perhaps being rather disingenuous here in suggesting that hitherto such decisions had never been her own to make. But in reality how far was this really the case?

The Edwardian coronation – August 1902

Edward VII was crowned on 9 August 1902. The nature of the actual event differed from original plans insomuch that Edward's illness in June had forced the postponement of the coronation, supposed to take place on 26 June. Edward had been feeling increasingly unwell as the preparations for the coronation reached their peak. He was diagnosed with appendicitis and operated on immediately but had been in grave danger for a time. Alexandra continued to fulfil her schedule on his behalf, keeping the real extent of his illness from the general public.

Edward, showman that he was, took the opportunity afforded by his recovery to conceive a spectacle that would do justice to the Empire. It was after all the moment he had waited for all of his adult life. In contrast to the short period of Edward and Alexandra's engagement in 1862/63, Edward scheduled eighteen months for the planning of the coronation. In centuries past, the anointing of the new monarch was a hurried affair as rights of ascendency risked being contested – a coronation would be organized quickly to ensure the new king's authority as God's ambassador on earth. Once such fears were unfounded and the line of accession unchallenged, the new monarch might take time to plan a more elaborate ceremony. That said, earlier coronations were not necessarily less magnificent, they were simply organized differently. Since there was less time to plan them, more of the court's resources were diverted to come up with the pageantry in a more concentrated fashion. Edward had little to work with from living memory. His mother's coronation in 1837 had been punctuated by uncertainty and poor planning, being the first coronation of a queen regnant since Queen Anne who came to the throne in 1702. The minister and diarist Greville noted after that event: 'There was a continual difficulty and embarrassment and the Queen never knew what to do next' (cited in Staniland 1997: 115). Edward intended to ensure that no such confusion attended his own ascension to the throne (Magnus 1964: 276).

The reporter for the *New York Times* described the filling of the streets from sunrise as crowds jostled for the best positions. Westminster Abbey itself played host to the nobility by 10 o'clock, almost two hours before Edward and Alexandra left Buckingham Palace. At 11.15 the Prince of Wales arrived, and soon after fanfares announced that the King and Queen had reached the Abbey (Battiscombe 1969: 249 and Ridley 2012: 367–69). A second fanfare preceded Alexandra who entered first, the boys of Westminster School singing 'Vivat Regina' as she processed to her seat in the chancel. Similarly 'Vivat Rex' was chanted as the King made his way forward in his crimson robe of state made by Ede & Ravenscroft and a scarlet military uniform similar to that worn to his wedding in 1863 (Campbell 1989). Edward, Duke of Windsor, recalled the ceremony: 'The Coronation service lasted almost three hours, an interminable time for small boys to be expected to keep still' (Windsor 1954 np).

The anointing of Alexandra as queen consort was a significant moment for her. Her strong beliefs in the power of the anointment had to be addressed before the ceremony, when she summoned Archbishop Maclagan to explain her anxieties: 'Like most women of her age and generation, she augmented her own hair with a *toupet*. If she were to be properly anointed she felt that the holy oil must touch her own body, not merely this erection of false hair; she therefore begged the Archbishop to be sure that some of the oil ran down onto her forehead' (Battiscombe 1969: 249–50). This duly took place, according to the account of the Duchess of Marlborough: 'From my place on her right, I looked down on her bowed head, her hands meekly folded in prayer, and watched the shaking hand of the Archbishop as, from the spoon which held the sacred oil, he anointed her forehead. I held my breath as a trickle escaped and ran down her nose. With a truly royal composure she kept her hands clasped in prayer; only a look of anguish betrayed concern as her eyes met mine and seemed to ask "Is the damage great?"' (Vanderbilt Balsan 1973: 132).

The choice of the American Consuelo and three other tall duchesses was orchestrated by Alexandra for effect rather than tradition, as the biographer Tisdall related:

> Four of these ladies who were to stand by her throne in the Abbey and 'arrange' her crown, she was going to pick for herself. She was not interested in dusty claims or precedents and was sorry to cause disappointment if somebody had already selected them for her. She would have four Duchesses. The really important thing was that they should all be tall like herself. They must all be beautiful and they must all have a certain similarity of appearance. She was not going to have the effect spoiled by some lady who did not match the rest. (Tisdall 1953: 201)

According to Edward himself, it was successful, and he wrote that the synchronization of these ladies as they placed their coronets upon their heads when Alix was crowned was 'like a scene from a beautiful ballet' (Fisher 1974: 169).

A gown fit for a queen – The coronation gown and robes of Queen Alexandra

Where Alexandra's wedding dress almost forty years earlier shimmered in silver, so the coronation gown dazzled in gold. It is, in a sense, less complex as a garment compared to the wedding dress, in so much that it is unaltered and so its composition now is just as it is featured in the many contemporary photographs capturing the occasion and the appearance of the new queen (Figure 8.1). Consisting of a separate bodice and skirt, the dress is made from a heavy and plain gold silk gauze. This is surmounted with a layer of silk net, across which are sewn thousands of round gold spangles at regular intervals. Close scrutiny of the coronation gown suggests again conclusions that would otherwise be impossible were it not for the survival of the garment itself. While photography progressed enormously in the years between Alexandra's wedding and her coronation, still the black and white images, detailed and numerous though they are, fail to convey the garment and its impact, Luke Fildes' portrait the only contemporary image in colour. (See Plate 14.) Three elements of the gown most immediately apparent are the long over-sleeves, the wired collar and the colour.

Figure 8.1 Photography of Alexandra in her coronation gown and robes that captures the drama of the falling net sleeves and the wired collar, 1902 (original postcard, author's own collection).

The overarching effect of each of these elements is pure drama. The sleeves are long and decorative only, falling over the short puff sleeves at the shoulder. The wired collar, reminiscent of her costume ball gowns of earlier years, is topped at each point with a faux pearl, more redolent perhaps of Tudor royalty. The impact of the colour is most striking of all. The sheer abundance of gold from the gold spangles, embroidery and lace trim on the overdress and the more sombre gold of the underdress is impressive even now, lying flat and two dimensional over a hundred years after the event. A striking cloth of gold garment certainly featured among Queen Victoria's range of coronation garments fit for a queen regnant in 1838. As with Alexandra's dress at the turn of the twentieth century, Victoria had popular symbols of national identity woven into the figured silk of the dalmatica including thistles, shamrocks and Tudor roses. The difference I would suggest is a spiritual one between queens regnant and consort. Queen Victoria's garments did show some concession to fashionable female dress of the late 1830s, but they are predominantly garments reminiscent of ecclesiastical tradition in keeping with the anointing of the monarch. While Alexandra took her role as anointed consort very seriously, her clothing was able to refer to tradition with embroidered cloth of gold, but chose a more contemporary style. To see Alexandra's dress now, however, is to realize the impression then. The effect of such rich textures under candles and electric lights in its three-dimensional life is a testament to Alexandra's eye for an occasion. Her choice of fabric and embellishment ensured that all of the pomp and drama of the coronation was captured and personified in one dramatic garment.

An early indication that Alexandra would take her lead, at least in part, from history when it came to the planning of her own part in the coronation came in the frail shape of the Grand Duchess of Mecklenburg-Strelitz, the only remaining royal personage to have attended the coronation of William IV, and therefore well placed to observe the behaviour of the last queen consort. Queen Mary's biographer James Pope-Hennessy recorded: 'Princess May's Aunt Augusta was much perturbed by all the innovations instigated by the new King. Was it true that Peeresses were no longer to wear diadems in the Abbey? Why had the colour of the Princesses' robes been changed? She had written down her memories of William IV's coronation for Queen Alexandra's benefit: "I put down in writing for her, of what I recollect of the old Court: this she was glad to have, as it shows what the Queen Consort had to do and where she stood and walked."' She went on to observe to her niece, the future queen Mary, however: 'Now, it appears, this is to be altered, yet she hopes to put it right for you some day, when you take her place' (Pope-Hennessy 1959: 370–71). While Alexandra was happy to consult and consider the events of the past, she clearly meant to adapt the occasion to suit her own ideas of the appearance and actions of a consort.

It was, however, the choice of gown and robes which would mark the significance of the day, both in the eyes of Alexandra herself and those of the many spectators expecting all of the pageant and splendour of the Empire. Highly ritualistic garments were worn by the monarch only, and not the consort, but Alexandra intended to ensure that her own appearance mirrored in splendour, that of her husband.

It is through the detailed planning of these garments – the velvet coronation robe and the gown – that the degree of Alexandra's agency, but also her delegation, is revealed. The velvet robe was composed of a variety of structural elements. The maker is given as Ede & Ravenscroft and they did indeed conduct the making up of the robe, but this belies the more complex story behind the hand stitching (Figure 8.2).

Figure 8.2 Alexandra in her coronation garments, showing the full embroidered splendour of the velvet robe that was put together by Ede & Ravenscroft but consisted of components by many makers, from a drawing in the *Daily Telegraph* (original postcard, author's own collection).

The design incorporating nationally symbolic emblems was conceived, at the request of Alexandra, by Frederick Vigers.[1] The design itself was not uncontroversial: 'As Queen Consort, not Queen of England in her own right, the Queen was not strictly speaking supposed to have all the Royal emblems on her robe – for instance the Crown and the Star: she desired them however and the design incorporating them all was drawn by Mr Frederick Vigers, FRIBA, and executed by the Ladies' Work Society, presided over by Princess Louise' (Halls 1973: 53). The liberal scattering of gold embroidered crowns across the surface of the robe, which are more ornate than other coronation robes in the collection, bear more than a passing resemblance to the decorative tradition of Danish coronation robes (Johansen 1990). Perhaps for the first time now that her position had changed, she felt able to incorporate an element of her own cultural heritage into the garments which held such spiritual significance for her. Maybe this was the subversion which had been denied Alexandra for so long and to which she was referring in her conversation with Sir Arthur Ellis – the chance to openly pay her respects to the country of her birth and acknowledge her cultural antecedents through dress. After years of championing British wares, and bearing British emblems, the decorative influences on the robe of her coronation could at last celebrate Denmark. Stylistically this meant embellishment with many crowns. The Danish custom was to wear 'velours de soie rouge, entièrement brodé de motifs de couronnes d'or' [red silk velvet covered with embroidered gold crowns] (Johansen 2009: 140).

The robe in its entirety cost almost £1400. A manuscript, also held by the London Museum at this time, detailed some of the other contributors to the robe; the gold borders were woven by Warners & Co, the velvet was woven by an old Huguenot weaver, M Dorée, and the velvet was supplied by Marshall & Snelgrove, Ede & Ravenscroft then bringing the various elements together. A small column towards the end of the first surviving volume of Alexandra's wardrobe accounts reveals the cost of such luxury. For the embroidery the Ladies' Work Society received £860, Frederick Vigers was paid £54 for his designs, the braid woven at Warners cost £37.9.5, Marshall & Snelgrove charged £26.5 for the velvet and at the end of it all Ede & Son were paid £410 to create the finished article.[2] Over half of this amount was accounted for in embroidery alone, owing to the sheer volume of metal thread and bullion required to execute the many emblems represented. That these symbols alone cost so much indicates Alexandra's vision of a patriotic queen and her determination to display to all her role as consort.

Even the colour of the velvet was not without complications: 'The colour of the velvet is not the velvet shot with crimson in the warp, traditional for a Queen of England, but a different purple shade, chosen by the Queen and called 'petunia' by Princess Louise' (Halls 1973: 53). That even the colour of the velvet was not immune to Alexandra's departure from tradition is a further gauge of her resolve to reinforce nationalistic tradition while simultaneously stamping her own authority across it. This robe was designed to speak volumes – more ornate, according to curators – than most of the other coronation robes in the collection, including those of monarchs themselves. It spoke of Britain and her Empire. But it also spoke of personality and the power of the individual.

Images of the newly crowned queen show little of the velvet robe, by the nature of its attachment to the back of the shoulders, so that the eye is drawn to the principal garment of the day – Queen Alexandra's coronation gown. This was a garment designed for maximum impact; it is a theatrical garment in so many of its elements, illustrative of careful planning and attention to detail. The wired collar was a bold adornment to include, as Zillah Halls remarked upon from the London Museum collection: 'Queen Alexandra's high-standing wired collar has a certain affinity with the Scandinavian and "Henry IV" not to speak of one of the last stage costumes worn by Adelina Patti in 1895 and also in the museum's collections' (Halls 1973: 16). She clearly recognized that beyond the religious aspect of the coronation, it was essentially a piece of theatre and with a collar reminiscent of Elizabeth I, dazzling fabric and long sweeping medieval sleeves, she would play her part.

Alexandra was, as with the robe, fully engaged with the design and realization of this gown. The commission, however, was to take shape far from her realm of control, and was overseen by another. Mary, Lady Curzon was, in 1902 the vicereine of India. She was feted for her style and beauty: 'She never made the mistake of overloading her outfits with too much fussy and distracting decoration, preferring to leave her exquisitely embroidered gowns to make their own dramatic, yet suitably regal, impact' (Ashelford 1996: 252). It was this approach which appealed to Alexandra's own sartorial tastes, and she felt confident enough of Lady Curzon's flair to call on her assistance prior to the coronation. Mary herself recounted this request in a letter to her husband dated 9 June 1901: 'This afternoon the Queen sent for me and I went to see her at Marlborough House and absolutely nothing could exceed her kindness – kissed me! – patted me – admired me! And wished to see me again. I brought her a black & silver piece of embroidery to shew her and she wants me to order a similar dress for her Coronation pageants – one is to be black & silver, another mauve & gold with great train. She said she would leave it all to me which I don't much like – but I shall do my very best to get her something beautiful embroidered at Delhi' (cited in Bradley 1985: 107). This is followed by another letter written a month later from London: 'I am waiting here for Queen's command. Charlotte Knollys has written she wished to see me about ordering Coronation dress in India' (Bradley 1985: 117).

Lady Curzon and her new queen inhabited different worlds; they shared little in common, yet there is a curious synergy of experience that validates Alexandra's choice in handing so important a task to a woman so far away. Like Alexandra, Mary Curzon presided regularly over a kind of court presentation ceremony not dissimilar to that of the Royal Drawing Rooms; fancy-dress balls at which the vicereine had to maintain a certain regal standard were common and her styling of her famous peacock dress for the Coronation Durbar in 1903 rivalled Alexandra's coronation gown for sheer magnificence. Her ability to correctly assess the requirements for her public appearance was one of the attributes so prized by Alexandra.

Suppressing her earlier fears over so daunting a commission, Mary Curzon embraced the challenge. Her communications via Charlotte Knollys reveal Alexandra's hand in the design from the outset. Less than a week after she had reported the news in her letter to her husband, Lady Curzon received instructions from the Queen: 'The Queen has instructed me to write and say that she thinks the dress for the Coronation would look very well net embroidered in gold and silver with rose, shamrock and thistle. Could you therefore have a design made and send it to Her Majesty to look at. It must not be "too conventional" or stiff but something in the "flowery" style of your dress ... . I am sure it would be a very popular thing for the Queen to have her Coronation dress made in India and I think the effect would be lovely' (Thomas 2007: 388). The text appears to suggest that Charlotte is quoting the Queen verbatim over the charge that the embroidery not be 'too conventional' but 'flowery' like the vicereine's, allowing the smallest glimpse of Alexandra's personal wishes. That this most anticipated and visible of gowns should not be too conventional is a declaration of the new queen's intentions. She was determined that her appearance on the day the world was watching her should not be mired in the establishment's expectations and so ensured enough of the exotic Far East in the design to stamp her individuality while remaining within the bounds of taste.

One of the deciding factors which influenced Alexandra's decision to have the overdress made in India was 'as a tribute to the sub-continent she knew that she would now never see' (Hough 1992: 241). One of the regrets of her life was that she had been forbidden by Queen Victoria to travel with Edward on his state visit to India in 1876. The correspondence which flashed between the two women at the time, revealed deep determination on both sides to have her way. The ruling matriarch prevailed, however, and Alexandra remained in England. Now, when the choice was hers to make she ensured that she would be crowned in a dress that hailed from that distant corner of the world, both as a statement of Empire and her own personal desires.

It was not only the lure of Indian design which attracted Alexandra to order her designs so far overseas, but also a more pragmatic consideration. Three letters, from Charlotte Knollys to Lady Curzon between August and October 1901, are emphatic on one point: '*Private* My Dear Lady Curzon, The Queen wishes me to write and ask you not to tell anyone in *England* about the dresses ordered in India, or else they will be wanting to have some also, whereas HM would like to have something *original* for her Coronation dress.'[3] Clearly the risks of handing the commission to a London-based embroidery firm were apparently too great in Alexandra's estimation. Less than a week later, Miss Knollys writes again: 'I do not think the Queen has the slightest objection to letting it be known in *India* that her Coronation dress is to be made there. She only thought (entre nous) that if the London Ladies got hold of it they would be wanting to copy hers!'[4] Any feelings of patriotic patronage were overridden by the more pressing concern of ensuring utter originality. After forty years of mixing with the 'London Ladies' the Queen opted to put as much distance as possible between the designs and any potential copycats. Even after the coronation was over, Alexandra still valued her originality, and a letter from Sir Dighton Probyn to Lady Curzon containing a bank draft for the embroidery firms, contains the following warning quoted, he says, from the Queen: '"Be sure and tell Lady Curzon to see that the natives to whom I am going to give my warrant do not let the Duchess of Connaught or any of the Ladies now going out to India, copy my dresses"!! How this is to be managed quietly I cannot think!'[5] It was worth the absence of complete control in order to achieve this, besides which the Queen trusted in Lady Curzon's abilities to discharge her duty with elegance and flair. Mary's efforts were given the royal seal of approval, with Charlotte Knollys again reporting for the Queen that 'HM is enchanted with them'.[6] Mary wrote in a letter to her mother of the personal approach she had taken to the execution of the design: 'I have cut them all out on the floor & traced the design through marking paper on to the stuff till my back has nearly cracked' (Thomas 2007: 388).

As with the velvet robe, the various elements that together constituted the dress, were made up elsewhere, this time left in the trusted hands of arguably Alexandra's favourite couture house of this period, Morin Blossier. It is their name woven into the silk waistband of the bodice and skirt and it was to them that the sum of £996.2.6 was paid.[7] It was a brave choice on Alexandra's part and is indicative of her trust in the French firm's abilities to create the perfect gown for her. Queen Alexandra herself wrote to Lady Curzon, expressing her thanks and updating her with the progress of the gown at the dressmaker's: 'And now I must tell you about my Indian Coronation robes which you so kindly *designed* and carried out. I have had the white and gold embroideries made up over a *Cloth* of *Gold* which makes a brilliant effect.'[8] This inherent sense of what would work for her overcame any qualms of loyalty to British manufacture. Despite the nationalistic symbolism embroidered all over the gown, not a part of it was constructed in the UK.

On 9 August 1902, the postponed coronation of Edward VII and Queen Alexandra took place; it is from accounts of the ceremony that the new queen's shrewdness and awareness of what the occasion warranted becomes more apparent. The choice of the all-gold gown, in addition to the obviously regal overtones, made perfect sense given the theatre of the crowning ceremony. The *New York Times* described the moment: 'When the tottering Primate, who almost fainted in the act, placed the diadem on the head of him whom he had just anointed in the name of the Lord to be "a Captain over his inheritance", electric lights suddenly blazed in the sanctuary behind which the bones of St Edward repose.'[9] The effect of the ultra-modern electric lights on the Royal couple, and their glittering attire, must have been tremendous and almost certainly premeditated.

Queen Alexandra had made her entrance first and her emergence from a darkened area of the Abbey must also have been calculated for maximum effect. One of the peeresses, Lady Jane Lindsay wrote: 'When the Queen appeared, it was like a vision coming through the dark archway of the screen. I never saw anything more beautiful' (cited in Hough 1992: 242–43). Consuelo, Duchess of Marlborough, one of the four of the Queen's canopy bearers, wrote of the loveliness of the Queen as she processed forward: 'I felt a lump in my throat and realised that I was more British than I knew' (Vanderbilt Balsan 1973: 132).

Alexandra had ensured through careful planning, fine detail and her now well-practised flair for what an occasion demanded in terms of dress, that she shone – spiritually and materially at this most splendid of events (Figure 8.3). The reporter for the *New York Times* was effusive in his praise as he looked at Alexandra on her throne: 'No wonder the whole nation admires her, for surely a younger looking woman of her years was never seen, or a more graceful one. She is endowed with that natural grace and instinctive knowledge of the fitness of things which the most laboriously acquired manners can never equal.'[10]

Figure 8.3 Alexandra depicted in a Punch engraving as the fairy queen for her provision of a tea for maids of all work to celebrate the coronation. The image creates a vision of Alexandra in a garment that was surprisingly accurate in its dramatic and theatrical elements, 18 June 1902 (author's own collection).

Conclusion

Compared to the decades lived as Princess of Wales, Alexandra was only to occupy the throne as consort for nine years. She was determined that her appearance at the coronation was to be one that might live up to the expectations of a watching world and also one that adheres to a sense of tradition and spirituality which was also important to her. It is an ensemble of two halves – the velvet robe could be described as the ceremonial object, the garment bound up with the traditions of monarchs past with its regal purple velvet, gold embroideries and ermine border. The gown, on the other hand, is perhaps the temporal world embodied in the fashionably styled bodice and skirt, the dramatic collar and sleeves and the consistency of the gold across its surface from underdress to elaborate overdress. It embodies too her approach to dress more broadly, this sartorial duality she was able to bring to her appearance. She simultaneously satisfied British sensibilities having her robes made entirely in the UK displaying British workmanship, ceremonial motifs and all made by the charitable foundation of the Ladies Work Society. Underlying the design more discreetly, however, was the stylistic nod to the country of her birth with the aesthetics drawn from Danish coronation robes.

The dress itself was an entirely different matter. Not a stitch of it was fabricated in Britain. From the design of the overdress that was conducted in India by the American vicereine Lady Curzon to the construction of the underdress by Morin Blossier in Paris it was a vision of French couture. This was not widely disseminated at the time and as usual Alexandra had managed to negotiate carefully the official protocols amid the wider expectations of how her imperial royal body should appear. The similarity between her coronation gown and the other dresses worn in a fantasy/performance context is noticeable. The high-wired collar is a feature shared by all three garments as is the profusion of gold embroidery and the historicism of the falling sleeves. She had practised her appearance as a queen at the Waverley Ball and the Devonshire House Ball and she brought these aesthetics to bear in the execution of her coronation dress, complete with well-timed electric lighting and her theatrical emergence from the gloom of a darkened archway in Westminster Abbey. While she was already suffering with certain physical difficulties, including the scoliosis of her spine and profound deafness, she dazzled observers with her supposed youthfulness. It is no accident that the unretouched image of her never went into circulation but rather the unlined face wearing the glittering robes that clothed her still slender 23-inch waist. On that August day in 1902, through artistry, clever design and a smoke and mirrors display, Edward and Alexandra gave the nation all of the pomp and ceremony that Queen Victoria had for so long rejected.

9
DISPERSAL OF A ROYAL WARDROBE

The auction

On 30 April 1937 the luminaries of New York society and patrons of the arts were invited to the preview of an auction. An afternoon of refreshments would be punctuated by young women modelling those items up for auction which numbered some seventy lots. The sale excited enough interest to merit a report in the *New York Times*: 'Royal robes and state gowns of Alexandra, consort of Edward VII, were paraded by models and sold to the highest bidders yesterday afternoon at auction at the American Art Association Anderson Galleries Inc.'[1] The auction of Queen Alexandra's clothing represented the largest single dispersal of her belongings and demonstrates how far flung her surviving garments were to become after her death and the death of those to whom she gifted items of dress during her lifetime. Between the bequests of dressers and their descendants and the acquisitions of museums from auction the dissemination of this royal wardrobe is both a tale of the social biographies that objects acquire and a lesson in the perseverance required in tracking down these disparate pieces in locations around the world. As a cautionary note, these survivals represent the accidents of history. There is no pattern to their existence, no logical interpretation of their place within museum storage.

The selling and exhibition of royal dress had a long precedent (Figure 9.1). In June 1831, 120 lots of George IV's sumptuous wardrobe were put up for public sale by Mr Phillips at his rooms in New Bond Street. The *Caledonian Mercury* reported on the outcome: 'There was very slight competition for any of the articles, and we did not observe that they were knocked down to persons of distinction. The proceeds of the sale could not have amounted to any considerable sum.'[2] The poor return on this public sale may have been indicative of George IV's unpopularity but its report in the national press suggests that such a public auction was socially acceptable. One of the most significant pieces from this auction was the King's magnificent velvet and ermine coronation robes. Originally

Figure 9.1 Postcard of an early display of Edward and Alexandra's and George and Mary's coronation robes in the London Museum. Mary was an early supporter of the collection of royal dress, 1912 (original postcard, author's own collection).

costing over £24,000, they were purchased by Madame Tussaud in 1831 for public display where it remained until the 1860s when the London pollution was deemed detrimental to its continued exhibition (Taylor 2002: 39). Queen Alexandra's own mother-in-law would have provided a blueprint for the disposal of garments since so many of her unwanted clothes were gifted to loyal members of the royal household and have subsequently landed in collections around the world. Many museums, besides that of the Royal Ceremonial Dress Collection, own one of the distinctively proportioned black dresses that were such a staple of her widow's wardrobe. It was not just dresses that were given or acquired by staff in the royal household but other more intimate objects as well, including silk stockings embroidered with the royal cipher and even fine linen drawers.

Another comprehensive royal wardrobe to have survived is also associated with Alexandra, that of her daughter Maud who became queen of Norway. These survivals are arguably easier to follow since the contents of her wardrobe were kept as part of a much more conscious collection policy on the part of the Norwegian royal family. Outfits from her marriage through to her death, including daywear, sportswear, accessories and associated ephemera of the consumption of dress, form a coherent narrative of one woman's relationship with her clothes. This is not the experience of Alexandra's wardrobe, however, which was never collected with any eye to posterity meaning that the survivals are accidental, random with many holes in the story.

In more recent years, the sale of royal dress to raise money for charitable foundations, most notably Diana the former Princess of Wales' garments, has received a great deal of publicity. In 1997: 'Diana decided to auction seventy-nine of her past evening gowns to raise money for the Royal Marsden Hospital Cancer Fund and the AIDS Crisis Trust. She would turn couture into hard cash that could do some practical good' (McDowell 2002: 222). There is much similarity of experience between Alexandra and Diana, not least for the shrewdness with which they managed their public appearance, centred around clothing choices, using dress as a non-verbal communicator at times in their lives when they might not articulate verbally but could convey their situation through dress. Diana, of course, chose the garments that she was going to relinquish and so these represented a set of conscious sartorial choices over which she retained control. The 1937 auction of Alexandra's clothes, on the other hand, were purely accidental survivals. They happened to be the garments that remained in her various wardrobes after her death, some of which came into the possession of a court furrier, Samuel Wilson Soden, under whose instruction the gowns came to be auctioned. Public sales of dress were not confined to royalty alone. Aristocratic families would also auction off their finery as in the example of Mrs Arthur Paget, a contemporary of Alexandra's: 'After she died in 1911 her clothes were sold by auction. All her beautiful dresses went for very little, and her Cleopatra costume fetched only £9. One newspaper account ends its description of the sale with the sad comment, "The frocks which once graced a society leader will soon perhaps be found in the second hand clothes shops of Bayswater and Whitechapel"' (Murphy 1984: 118).

Recycling dress

During her lifetime, there were methods of disposal open to Alexandra that facilitated the never-ending cycle of the royal wardrobe. Public expectations centred on her appearance demanded a disciplined approach around recycling the contents of this wardrobe. The role of the dresser within the cycle was key, a factor that will be examined at length in this chapter. There were other creative ways, however, of disposing of garments deemed no longer suitable for the royal body. One method of offloading royal garments actually generated an income and was reported in the *New York Evening Mail* of 28 February 1920: 'Most of the ladies from any royal family buy at least two dozen court gowns in a year and they do not wear any of them more than twice. What becomes of them? Do they accumulate in wardrobes or are they stored away? Certainly not! These are practical times. They are disposed of through a dress agency.'[3] The article goes on to outline the logistics of the process which was negotiated by the dresser: 'It is customary for all foreign royalties to allow their dressers a commission of at least 15 % so that they are able to make from $500–$1500 a year. English royalties don't allow their dressers any commission, but give them much higher salaries.'[4] For the British monarchy, the existence of the agencies overseas may have offered a welcome discretion to the transaction: 'There is a well known one in Paris where the Queen of Spain, Queen Alexandra, the Queen of Norway and many other royal ladies dispose of their left-off gowns.'[5] This pragmatic approach to the disposal of dress may well have evolved from the age-old traditions of perquisites enjoyed by members of a royal household, but its existence here as a commercial enterprise via an established dress agency is instructive. None of the surviving garments now in collections that are associated with Alexandra have any provenance linked to a dress agency and so it seems entirely feasible that there will be garments of hers around the world that have lost their original context with no connection now to a long dead princess and queen.

Alexandra herself took a slightly different approach to the reuse of unwanted garments as demonstrated in a document written by her dresser Mrs Giltrap in 1926. Following the death of Alexandra, and at the request of Queen Mary, Mrs Giltrap compiled a list of surviving dresses belonging to her former mistress. Within this list she writes: 'Between 1888 and 1890 The Queen had 6 good brocade dresses unpicked and cleaned and handed over to R_____[illegible] at Sandringham to cover furniture. The Gold dress with bunches of lilies covered the chairs in the Boudoir at Sandringham. I enclose patterns of some that were cleaned.'[6] This short vignette offers a slightly different version of a queen in possession of a significant dress allowance. It is a woman not only in complete control of her possessions and the wardrobe that so defined her, but also of a woman thinking laterally about the reuse of garments and their usefulness beyond their original purpose. Significant though her spending was, it is perhaps an echo of her former life in Denmark – the childhood in which she learnt to sew her own clothes, refashion her own hats and to value cloth as a commodity. The fragments of silk still survive attached to the document, a fragmentary relic of a garment now long lost. However, the fragments happened to match up to some samples kept in the Royal Ceremonial Dress Collection, labelled as pieces from court gowns once belonging to Queen Alexandra, some of which had been made up into a small drawstring bag, presumably by a dresser. They are tantalizing glimpses of parts of the royal wardrobe now lost to view, kept as souvenirs perhaps for their royal association but divorced from their context of use, their association with a public figure key to their survival. (See Plate 15.) Kay Staniland observed in her volume *In Royal Fashion*: 'Historic royal clothing of any period holds a fascination for the visiting public … it offers an actual contact with its original owner, an outer skin which is still strongly permeated with the bodily characteristics of that personality' (Staniland 1997: 134).

The auction

The auction of Queen Alexandra's garments in New York received no press coverage in the UK.[7] The reasons for this are purely conjecture based since little is known about the vendor or how he came to acquire so many garments of royal origin. The cover of the auction catalogue reads: 'Property of Samuel Wilson Soden, Esq, Sold by his Order.'[8] Soden was a furrier with premises on Regent Street and according to his shop sign a 'court furrier' at that.[9] This may explain a royal connection although not his acquisition of the garments. Alexandra's daughter Princess Victoria had died in December 1935 and it is possible that the clothing came from this source. Certainly one of the garments in the auction was directly related to Victoria – her velvet robe from the coronation of her father Edward VII in 1902. The sale of royal memorabilia was perhaps a sensitive issue given the wider context at this time. Edward VIII had abdicated only six months earlier with the coronation of his brother George VI taking place during the same month as the New York auction. The Anderson Art Galleries exhibited the garments for four days prior to the sale, their showrooms open daily from 9.00 to 6.00 according to the catalogue.[10]

With thirty lots accounted for, the remaining forty were sold to persons not now known, although the occasional clue might be gleaned from a variety of sources. The *New York Times* reported that Mrs S. Stanwood Menken[11] 'gave $100 for a silver-embroidered light grey wool cape which was a part of Queen Alexandra's trousseau and $77.50 for a black sequin and tulle State gown'.[12] This black gown next appears in 1939, modelled by the socialite Babe Paley for a feature entitled 'The Queenly Figure': 'Now that we are going to wear "Queen Alexandra" dresses – and the four preceding pages prove that we are – what shall we do about our figures?'[13] The whereabouts of the black embroidered tulle gown now are not known but this single gown stands as an example of the difficulties research of such disparate objects as these can encounter.

A dress that does still exist, associated with Queen Alexandra and possibly the New York auction, has travelled along a complex route from royal evening dress to wartime wedding gown. In 1944 an auction took place at the Queensbury All Services Club to raise money for the war effort.[14] One of the lots was an Edwardian evening dress that formerly belonged to Queen Alexandra that was donated to the auction by the famous big band leader Jack Hylton. The dress was purchased by a serviceman for his sister's wedding – he paid £300 pounds for it. The dress was remodelled and worn by his sister later that year. The dress still survives although is in a fragile state now and is still in the possession of 'Vicky' whose wedding dress it was. I have never seen the dress as Vicky is very elderly but enjoyed a regular correspondence with her best friend who gave me many details as to its origins. Hylton did tour around America during the 1930s – he was there in 1936 – but came back to tour Europe and Britain in 1937, meaning that he did not acquire the dress through the New York auction. Its origins therefore remain a mystery at this point and yet form a part of the multifarious survivals from collections both public and private that underpin this entire project. A similar story of wartime fundraising accompanies a black silk taffeta and blue silk chiffon dress of Alexandra's that is now in the Canadian War

Museum, Ottawa. The curator told me: 'According to the information provided by the donor, his parents received the dress in appreciation for participating in a fund-raising auction sometime in 1941 for British War Relief. The donor indicated that the dress was included in a consignment of forty to fifty items sent from the UK for the auction.'[15] The description shares some similarity with that given in the New York auction of 1937, number 44 is a gown of 'black chiffon overlaying light blue chiffon on a black satin foundation'. It is possible, given that some of the New York garments were purchased by a Canadian collector whose ultimate destination was the Royal Ontario Museum, that this dress was a part of the original auction and then was given once again as part of the war effort but at this stage without records or even images, it is impossible to verify.

The different documentation associated with some garments at the 1937 auction offers a longer biographical trajectory from commission and wear through to inhabiting an entirely different place as museum object. This kind of historical tracking can be extremely illuminating, what Kopytoff described as the 'cultural biography of things'. The inanimacy of the object does not prevent its existence in different contexts 'speaking' to us, the observer, of its path and its story: 'Biographies of things can make salient what might otherwise remain obscure' (Kopytoff 1986: 65). On 1 August 1901, Mary Curzon wrote to her father in great excitement:

> I am being kept in London by such an unexpected duty – it is this – the Queen has asked me to undertake and making and design of her Coronation robes to be embroidered in India … . She told me to use my own judgement in every way as she had absolute confidence in my taste and not only have I got the making of the actual Coronation dress *but* 3 others besides for all the great State functions and these too are to be worked in India.[16]

Almost six months later she wrote again, this time to her mother, of one of these state robes: 'The black dress I ordered for the Queen is magnificent, it costs 450R or £32. It is black with a trailing design of flowers in gold and silver.'[17] There is a very short entry in *The Times* for Tuesday 30 May 1905 that may or may not be the dress in question during its period of use: 'Her Majesty the Queen wore a black dress embroidered in silver: train to correspond.'[18] It was describing one of 'Their Majesties Courts' and so would be entirely in keeping with the occasion.

A description of this dress next appears in Mrs Giltrap's inventory of surviving garments written in the months after Alexandra's death as 'Indian Black and Silver Lotus Flower'[19] How the garments were distributed after 1926 is difficult to ascertain but by 1937 this dress had come into the possession of Samuel Wilson Soden and was one of the items listed for auction at the Anderson Art Galleries, number 38 in the catalogue with the description: 'Black tulle appliqué-embroidered with an allover design of curling silver floral branches, the blossoms heightened with gold; black satin foundation. Separate bell-form skirt with train, hem with tulle flounces; two printed bodices with puffed sleeves of tulle pique with sequins'.[20] The gown was purchased by Irene Lewisohn, founder of the Museum of Costume Art that was to merge with The Metropolitan Museum of Art in 1937. She did, in fact, purchase almost a quarter of the entire catalogue to create a collection of Alexandra's garments at The Met that is now the largest in the world. The original entry card notes the purchase, describing it as 'silver and gold embroidered black tulle STATE GOWN: skirt, two bodices and long train'.[21] It was received by the museum on 5 May 1937, the day of the auction itself.

A similar route can be traced for another state gown of the period, whose order first appears in the wardrobe accounts of 1903. Although the garment itself is not described, the amount as charged by the Paris couture house of Morin Blossier is listed. The distinctive design of yellow satin, diamante embellishment and painted purple irises allows the dress to be identified as that worn to a state ball at Buckingham Palace in July 1904: 'Her Majesty the Queen wore a dress of primrose satin embroidered with silver and mauve orchids.'[22] It too is noted in Mrs Giltrap's inventory before appearing once again in the New York auction catalogue as number 31. This particular dress was purchased by the Canadian collector colonel Flanagan and he eventually donated the dress, among others from the same collection, to the Royal Ontario Museum, Toronto.

It is rare that the existence of a single garment can be followed along so many different tangential paths, and in the case of these two garments alone, the differing descriptions and destinations reveal the potential pitfalls of object-based dress history. It is part of the remarkable ebb and flow of garments into and out of one wardrobe after another, from that of the maker to the royal patron; from the royal patron to the furrier; from the furrier to the collector and ultimately the museum store.

The gift

The easiest route of dispersal to follow is that of the staff to whom Alexandra made gifts of her clothing. Dressers were perhaps an obvious choice given their daily association with Alexandra's wardrobe and the choices she made from it. Their duties of repair and maintenance also meant that they were ideally placed to receive gifts of those items deemed no longer suitable for royal wear. They were not the only staff members to benefit from her generosity, however. The garments now in the National Museum, Liverpool's collection, form part of the Nunn Trust but were originally given by Queen Alexandra to Mrs Dodds, her housekeeper at Sandringham. Although her role operated away from the royal wardrobe, the gift of royal clothing by her mistress was presumably well received. Without documentary evidence to illuminate the motives of such gifts it is impossible now to ascertain whether this was practical patronage or purely souvenir. The whole of the Nunn Trust collection speaks of royal knick-knacks being distributed by the royal family and accumulated by members of the royal household perhaps in a souvenir or talismanic capacity. There are buttons, garments, all sorts of baby memorabilia given to Phyllis Swallow, head of the royal nursery as well as children's garments, a bouquet holder, dresses, slippers, a pen, nightdress, chemise, stockings and handkerchiefs. Many include an additional note in the museum documentation such as 'much worn' or 'mended' speaking of careful management.[23] These were items that had been well worn, repaired and then passed on, often kept in families by the subsequent generation who then made a gift or sale of the items to museum collections. Dressers often stayed in post for long periods of time and were much lamented if they left. Alexandra clearly took pleasure in the relationship she had with her dressers and enjoyed giving items of clothing to them, even at times when the garment itself was felt to be inappropriate on the part of the recipient. One such occasion was recorded as relating to her dresser Bessie Temple:

On one occasion [Alexandra] presented Bessie with a beautiful grey silk frock, remarking that she herself no longer needed it as she had a new one almost exactly similar. For that very reason Bessie took great care never to wear the frock when she was anywhere near the Princess. One day, however, she was faced with the question 'Why do I never see you in that pretty frock?' 'Because, Ma'am, I do not want to appear dressed the same as Your Royal Highness.' 'Nonsense! That is exactly why I gave it to you; I *want* us to look just alike.' (Cited in Battiscombe 1969: 203)

Certainly the garments associated with Alexandra that survive in the Royal Ceremonial Dress Collection in London came from descendants of the Temple family and attest to the position that they occupied in their mistress's affections. Similarly a number of the garments in the collections of the FIDM Museum in Los Angeles also originated via the dresser Mrs Giltrap's family as a letter written by M. Deane explains:

The Clothes, Photographs & other items that I have sold to Mrs Doris Langley Moore were the property of the late Harriet Giltrap who was Dresser to Queen Alexandra when she was Princess of Wales and after Queen Alexandra, the clothes were worn by Queen Alexandra and the Photographs were given to my Wife by Mrs Cook as promised by Mrs Giltrap, the Skirts and other parts of the costumes were made into dresses by Mrs Cook who was Mrs Giltrap's niece with whom Mrs Giltrap lived in a flat on Duchy of Cornwal Estate, the flats were for Pensioned Servants of the Royal Family only.[24]

Mrs Deane helped Mrs Giltrap, who suffered from arthritis, when Mrs Cook was not available, hence her association with the former dresser.

This recent acquisition by the Fashion Institute of Design and Merchandising Museum of the Helen Larsson collection includes several items of Alexandra's clothing. The objects were acquired by a private collector, Helen Larsson, in the 1960s through her association with the British arts and dress history patron Doris Langley Moore.[25] Langley Moore was a founding light of the Fashion Museum, Bath and as a result of her connection with Helen Larsson and Bath, the two collections on either side of the Atlantic Ocean now share a number of similar garments formerly belonging to Queen Alexandra, including tailored waistcoats and jackets. How she came to acquire these in the first place is not a well-documented story.

One of the accession cards in the Fashion Museum records a note from Mrs Langley Moore:

> This dress was one of eight which were found among the effects of a shop in Margaret Street – 'Baroque'. They all appear to have belonged to Queen Alexandra, some had the typical black label as in our other Queen Alexandra specimen. I was given the choice of two and selected this one because we have no other model by this couturier. As King Edward VII died in 1910 and six of the dresses found were made in this year, it is to be assumed that these were made before his death and were discarded for mourning.[26]

Corroboration of the shop 'Baroque' and its Alexandra dresses comes from an unlikely source. A 1950s advertisement newsreel entitled 'Look Back For Inspiration' intersperses models wearing contemporary gowns by 'Baroque's' dressmakers with original dresses of Queen Alexandra's.[27]

How a small independent dressmaker in London came to own eight of Queen Alexandra's dresses is unknown. Their subsequent perusal by Doris Langley Moore is indicative of her own very active sourcing of royal and historic dress both for herself and her clients such as Helen Larsson. This activity is revealed in correspondence between the two women. A letter from Langley Moore to Helen Larsson dated 6 October 1963 describes such purchases: 'Now I must tell you that I lately bought some clothing of Queen Alexandra's, when Princess of Wales. It is of absolutely guaranteed authenticity.'[28]

Unknown survivals and unexplained dispersal

There is an entire grouping of garments associated with Alexandra and dispersed either during her lifetime or after her death, that at this point in time cannot be quantified. As the dress agencies disposed of garments, possibly anonymously and as pieces were auctioned, time separates the object from its provenance. Like a game of Chinese whispers the original context of the object can be diluted and muddled over time. Just occasionally there might be an oblique reference in a record that hints at survivals: Mrs Giltrap writes in her document to Queen Mary that 'Her Majesty's Dresses at Sandringham were sent to The Empress'.[29] This presumably refers to Empress Maria Feodorovna, Alexandra's sister Dagmar. These may have been sent to their holiday home in Denmark, Hvidovre, but if so then there is no longer any record of their route to her homeland. It is possible that without any further note of their original owner, they have been miscataloged as belonging to Dagmar. It is equally possible that at some point after Dagmar's death the garments were simply subsumed into the royal collection or sold with no known provenance and therefore may still exist somewhere but with their original context long forgotten.

While a large number of the lots at the 1937 auction have been accounted for, over half are still in locations unknown, purchased perhaps in their ones and twos and now in private collections or small public historic collections, their provenance unrecorded. Even now, garments continue to emerge, a recent discovery being that of up to four court gowns associated with Alexandra in the study collection of a TV and film costume designer.

Creating a similarly frustrating angle for the researcher are the garments that appear to wash up unexpectedly in the most unlikely places with little documentation and even less explanation. A pair of Alexandra's fine linen under-drawers, complete with her crowned cipher, were discovered in the collection of the Kent State University Museum in Ohio, the curator stating: 'I thought you were brave but it turns out we have one garment so I guess your detective works has paid off, if only a little. Our founders, Shannon Rodgers and Jerry Silverman, collected mostly through auction houses and dealers in the 1970s & 1980s in New York and London, in case that helps you.'[30] It didn't really, although their survival is fascinating. There are her boots in the Powerhouse Museum, Sydney and a fur coat in Oslo. Most strange of all perhaps is a photograph now in the FIDM Museum of an Edwardian reception dress supposedly belonging to Queen Alexandra that was displayed for years in Disneyland Florida before being purchased by the Californian collector Helen Larsson. The picture remains but the dress does not, sold on presumably by Larsson at a later date, destination unknown.

A dress now in the collection of the Bunka Gakuen Museum, Tokyo, underscores the continually shifting outcomes associated with studying objects that are disparate, changing the accepted narrative as new knowledge becomes available. Mamiko Matsumura, MA student at the Textile Conservation Centre, Winchester School of Art, undertook her final project conserving the c1908 bodice of the dress from Tokyo in 2000. The garment was not mounted and photographed until relatively recently, however, and added to a digital collection that was disseminated more widely around the world. It was only when the photograph came to light and after watching once more the British Pathé footage of Alexandra's dresses at the Margaret Street dressmaker that it became apparent the dresses were one and the same. A garment that had been recorded separately in research terms was united. The journey from a small West End 1950s dressmaker to a large Japanese decorative arts museum is unclear. The museum's acquisition notes simply refer to the dress being purchased from a European owner. Perhaps Doris Langley Moore purchased a number of the items for sale at 'Baroque' and sold to other collectors or perhaps it is somebody else now entirely unknown. The dearth of records means that although the dress is identified from the film and the photograph, this new connection still leaves an incomplete picture and one that is unlikely to be fully understood.

Doris Langley Moore's hand in the dissemination of Alexandra's wardrobe is similarly apparent in another discovery relating to objects now separated geographically but connected sartorially. Langley Moore was strategic in her purchasing and subsequent selling of royal dress. Some pieces she kept for the growing collection in Bath and others that she felt replicated objects they already had she then sold on – this is apparent in the similarity of certain objects in the two collections – spotted waistcoats by the tailor Busvine, two of which are in Los Angeles and one in Bath. (See Plate 16.) Tailored jackets by the celebrated Vernon – two in Los Angeles and one in Bath. Two garments, however, had not been connected until very recently when a letter Doris wrote to Helen came to light.

On 12 October 1963 she wrote: 'I have sent you one of her silk blouses with matching jacket, as mentioned, and I am keeping another *exactly* similar, except that it is pink and not blue, for Bath.'[31] Having studied the Bath collection of Alexandra's clothes carefully over the years I had never encountered a blouse or jacket fitting this description that was associated with Alexandra. However, passing this information onto the curator Rosemary Harden, she immediately recognized it as a garment that had been catalogued as belonging to Queen Mary. Studying snapshots of the two garments in question reveals that they are indeed the same piece in two colourways (see Plate 17).

Doris Langley Moore's careful garment selection was very typical of its day in terms of the collection policies of historic dress which tended towards the collection of well-preserved aristocratic and if possible quite splendid garments. She notes in one of her letters to Helen Larsson that the Alexandra garments are 'not spectacular but worth having'.[32] By not spectacular, Doris Langley Moore presumably meant that they were garments devoid of an obvious queenly association – they are not glittering ball gowns or court robes. Dress history scholarship has changed in the interim and now the objects both in Bath and Los Angeles represent elements of Alexandra's wardrobe that are not found anywhere else and so they are of great significance – including pieces from her trousseau now long gone, items of tailoring for which she was perhaps best known but of which very little has survived – and have a great deal to offer this study of Alexandra's life in dress, separated though they are geographically.

This separation did not concern Doris when she made her selections and there is no sense in the correspondence that she felt collections associated with one person should remain together. Her greatest frustration was in the customs bureaucracy and she went to some lengths to try and reduce the duty she would pay on the garments, stating in one letter: 'This morning I posted yet another parcel which I have declared as a wedding and bridesmaid's dress in the hope that some tender hearted customs official will suppose it is for a current wedding and let it through.'[33] What these examples do serve to emphasize is that even now Alexandra's wardrobe is evolving and expanding with new tales to tell and new paths to follow. While so many of these objects remain unaccounted for there remains the probability that this will remain an unfinished story.

Conclusion

Disposing of objects from a royal wardrobe evidently had precedents that made the auction of Alexandra's clothing acceptable albeit in an American setting. These waves of dispersal punctuated Alexandra's life, frequently giving items of clothing away to members of her household or disposing of them discreetly via an established European dress agency. Like driftwood, however, the objects that have washed up as a result are accidental, random survivals that do not therefore create a coherent picture. Trying to bring together this fractured record of survival poses a challenge to the researcher. From a pair of Alexandra's drawers in Ohio to her boots in Sydney, a fur coat in Oslo and a sequinned gown in Copenhagen to the larger collections of garments in the UK, New York, Toronto and Los Angeles, weaving together this wardrobe and analysing its contents is as much about detective-like legwork as it is historical enquiry. Altogether it is an eclectic mix of objects difficult, therefore, to quantify. They are from different decades, on different continents, in different collections and in different conditions. The only thread that connects them is one-time ownership by the same woman.

CONCLUSION

Alexandra's spending on clothes reduced dramatically in the decade after Edward's death.[1] French couture no longer featured among her wardrobe accounts and the suppliers mostly comprised the larger department stores, drapers and favoured tailors.[2] These years were punctuated by periods of extreme grief for Alexandra – friends and family members dear to her heart died in quick succession: her oldest friend and lady-in-waiting Lady Macclesfield, her brother king George of Greece, her grandson John. Such losses contributed to her choice of dress. In 1911, less than a year after Edward's death, Queen Mary described her mother-in-law as 'hopeless and helpless' (cited in Battiscombe 1969: 278) and a few years later wrote, 'It is so hard to see that beautiful woman come to this' (Pope-Hennessy 1959: 537). She also felt keenly her loss of status and of appearance. Clothes ceased to matter much. Unlike Queen Victoria before her, whose widowhood was played out at the prime of her life, Queen Alexandra experienced the loss of her spouse, siblings, friends and beauty in a short space of time.

She despised her agedness, often referring to herself as 'ugly old woman'; in a letter to her friend Lord Knutsford she implored him to 'think of me as I used to be, now I am breaking up' (cited in Battiscombe 1969: 302). T.E. Lawrence wrote movingly of an audience with the old queen at Marlborough House which he recalled on the day of her funeral:

> When we reached the presence, and I saw the mummied thing, the bird-like head cocked on one side, not artfully but by disease, the red-rimmed eyes, the enamelled face, which the famous smile scissored across all angular and heart-rending: – then I nearly ran away in pity. The body should not be kept alive after the lamp of sense has gone out. There were the ghosts of all her lovely airs, the little graces, the once-effective sway and movement of the figure which had been her consolation. (Lawrence 1973: 181)

Clearly Lawrence himself could recall Alexandra in her heyday, her 'lovely airs' and 'once effective sway' still present but a caricature of what they once represented. His reference to her 'enamelled face' suggestive of the wearing of a mask and her movements that hinted at long-gone grace of movement seem to describe a woman no longer in touch with much of reality but endeavouring to appear regal all the same. Her life at this point was rarely a public one (Figure 10.1).

Figure 10.1 Photograph of Alexandra in old age, still wearing the embellished garments that came to distinguish her later years, here a spangled jacket and pearls (original postcard, author's own collection).

As with so many of her sartorial choices from a fifty-year career, these later public outings that were so much a trial to her had to be managed astutely. The sparkling jackets, satin skirts and embellished veiled hats of her old age were nothing if not armour. She protected herself from the public and attempted to shield the public gaze from her true self through a shimmering sartorial display that by the 1910s and 1920s were more suited to evening wear and not these daytime outings. Where once Alexandra as a celebrated member of the monarchy dressed in evening finery to be noticed, her motives were altogether different in the last years of her life. Her fine clothes were intended to distract from the fragile corporeal reality. It could be argued that she was still dressing shrewdly, taking the measure of the occasion and how she wished herself to be seen, or rather ironically *not* seen. They were not, however, the decisions that the young Alexandra or even the stately queen Alexandra would have taken at the peak of her career and are thus not a reflection of her true sartorial self.

The surviving material culture of the younger woman's wardrobe *does* add significantly to what was already known about a biographical subject. In this project specific items of clothing have revealed previously unknown facets of Alexandra's life, as well as have added a significant depth to the balder facts already known. In certain cases, the garments and ephemera associated with them actually revealed previously unknown data – the iris motif evening dress literally exposed the secrets of Alexandra's physicality, its construction highlighting a curvature of the spine significant enough to warrant its disguise in a public setting. Although Alexandra's rheumatic fever was well documented and the resulting limp was impossible to hide, the wider implications of this in the long term had never before been considered. Only through this dress and its apparently mismatched embellishment did the reality of her physical impairment emerge.

The evidence of the wedding dress also suggested a facet to Alexandra's character, aged 19, that contradicted the accepted assertions of the biographers. The presence of the European lace panel roughly stitched to the underside of the wedding gown's skirt might indicate an element of subversion. While publicly adhering to Queen Victoria's demand for a British lace dress, the surreptitious addition of this European lace where nobody but the wearer might know of its presence hints towards a more wilful character who was already beginning to assert herself, albeit ever so slightly at this early stage.

At the other end of her career as Princess of Wales resides the coronation dress, the gown in which she might exhibit all of her own free will. In complete contrast to the wedding dress, not a stitch of this garment was of UK manufacture. The accepted story of its creation abroad was that of an imperial tribute to the romance of an imagined India. Examining papers that no other biographer had studied told a quite different story – one of pragmatism forged over decades of dressing alongside the 'London Ladies' and demonstrating her determination for originality. In a recognizably modern bid to ensure that the British press and public did not know what her dress would look like, she had the design and fabrication conducted thousands of miles away.

That the dress was completed in Paris by the couture house Morin Blossier, dispelled a myth that was oft-repeated in subsequent biographies – that Alexandra bought British and, like her mother-in-law before her, eschewed Parisian couture. The coronation gown and indeed every single surviving evening dress after 1880, of which there are seventeen, were all French. When it came to the construction of her public appearance, Alexandra was not going to be mired in expectations of all-British sartorial consumption. The French made, in her opinion, better evening gowns and so French evening gowns she would wear. In contrast the British were tailors par excellence and so all of her tailoring was

British. She negotiated these choices sensitively. There was no backlash in the British press about her Parisian preferences and so it appears that her purchasing was conducted sensitively. So sensitively, in fact, that without consulting any of the gowns associated with her, traditional biographers upheld the apocryphal stories of her patriotism.

In tandem with the garments themselves are those areas of Alexandra's royal wardrobe that have remained almost completely in the shadows until now. Although there were general acknowledgements of her stylishness and interest in fashion among the pages of the existing biographies, the realization of her clothed royal body was given no consideration. Her appearance was never subject to any analysis prior to this research, less so the logistics of achieving and maintaining that appearance. The dressmakers, messengers, dressers and launderers who were all a part of Alexandra's managed appearance have been erased from any account of her life to date. In part this is because they have left no written record themselves but this only made the details of their roles even more tantalizing. These are the nuts and bolts of her daily life – the flesh that bulks out the barer bones of the known biography of dates and events. Such practical arrangements were not supposed to be visible – notions of discretion ensured that details about the royal laundry were scarce, dressers were shadowy figures on the fringes of the written records and travel arrangements were peripheral to the destinations themselves. There is little published material relating to these features, most of the material gleaned from primary sources. This suggests an area for future development – those roles that inhabited a hidden facet of royal life beyond even the royal household, which was still one of relative privilege. This question did, however, underscore the importance of the multidisciplinary approach adopted throughout, supporting the blend of object and text-based evidence that 'show how the material and textual illuminate and reinforce each other' (Burman 2007: 157).

Examining the duties of the dresser and how laundry was managed on the scale of that exhibited by the royal family highlighted some of the realities of public dressing. The degree of travel involved and the luggage that accompanied it was an area almost totally devoid of research and yet it was a crucial part of Edward's and Alexandra's lives together. Hers was a carefully managed persona. She certainly made her own decisions about the fitness of her appearance for any given moment but once that decision was made a whole operation swung into action that involved many people from those making the garments to those managing and repairing them, to those responsible for their transport.

This persona was carefully constructed. Alexandra's clothing displayed important elements of her royal image making that could both reveal and disguise as she saw fit. When performing in public at ceremonial occasions she played the part expected of her in a way that Queen Victoria refused to do. With her high-wired collars and an eye to dramatic detail and colour, her appearances as Queen were suitably queenly. When dressing for different parts, including fancy dress, she revealed an aspiration for such majesty, which was fully realized on Victoria's death. Yet at other times when she was not making such a public performance, she took interpretations of tailored yachting gowns into a different worn context. She challenged the critics of her extreme slenderness by accentuating her shape in unadorned, feminized versions of a male suit, displaying a strong sporting body at odds with the prevailing trend of soft femininity. Dress was power, disguise, depending on the requirements of any given day.

Alexandra was not a trend-setter. The tailor-made aside (which was perhaps the only instance whereby she ignited a new fashion), she dressed safely and in such a way that ensured admiration and positive press. However, the surviving objects and archival material such as the wardrobe accounts reveal that she did like to exhibit an element of difference in her appearance. As established earlier with her plans for the coronation gown, she did not want to dress alongside the London ladies. Thus when John Redfern was an unknown draper, he enjoyed the Princess of Wales' patronage but as his star rose ever higher so her interest waned and she chose other less familiar tailors. She did not shop with Worth but with less celebrated couture houses such as Morin Blossier. She conformed at the same time as she dissented and it was perhaps this chameleon-like approach which was her greatest strength. This assessment of Alexandra's working royal wardrobe when the clothes are, as Banim, Green & Guy have termed it, 'active', passing through stages of use and usefulness, shines a light into previously unexplored corners (Guy, Green and Banim 2001).

Alexandra recognized the efficacy of dress in projecting a particular image given the limitations of the period and her position, a form of communicative power considered by Diana Crane: 'Lacking other forms of power, [nineteenth-century women] used nonverbal symbols as a means of self-expression' (Crane 2000: 100). She did so in a way that is very recognizable among certain other twentieth and twenty-first-century royal women. Princess Margaret, whose life was one of complexity played out in the public eye, knew how to dress effectively as a princess of the British monarchy. As an exhibition featuring Princess Margaret's clothes stated: 'Her clothes reflect the rule-breaking of a more liberal era and the greater freedoms of her role.'[3] In this sense she had greater choice allowed to her but her ability to create a sensation in the public spaces she inhabited based upon her appearance was something she shared with Alexandra. Such astuteness was by no means universal. As recorded elsewhere, Queen Mary was not known for her fashionable flair but, according to a lady-in-waiting, this was not necessarily out of choice but in deference to her husband George: 'She never even wore a colour that the King did not like. Her style of dressing was dictated by his conservative prejudices' (Airlie 1962: 128). Her clothing was purchased from British companies with a business-like acceptance but little flair in the resulting appearance.[4]

Overall this is the tale of the sartorial diaspora that Alexandra's surviving wardrobe represents. There is no pattern to any of the garments' accidental survival and no logical reason for their geographic spread. This has made the search for garments both a frustrating and a fascinating exercise. It is indicative of the curiosity that such garments and their association with royalty can hold for collections and collectors as their final home lies far from their original worn context. This research started as a study of Queen Alexandra's scant surviving clothing encountered in the Royal Ceremonial Dress Collection in London. It evolved into a great deal more. As more and more garments were discovered in museums around the world, the full range of the working royal wardrobe began to emerge from the shadows. Not only did it begin to allow for a serious analysis of the material culture and what it might reveal about the woman who wore it, it shone a light onto previously unrecorded areas of royal life. The practical realities of the office of robes, its staff, the maintenance, the couture houses, department stores, photographers and journalists and the general public were all areas that had existed at the margins of academia or in some cases never been studied before. Bound together in the wardrobe of one woman, it has cast a brighter light upon Queen Alexandra's image, her household, her suppliers and the clothing of her royal body.

NOTES

Introduction

1   The Oxford English Dictionary defines the term 'material culture' as: 'The physical objects, such as tools, domestic articles, or religious objects, which give evidence of the type of **culture** developed by a society or group.'

Chapter 1

1   Royal Archive, Windsor, RA/Z/463/123.

2   Letter from Queen Victoria, Royal Archive, Windsor, RA/Z/449/51.

3   *The Waikato Times*, 18 October 1884, p. 2, http://paperspast.natlib.govt.nz/cgi-bin/paperspast?a=d&d=WT18841018.2.43&l=mi&e=. Accessed 23 March 2013.

4   The randomly selected folio is Royal Archive, Windsor, RA VIC/Add A21/219A, Folio 28.

5   The Royal Collection, RA/VIC/Add A 8/1425.

6   One example is now in Norfolk Museums Collections, Carrow House, NWHCM: 1910.7.

7   The National Archive, Kew, LC13/5, p. 31.

8   *The Queen*, Saturday, 19 June 1897, p. 1.

9   The National Archive, Kew, LC13/5 p. 382.

10 The list of royal warrant holders was published annually in the *London Gazette*.

11 The National Archive, Kew, LC12/1-5 & LC13/1-5.

12 Office of Robes Ledger, The National Archive, Kew, LC13/3, Folio 132.

13 Royal Archive, Windsor, RA/VIC/Main/Z/202/55, 60-62, Folio 55.

14 Royal Archive, Windsor, RA/VIC/ADDJ/1591, 1592.

15 Royal Archive, Windsor, RA/VIC/ADDA21/219A, Folio 9.

16 Royal Photographic Collection, Windsor, RPC 03/0064, p. 14.

17 Royal Photographic Collection, Windsor, RPC 03/0069, p. 46.

18 Royal Photographic Collection, Windsor, RPC/03/0069, p. 4.

19 Royal Archive, Windsor, RA/VIC/MAIN/Z/202/55, 60-62, Folio 55, March 1866.

20 Kew Foot Road and Sheendale Road Conservation Area Studies, London Borough of Richmond Upon Thames, 2004, www.richmond.gov.uk. Accessed 24 March 2012.

21   The National Archive, Kew, LC11/172.

22   The National Archive, Kew, LC11/172.

23   Royal Archive, Windsor, RA/VIC/ADDA21/219A, Folio 40.

24   Royal Archive, Windsor, RA/VIC/ADDA21/219A, Folio 99.

Chapter 2

1   Royal Archive, Windsor, Lady Geraldine Somerset's diary, 1863.

2   Royal Archive, Windsor, RA Z31/45, V to QV, 8/29/77.

3   Royal Archive, Windsor, RA Z463.

4   Letter from Samuel Tucker to Mary Tucker, Devon Record Office, 1037M/F2/1.

5   Letter from W Wills to Mary Tucker, Devon Record Office, 1037M/F2/1.

6   The Royal Archive, Windsor, Diary of Lady Geraldine Somerset, 1863. She was lady-in-waiting to the Duchess of Cambridge and so centrally placed as an observer during the wedding preparations.

7   *The Marriage of the Prince of Wales and Princess Alexandra of Denmark*, William Powell Frith, Oil on canvas, Royal Collection RCIN404545.

Chapter 3

1   *Night & Day*, The Fashion and Textile Gallery in The Museum at FIT, New York, 3 December 2009 to 11 May 2010 and *Dressing Up, Dressing Down*, The National Trust, Killerton House, Devon, February to October 2011.

2   *The Queen, the Lady's Newspaper and Court Chronicle*, January to June 1882.

3   *The Queen, the Lady's Newspaper and Court Chronicle*, Saturday 17 April 1897, p. 755.

4   *The Times*, 9 June 1863, p. 10c.

5   Royal Ontario Museum, Toronto, accession number 942.12.1.A-E.

6   The Fashion Museum, Bath, accession number BATMC1.17.10A-D.

7   *The Glasgow Herald*, 31 August 1863, Issue 7376, p. 4a.

8   *The Times*, 9 February 1870. p. 15c.

9   *The Times*, 22 March 1870.

10   *The Queen, the Lady's Newspaper and Court Chronicle*, 19 June 1875, p. 409.

11   *The Times*, 6 May 1875, p. 10a.

12   The Fashion Museum, Bath, BATMC 1.17.11 & A.

13   Accession card note for object BATMC 1.17.11, Fashion Museum, Bath.

14   Letter from Charlotte Knollys to Lady Curzon, 20 May 1902, British Library, Asian & African Dept, Lady Curzon Papers, F306/35 No 86.

15   Royal Archive, Windsor, RA/VIC.ADDA2/219B, Folio 42.

16   Royal Archive, Windsor, RA/VIC.ADDA2/219B, Folios 44 & 46.

17   Royal Archive, Windsor, RA/VIC.ADDA2/219C, Folio 95.

18   Email received from Jean Druesedow, 2 November 2011.

Chapter 4

1   Letter from Charlotte Knollys, The Knollys Papers, 2IM69/25/5, Hampshire Record Office.

2   Royal Archive, Windsor, RA/VIC/ADDA21/219A, Folio 110.

3   *Newcastle Evening Chronicle,* 20 August 1884, np.

4   Royal Photographic Collection, Windsor, RPC 03/0065, p. 1.

5   National Archive, Kew, Ordinary and Extraordinary Bills, LC11/172.

6   Royal Photographic Collection, Windsor RPC 03/0064/37.

7   Royal Photographic Collection, Windsor RPC 03/0064/25.

8   Royal Photographic Collection, Windsor, RPC 03/0064/12.

9   Royal Photographic Collection, Windsor, RPC/03/0069/5.

10 Royal Photographic Collection, Windsor, RPC/03/0069/9.

11 Anderson Galleries Inc, *A Unique Assemblage of Royal Robes and State Gowns Formerly Belonging to HM Queen Alexandra*, American Art Association, New York, 1937, p. 15.

12 Royal Photographic Collection, Windsor, RPC/03/0069/10.

13 *The Queen, the Lady's Newspaper and Court Chronicle*, 14 December 1878, p. 459.

14 Royal Archive, Windsor, RA Vic/Add A21/219A, Folio 28.

15 Map 87, Huntingdon Record Office.

16 *The Newcastle Daily Chronicle*, 18 August 1884, np.

17 Royal Photographic Collection, Windsor, RPC 04/0004/1.

18 Royal Archive, Windsor, RA/AA/33/7.

19 *The Queen, the Lady's Newspaper and Court Chronicle*, 29 April 1899, p. 702.

20 Royal Photographic Collection, Windsor, RPC 04/0004/27.

21 Royal Photographic Collection, Windsor, RPC 04/0004/35.

22 Royal Photographic Collection, Windsor, RPC 04/0004/35.

23 *The Times*, 9 April 1885, p. 12B.

24 *The Times*, 12 April 1885, p. 6A.

25 *The Times,* 22 April 1885, p. 6B.

26 *The Times*, 18 May 1885, p. 11D.

27 *The Queen, the Lady's Newspaper and Court Chronicle*, 7 May 1904, p. 770.

28 Royal Photographic Collection, Windsor, RPC 03/0064/4.

Chapter 5

1   The red velvet gown is now in the Royal Ceremonial Dress Collection, Kensington Palace, and the white satin gown is held at the Museum of London.

2   At the 1897 Devonshire House Ball, there were no less than three Cleopatras, Queen Esther of Persia and an African queen among the guests. See also Kirk

A, 'Japonisme and Femininity: A Study of Japanese Dress in British and French Art and Society c.1860-c.1899', in *Costume*, Number 42, 2008: 111–29 for an analysis of the Japanese influence on fancy dress.

3 For example, the Lafayette collection of the Devonshire House Ball in 1897 found at http://www.vam.ac.uk/vastatic/microsites/1158_lafayette/categories. php?category=dhb&&page_number, the album of costumes from Victoria and Albert's fancy-dress balls of 1842, 1845 and 1851 as well as individual images that can be found in a wealth of archives and record offices.

4 *The Queen, the Lady's Newspaper and Court Chronicle*, 25 July 1878, p. 80C.

5 *The Liverpool Mercury*, Thursday 10 September 1863, p. 1.

6 *The Liverpool Mercury*, Thursday 10 September 1863, p. 1.

7 *The Era*, London, Sunday 5 November 1863, np.

8 *The Times*, 23 July 1874, p. 10.

9 *Court Journal*, July 1871, np.

10 Ardern Holt's advice regarding Mary offered two alternatives, both illustrated in her manual. Holt, Plate VIII, p. 147.

11 By 1871, Edward had been involved in a number of public scandals, Alexandra had suffered a serious illness and her final pregnancy had resulted in the death of her son only 24 hours after his birth.

12 Royal Archives, Windsor, RA VIC/Add A 21-22/A Folio 27.

13 A typical example appeared in *The Pall Mall Gazette*, Saturday 3 July 1897, Issue 10069, p. 7.

14 *Freeman's Journal and Daily Commercial Advertiser*, Dublin, Monday 5 July 1897, p. 6.

15 *The Queen, the Lady's Newspaper and Court Circular*, British Library Colindale, LON MLD 45, 1873, vol. 2, p. 101.

Chapter 6

1 The Henry Poole & Co, 15 Savile Row, London, Prince of Wales' Measurement ledger, no number.

2 Henry Poole & Co, 15 Savile Row, London, Livery Ledger 1863–1869, Folio 25.

3 Henry Poole & Co, 15 Savile Row, London, Livery Ledger 1869–1874, Folio 709.

4 Henry Poole & Co, 15 Savile Row, London, Livery Ledger 1863–1869, Folio 25.

5 For example, 7 June 1863 – a grey barathea cashmere dust coat was ordered by Alexandra, Henry Poole & Co, 15 Savile Row, London, Livery Ledger 1863–1869, Folio 25.

6 Turnbull & Asser, http://store.turnbullandasser.co.uk/Materials_and_styling/ Barathea_Weave.html. Accessed 27 September 2012.

7 Royal Archive, VIC/Add A21/219B Folio 120.

8 First advertised in *The Queen*, 26 August 1876, p. 56.

9 National Archive, Kew, LC11/172.

10 National Archive, Kew, LC11/172, top of page.

11 National Archive, Kew, LC12/1.

12 *The Queen*, 22 November 1879, p. 489.

13 The earliest illustration of a jersey bodice appears in *The Queen*, 6 August 1881, p. 144.

14 Royal Archive, Windsor, RA VIC ADD A 21 219A Folio 30.

15 Accession number 966.295 a&b – Royal Ontario Museum, Toronto. This suit is not associated with Alexandra but is of a comparable date and style to those that are.

16 Royal Photographic Collection, Windsor, RPC 03/0069, Mediterranean Cruise Album 1905, Vol 1, Folio 28.

17 Royal Photographic Collection, Windsor, RPC 03/0069, Mediterranean Cruise Album 1905, Folio 30.

18 Uncatalogued letter: 13 October 1963 from M Deane, acquired by Mrs Doris Langley Moore and sent to America with the suit jackets. The letter is now part of the collections at the Fashion Institute of Design Merchandising Museum, Los Angeles.

19 Red spotted waistcoat c.1890 accession number BATMC 1.17.13, The Fashion Museum, Bath; blue spotted waistcoat c.1890 accession number L2011.13.29, Fashion Institute of Design Merchandising Museum, Los Angeles; black spotted waistcoat c.1890 accession number L2011.13.30, Fashion Institute of Design Merchandising, Los Angeles.

Chapter 7

1 Royal Archive, Windsor, RA QM/PRIV/CC 58/168.

2 Royal Collection, RCIN65710.

3 Royal Collection RCIN65282.

4 Royal Ceremonial Dress Collection, London, 1994.194/1&2 two-piece dress by Mme Fromont, Paris, c.1894 and Museum of London, 66.93 two-piece dress by Henriette Favre, c.1911.

5 Author's own collection – Queen Alexandra's Letter to the Nation Postcard.

Chapter 8

1 Frederick Vigers was an avant-garde designer, who was later to win awards for wallpaper design.

2 Royal Archive, Windsor, RA VIC Add A21/219 A, Folio 146.

3 Lady Curzon Papers (LCP), British Library, East India Papers, F306/35 No71, 3 August 1901.

4 LCP, British Library, F306/35 No 76, 9 August 1901.

5 LCP, British Library, F306/35 No 108, 6 November 1902.

6 LCP, British Library, F306/35 No 86, 20 May 1902.

7 Royal Archive, RA/VIC/Add A21/219 A, Folio 146.

8 LCP, British Library, F306/35 No93A, 23 July 1902.

9 E.A.D, *New York Times*, 10 August 1902, np.

10 E.A.D, *New York Times*, 10 August 1902, np.

Chapter 9

1 *The New York Times*, 6 May 1937, np.

2 *The Caledonian Mercury*, Monday 13 June 1831, p. 2d.

3 Anon, *New York Evening Mail*, 28 February 1920, np.

4 Anon, *New York Evening Mail*, 28 February 1920, np.

5 Anon, *New York Evening Mail,* 28 February 1920, np.

6 Royal Archives, Windsor, RA QM/PRIV/CC58/168.

7 A search of the UK British newspaper databases under a variety of search terms did not bring up any articles mentioning the US auction.

8 Auction catalogue, *A Unique Assemblage of Royal Robes and State Gowns Formerly Belonging to Queen Alexandra*, American Art Association Anderson Galleries, New York, 1937.

9 A short newsreel clip from the 1930s shows a parade passing along Regent Street. Soden's shop front is visible with his name and title of Court Furrier. See 'London' newsreel footage, 1930–9, British Pathé, film ID 1881.14, http://www.britishpathe.com/video/london-1/query/Roman. Accessed 24 April 2013.

10 American Arts Association Anderson Galleries, *Royal Robes and State Gowns*, 1937, https://archive.org/details/royalrobesstateg00amer Metropolitan Museum of Art Library.

11 Mrs Stanwood Menken was a well-known New York socialite, regularly featuring in *Life* magazine and the gossip pages of *The New Yorker.*

12 *The New York Times*, 6 May 1937, np.

13 *Vogue,*1 May 1939, p. 73. The previous article referred to here was entitled 'Curtsy to Queen Alexandra' and featured sketches of Edwardian style gowns drawn to appeal to the 1930s consumer.

14 Previously the Scala Theatre, it was renamed in 1942 and held concerts and charitable benefits during the war. It is now the Prince Edward Theatre.

15 Fernberg E, email sent on 11 October 2007.

16 LCP, British Library F306/10&11 No 58.

17 LCP, British Library, F306/10&11 No 88.

18 *The Times*, Saturday 30 May 1905, p. 11.

19 Royal Archive RA QM/PRIV/CC58/168.

20 American Arts Association Anderson Galleries, *Royal Robes and State Gowns*, 1937, np.

21 Original catalogue card for CI37.44.9a-d, Metropolitan Museum of Art, New York.

22 *The Times*, Saturday 9 July 1904, p. 14.

23 Original accession cards, National Museums, Liverpool.

24 11 October 1963, Larsson Papers, Museum at FIDM, Los Angeles.

25 Doris Langley Moore (1902–89) was a respected early female historian. She founded the Fashion Museum in Bath and made important contributions to early dress history scholarship, including publications such as *The Woman in Fashion* and *The Child in Fashion*.

26 Accession card for dress c.1910 by Douillet, The Fashion Museum, Bath.

27 'Look Back for Inspiration', newsreel footage, 1951, British Pathé, film ID 1475.27, canister 51/77, http://www.britishpathe.com/video/look-back-for-inspiration/query/ Queen+Alexandra. Accessed 23 October 2010.

28 Doris Langley Moore to Helen Larsson, letter, 6 October 1963, now part of the Larsson Collection in the Fashion Institute of Design Merchandising.

29 Royal Archive, Windsor, RA QM/PRIV/CC58/168.

30 Email from Anne Bissonette, curator, received 16 April 2007.

31 12 October 1963, Larsson Papers, Museum at FIDM, Los Angeles.

32 6 October 1963, Larsson Papers, Museum at FIDM, Los Angeles.

33 6 October 1963, Larsson Papers, Museum at FIDM, Los Angeles.

Conclusion

1 In 1910 Alexandra received £2500 per quarter from the privy purse as an allowance to cover wardrobe expenses. By 1917 this had reduced to £1500 but much of this covered pensions, implying that her spending on actual garments was much lower. Royal Archive, Windsor, RA VIC Add A21/22/C Folios 2&3.

2 Although her interest in clothes may have waned in these later years, it is also true to say that her privy purse allowance was reduced owing to her change of status.

3 The exhibition is entitled 'Fashion Rules', Kensington Palace, London, http://www. hrp.org.uk/KensingtonPalace/stories/palacehighlights/fashionrules/. Accessed 6 September 2013.

4 This was particularly noticeable when comparing two evening dresses in the Royal Ontario Museum, Toronto – one belonging to Queen Alexandra and the other to Queen Mary. Where Alexandra's French gown was made of chiffon and spangles, Mary's was a British design of heavy white satin, heavily embellished with faux pearls and diamante. The overall impression was of a heavy 'less graceful' as the technician described it, dress.

BIBLIOGRAPHY

A Memento of the Marriage of Albert Edward Prince of Wales With The Princess Alexandra of Denmark (1863), London, unknown binding.

Adamson, G. (2009), 'The Case of the Missing Footstool: Reading the Absent Object', in K. Harvey (ed.), *History and Material Culture*, London, Routledge.

Agar, A. (1959), *Footprints in the Sea*, London, Evans Bros.

Airlie, Mabel Countess of (1962), *Thatched with Gold*, London, Hutchinson & Co.

Amelekhina, S. and Levykin, A. (2008), *Magnificence of the Tsars*, London, V&A Publishing.

Anderson, F. (2006), 'This Sporting Cloth: Tweed, Gender & Fashion 1860-1900', *Textile History*, vol. 37, no. 2, pp. 166–86.

Anon (1840), *The Workwoman's Guide*, London, Simpkin, Marshall & Co.

Anon (1860), *Routledge's Manual of Etiquette*, London, Routledge.

Anon (1878), *Travelling and its Requirements Addressed to Ladies By A Lady*, unknown binding.

Anon (1895), *The Post Office London Directory*, London, Kelly & Co.

Anon (1899), *The Post Office London Directory*, London, Kelly & Co.

Anon (1910), *The Post Office London Directory*, London, Kelly & Co.

Anon (1935), *Costume*, London Museum Catalogues No5, Lancaster House.

Anon (2012), *Louis Vuitton – Marc Jacobs*, Musée les Arts Décoratifs, Visitor's Guide No 36.

Antrim Lady (1937), *Recollections of Louisa Countess of Antrim*, London, King's Stone Press.

Arch, N. and Marschner, J. (2003), *Royal Wedding Dresses*, London, Historic Royal Palaces.

Arnold, J. (1972), *Patterns of Fashion 2*, London, Macmillan London Ltd.

Arnstein, W. (2003), *Queen Victoria*, London, Palgrave Macmillan.

Ashelford, J. (1996), *The Art of Dress Clothes and Society 1500-1914*, London, The National Trust.

Battersea, C. (1923), *Reminiscences*, London, Macmillan & Co Ltd, London.

Battiscombe, G. (1969), *Queen Alexandra*, London, Constable & Co Ltd.

Baumgarten, L. (1998), 'Altered Historical Clothing', *Dress*, vol. 25, pp. 42–57.

Bayard, M. (1888), *Weldon's Practical Fancy Dress, Or Suggestions for Fancy and Calico Balls, also Fancy Bazaars*, London, Weldon & Co.

Beavan, A. (1896), *Marlborough House and Its Occupants*, London, White & Co.

Blackman, C. (2001), 'Walking Amazons: The Development of the Riding Habit in England during the Eighteenth Century', *Costume*, vol. 35, pp. 47–58.

Bradley, J. (1985), *Lady Curzon's India, Letters of a Vicereine*, London, George Weidenfeld & Nicolson Ltd.

Breward, C., Ehrman, E. and Evans, C., eds (2004), *The London Look, Fashion From Street to Catwalk*, New Haven and London, Yale University Press.

Brooks Picken, M. and Loues Miller, D. (1956), *Dressmakers of France*, London, Harper.

Buck, A. (1984), *Victorian Costume*, Bedford, Ruth Bean reprint.

Buckley, C. and Fawcett, H. (2002), *Fashioning the Feminine: Representation and Women's Fashion from the Fin de Siècle to the Present*, London and New York, I. B Tauris.

Burman, B. (2007), '"A Linnen Pockett a Prayer Book and Five Keys": Approaches to a History of Women's Tie-on Pockets', in M. Hayward and E. Kramer (eds), *Textiles and Text – Re-Establishing Links between Archival and Object-based Research*, London, Archetype Publications.

Butler, N. (2007), 'William Burn: Kimbolton's Forgotten Architect', *Kimbolton Local History Journal*, no. 11, Spring.

Campbell, U. (1989), *Robes of the Realm*, London, Michael O'Mara Books Ltd.

Cartwright, J., ed. (1915), *Journals of Lady Knightly of Fawsley*, London, John Murray.

Collier, E. C. F., ed. (1944), *A Victorian Diarist*, London, John Murray.

Cooper, C. (1997), *Magnificent Entertainments: Fancy Dress Balls of Canada's Governors General 1876-1898*, Montreal, Goose Lane Publications.

Cornwallis-West, G. (1973), *The Reminiscences of Lady Randolph Churchill*, London, Edward Arnold.

Craik, J. (1994), *The Face of Fashion*, London, Routledge.

Crane, D. (2000), *Fashion and its Social Agendas*, Chicago, University of Chicago Press.

Crosby Nicklas, C. (2009), *Splendid Hues: Colour, Dyes, Everyday Science and Women's Fashion, 1840-1875*, unpublished PhD Thesis, University of Brighton.

Cunningham, A. (1843), *The Life of Sir David Wilkie*, Vol. 2, London, John Murray.

Cunnington, C. Willett (1990), *English Women's Clothing in the Nineteenth Century*, New York, Dover Publications Inc reprint.

Curl, J. (2000), *The Victorian Celebration of Death*, Stroud, Sutton Publishing.

Dalton, T. (2001), *British Royal Yachts: A Complete Illustrated History*, Wellington, Halsgrove Publishing.

Davey, R. (1848), *A History of Mourning*, Jay's London, London, McCorquodale & Co Ltd.

Davidoff, L. (1986), *The Best Circles – Society, Etiquette and the Season*, London, Century Hutchinson Ltd.

De Marly, D. (1980), *The History of Haute Couture 1850-1950*, London, Batsford.

Dillon, M. (2001), 'Like a Glow-worm who had lost its Glow', *Costume*, vol. 25, pp. 76–81.

Duff, D. (1970), *Victoria Travels*, London, Frederick Muller.

Duff, D. (1980), *Alexandra Princess and Queen*, London, Collins.

Entwistle, J. (2000), *The Fashioned Body – Fashion, Dress and Modern Social Theory*, Cambridge, Polity Press.

Erskine, S., ed. (1916), *Twenty Years at Court from the Correspondence of the Hon. Eleanor Stanley*, London, Nisbet & Co Ltd.

Esher, R. (1927), *Cloud Capp'd Towers*, London, Murray.

Esher, R. (1934), *Journals and Letters Vol 1*, London, Nicholson & Watson.

Ewing, E. (1975), *Women in Uniform*, London, Batsford.

Fine, B. and Leopold, E. (1993), *The World of Consumption*, London, Routledge.

Fisher, G. H. (1974), *Bertie & Alix: Anatomy of a Royal Marriage*, London, Robert Hale & Co.

Fulford, R., ed. (1968), *Dearest Mama – Letters between Queen Victoria and the Crown Princess of Prussia 1861-1864*, London, Evans Brothers Ltd.

Fulford, R., ed. (1971), *Your Dear Letter – Private Correspondence of Queen Victoria and the Crown Princess of Prussia 1865-1871*, London, Evans Brothers Ltd.

Greville Lady Violet (1897), *The Graphic*, Saturday 10 July 1897, Issue 1441, pp. 78–9.

Gupta, C. S. (2006), 'The Trade in Zardozi Textiles', in R. Crill (ed.), *Textiles from India: The Global Trade*, Chicago, Chicago University Press.

Guy, A., Green, E. and Banim, M., eds (2001), *Through the Wardrobe – Women's Relationship with Their Clothes*, Oxford and New York, Berg.

Hackett, H. (2001), 'Dreams or Designs, Cults or Constructions? The Study of Images of Monarchs', *The Historical Journal*, 44–3, Cambridge, Cambridge University Press.

Hall, C. (1999), *Little Mother of Russia*, London, Shepheard-Walwyn Ltd.

Halls, Z. (1973), *Coronation Costume 1685-1953*, London, London Museum. Harper & Bros.

Harmeyer, R. (2012), *Hairwork and the Technology of Memory*, unpublished MA thesis, University of Houston.

Hibbert, C. (1964), *The Court at Windsor*, London, Penguin Books Ltd.

Hibbert, C. (1964), *The Court at Windsor: A Domestic History*, London, Penguin Books.

Holt, A. (1984), *Fancy Dress Described Or What to Wear at Fancy Balls*, London, Debenham & Freebody, Fourth Edition.

Hon. Mrs Grey (1870), *Journal of a Visit to Egypt, Constantinople, the Crimea, Greece etc in the Suite of the Prince and Princess of Wales*, New York, Harper & Bro.

Hough, R. (1992), *Edward and Alexandra – their Private and Public Lives*, London, Hodder & Stoughton.

Inder, P. (1971), *Honiton Lace*, Devon, Exeter Museums Publications.

Jarvis, A. (1982), '"There was a Young Man of Bengal …" The Vogue for Fancy Dress, 1830-1950', *Costume*, vol. 16, pp. 33–46.

Jarvis, A. and Raine, P. (1984), *Fancy Dress*, Aylsebury, Shire Publications Ltd.

Johansen, K. (1990), *Royal Gowns*, Denmark, Rosenborg Palace.

Johansen, K. (2009), 'Magnificence des Rois Danois: Costumes de Couronnement et Habits de Chevaliers', in P. Arizzoli-Clémentel and P. Gorguet Ballesteros (eds), *Fastes de Cour et Ceremonies Royales*, Paris, Réunion des Musées Nationaux.

Kennedy, A. L (1956), *My Dear Duchess, Letters to the Duchess of Manchester*, London, John Murray.

Kinloch-Cooke, C. (1900), *A Memoir of HRH Princess Mary Adelaide Duchess of Teck*, London, John Murray.

Kirk, A. (2013), '"Composed of the same Materials": Like-dressing and the Doppelganger's Dress in Victorian Art and culture, c.1855-c.1885', unpublished doctoral thesis, London, Courtauld Institute of Art.

Kjellberg, A. and North, S. (2005), *Style and Splendour: The Wardrobe of Queen Maud of Norway*, London, V&A Publications.

Klausen, I. (2001), *Alexandra af Wales, Princesse Fra Danmark*, Danmark, Linhardt og Ringhof.

Kopytoff, I. (1986), 'The Cultural Biography of Things: Commoditization as Process', in A. Appadurai (ed.), *The Social Life of Things: Commodities in Cultural Perspective*, Cambridge, Cambridge University Press.

Lambert, M. (1991), *Fashion in Photographs: 1860-1880*, London, Batsford.

Lawrence, D. (2010), '"In a Hot Climate a Pretty Frock is a Great Assett": Finding, Changing and Exchanging Dress in Colonial Societies', paper given at the 2010 Pasold Research Fund and CHORD Conference, University of Wolverhampton, 8 and 9 September 2010.

Lawrence, T. E. (1973), *The Mint*, London, Jonathan Cape reprint.

Lepore, J. (2001), 'Historians Who Love Too Much: Reflections on Microhistory and Biography', *The Journal of American History*, vol. 88, no. 1, pp. 129–44.

Levitt, S. (1991), *Fashion in Photographs 1880-1900*, London, Batsford.

Lewis, J. E. (1998), *Mary Queen of Scots: Romance and Nation*, London, Routledge.

Lieven, D. (1993), *Nicholas II Emperor of all the Russians*, London, Pimlico.

Linkman, A. (1993), *The Victorians – Photographic Portraits*, London and New York, Tauris Parke Books.

Llewellyn, S. (1996), 'George III and the Windsor Uniform', *The Court Historian*, no. 2, pp. 12–16.

Longford, E. (1979), *Louisa Lady in Waiting, the Personal Diaries and Albums of Louisa Lady in Waiting to Queen Victoria and Queen Alexandra*, London, Jonathan Cape Ltd.

Maas, J. (1977), *The Prince of Wales' Wedding*, London, Cameron & Tayleur.

Maddox, B. (1999), 'Biography: A Love Affair or a Job?' *The New York Times*, http://www.nytimes.com/books/99/05/09/bookend/bookend.html (accessed 28 May 2013).

Magnus, P. (1964), *King Edward the Seventh*, London, John Murray, London.

Mallet, V., ed (1968), *Life with Queen Victoria: Marie Mallet's Letters from Court, 1887-1901*, London, John Murray.

Mansfield, A. (1980), *Ceremonial Costume*, London, A&C Black.

Matthews David, A. (2002), 'Elegant Amazons: Victorian Riding Habits and the Fashionable Horsewoman', *Victorian Literature and Culture*, vol. 30, no. 1, pp. 179–210.

Mayhew, H., ed. (1865), *The Shops and Companies of London*, London, Strand Printing and Publishing Company.

McDowell, C. (2002), *Diana Style*, London, Aurum Press.

Menkes, S. (1985), *The Royal Jewels*, London, Guild Publishing.

Millar, D. (1985), 'Quadrilles & All Kinds of Surprises: Queen Victoria's Costume Balls', *Country Life*, 10 October 1985, pp. 1024–6.

Miller, E. (1992), *Textiles: Property and Behaviour in Clothing Use*, London, Batsford.

Muller, H. (1980), *Jet Jewellery and Ornaments*, Aylesbury, Shire Publications Ltd.

Murphy, S. (1984), *The Duchess of Devonshire's Ball*, London, Sidgwick & Jackson Ltd.

Nathan, A. (1960), *Costumes by Nathan*, London, George Newnes Ltd.

North, S. (1993), Redfern, London, Courtauld Institute of Art, unpublished MA thesis.

North, S. (2008), 'John Redfern & Sons, 1847 to 1892', *Costume*, vol. 42, pp. 145–68.

Paget, Lady Walburga (1912), *Scenes and Memories*, London, Smith Elder & Co.

Painter, G. (1989), *Marcel Proust: A Biography*, London, Random House Publishing.

Pakula, H. (1997), *An Uncommon Woman – The Empress Frederick*, London, Orion Books Ltd.

Pepper, T. (1998), *High Society: Photographs 1897-1914*, London, The National Portrait Gallery Publications.

Plunkett, J. (2003), *Queen Victoria: First Media Monarch*, Oxford, Oxford University Press.

Pope-Hennessy, J. (1959), *Queen Mary*, London, George Allen & Unwin Ltd.

Pritchard, Mrs E. (1902), *The Cult of Chiffon*, London, Grant Richards.

Rappaport, E. (2000), *Shopping for Pleasure – Women in the Making of London's West End*, Princeton and Oxford, Princeton University Press.

Ridley, J. (2012), *Bertie: A Life of Edward VII*, London, Chatto & Windus.

Ruane, C. (2009), *The Empire's New Clothes, A History of the Russian Fashion Industry 1700 – 1917*, New Haven and London, Yale University Press.

Russell, W. H. (1863), *The Marriage of the Prince of Wales and Princess Alexandra of Denmark collated from the Description in The Times*, London, Redding & Co.

Russell, W. H. (1869), *A Diary in the East During the Tour of the Prince and Princess of Wales*, London, George Routledge & Sons.

Sala, A. (1859), *Twice Around the Clock or The Hours of the Day and Night in London*, London, Richard Marsh.

Sherwood, J. (2007), *The London Cut – Savile Row Bespoke Tailoring*, Florence, Fondazione Pitti.

Slater, A., Tiggemann, M., Firth, B. and Hawkins, K. (2012), 'Reality Check; An Experimental Investigation of the Addition of Warning Labels to Fashion Magazine Images on Women's Mood and Body Dissatisfaction', *Journal of Social and Clinical Psychology*, vol. 31, no. 2, pp. 105–22.

Smart Martin, A. (1993), 'Makers, Buyers and Users, Consumerism as a Material Culture Framework', *Winterthur Portfolio*, vol. 8, no. 2/4, Summer/Autumn, pp. 141–57.

Sorkin, M. (2009), *Night & Day*, The Fashion and Textile Gallery in The Museum at FIT, New York, 3 December 2009 to 11 May 2010.

Spence, J. (2001), 'Flying on One Wing', in A. Guy, E. Green and M. Banim (eds), *Through the Wardrobe – Women's Relationship with Their Clothes*, Oxford, Berg.

Staniland, K. (1997), *In Royal Fashion: The Clothes of Princess Charlotte of Wales and Queen Victoria 1796-1901*, London, Museum of London Publications.

Steele, V. (1998), 'A Museum of Fashion Is More Than a Clothes Bag', *Fashion Theory*, vol. 2, no. 4, pp. 327–35.

Stevenson, S. and Bennett, H. (1978), *Van Dyck in Check Trousers – Fancy Dress in Art and Life 1700-1900*, Edinburgh, Scottish National Portrait Gallery.

Stoney, B. and Weltzien, H., eds (1994), *My Mistress the Queen, Frieda Arnold, Dresser to Queen Victoria*, London, Weidenfeld & Nicolson.

Suoh, T., ed. (2002), *Fashion – A History from the eighteenth Century to the twentieth Century from the Collections of the Kyoto Costume Institute*, Koln, Taschen.

Tarlo, E. (1996), *Clothing Matters – Dress and Identity in India*, London, Hurst & Co.

Taylor, L. (1983), *Mourning Dress – A Costume and Social History*, London, George Allen & Unwin.

Taylor, L. (1999), 'Wool Cloth and Gender: The Use of Woolen Cloth in Women's Dress in Britain, 1865-1885', in A. de la Haye and E. Wilson (eds), *Defining Dress: Dress as Object, Meaning and Identity*, Manchester, Manchester University Press.

Taylor, L. (2002), *The Study of Dress History*, Manchester, Manchester University Press

Taylor, L. (2007), 'Object Lesson "To Attract the Attention of Fish as Little as Possible": An Object Led Discussion of Three Garments, for Country Wear, for Women, Made of Scottish Woollen Cloth, Dating from 1883-1908', *Textile History*, vol. 38, no. 1, pp. 92–105.

Taylor, L., de la Haye, A. and Thompson, E. (2005), *A Family of Fashion, The Messels: Six Generations of Dress*, London, Philip Wilson Publishers.

Thomas, N. (2007), 'Embodying Imperial Spectacle: Dressing Lady Curzon, Vicereine of India 1899-1905', *Cultural Geographies*, vol. 14, no. 3, pp. 369–400.

Tisdall, E. S. P. (1953), *Unpredictable Queen*, London, The Anchor Press.

Tobin, S. (2003), *Marriage a la Mode*, London, The National Trust.

Tomlinson, M. (1983), *Three Generations in the Honiton Lace Trade*, Sidmouth, Sovereign Printing Group.

Tooley, S. (1902), *The Life of Queen Alexandra*, London, Hodder & Stoughton.

Toynbee, P. (1903), *The Letters of Horace Walpole*, Vol. 1, Oxford, The Clarendon Press.

Twigg, J. (2010), 'How does *Vogue* negotiate age: Fashion, the body and the older woman', *Fashion Theory – The Journal of Dress, Body and Culture*, vol. 14, no. 4, pp. 471–90.

Vanderbilt Balsan, C. (1973), *The Glitter and the Gold*, Maidstone, George Mann.

Vane, H. (2004), *Affair of State, A Biography of the 8th Duke and Duchess of Devonshire*, London, Peter Owen.

Walkley, C. and Foster, V. (1978). *Crinolines and Crimping Irons: Victorian Clothes – How They Were Cleaned and Cared For*, London, Peter Owen Ltd.

Wyndham, H., ed. (1912), *The Correspondence of Sarah Spencer, Lady Lyttleton 1787-1870*, London, John Murray.

INDEX

Note: Page numbers in italics indicate figures and bold indicate tables.